# YOUNG ADULTS AND LONG-TERM UNEMPLOYMENT

# YOUNG ADULTS AND LONG-TERM UNEMPLOYMENT

**MICHAEL WHITE and SUSAN McRAE**

**Policy Studies Institute**

**PSI Publications are obtainable from all good bookshops, or by visiting the Institute at 100 Park Village East, London NW1 3SR (01-387 2171).**

**Sales Representation: Pinter Publishers Ltd.**

**Individual and Bookshop orders to: Marston Book Services Ltd, PO Box 87, Oxford, OX4 1LB.**

A CIP catalogue record of this book is available from the British Library

PSI Research Report 689

ISBN 0 85374 372 X

Laserset by Policy Studies Institute
Printed by BPCC Wheatons Ltd, Exeter

# Contents

Acknowledgements

Summary              i

1.   Introduction        1
2.   The Local Labour Market Context        22
3.   The Composition of the Young Long-Term Unemployed    56
4.   Patterns of Work        84
5.   Government Schemes in the Employment Process    113
6.   New Jobs        133
7.   The Value of Qualifications, Training and Experience    156
8.   Job Search        183
9.   Two Kinds of Flexibility        211
10.   Conclusions and Implications        232

Appendix 1    Sampling and Response        254
Appendix 2    Secondary Data Sources        258
Appendix 3    Multivariate Analyses        260

Notes and References        281

# Acknowledgements

The study reported here was funded by the Department of Employment, with additional funding by the Manpower Services Commission. However, the contents and conclusions of the report are entirely the responsibility of the authors, and do not represent the views of the Department of Employment or of any other organisation.

The study was assisted by a Steering Committee with Mr Peter Brannen as Chair. The liaison officer for most of the period of the study was Kathleen Greaves, a role assumed by Dennis Brooks in its latter stages. The authors are most grateful for the advice and creative contribution of the Steering Committee and liaison officers.

Permission to use data from the Census of Employment on the NOMIS database was granted by Statistics Branch, Department of Employment. Data from the Regional Office Information Systems were supplied by the Department of Trade and Industry.

The sample was drawn through the services of the National Unemployment Benefit System, Department of Health and Social Security.

The design of the interview questionnaire owed much to Gillian Courtenay of Social and Community Planning Research (SCPR). SCPR carried out the piloting and fieldwork for the interviews, under Gillian Courtenay's direction, and were responsible for coding, data preparation and preliminary analysis.

The analysis of local labour market data was carried out in collaboration with Michael Coombes and his colleagues at the Centre for Urban and Regional Studies (CURDS), University of Newcastle-upon-Tyne. Thanks to their generous help it became possible to expand this aspect of the study considerably beyond what was originally envisaged.

The secondary analysis made use of the Manpower Services Commission's National On-Line Information System (NOMIS), programmed and developed at the Department of Geography, University of Durham, by R. Nelson and P. Dodds.

Survey analysis was performed by means of the Quantum system on a PCS-Cadmus computer. For multivariate analysis, the Generalised Linear Interactive Modelling System (GLIM) was used, on a Research Machines PC-186 microcomputer.

Within the Policy Studies Institute, assistance was provided by Don Badendoch. The final report was laserset at PSI by Karin Erskine and Clare Pattinson.

The authors are grateful to all these for their help and most of all to the young people who took part in the interviews and the follow-up study.

# Summary

This summary is confined to a listing of the main findings of the research. Further integration and interpretation of the findings is provided in Chapter 10, 'Conclusions and Implications'.

## 1. The study
The report is based on a sample survey which has been weighted to give a nationally representative picture of those in the 18-24 age group who have spent six months or longer in their current registered unemployment. The aim of the survey has been to contribute to understanding of the influences upon labour market behaviour and outcomes in this group.

The analysis is based on interviews with 1620 young men and 852 young women. The response rate at fieldwork was 73 per cent. There was a particular emphasis upon collecting complete labour market histories from age 16, and upon analysing other objective labour market information such as individual qualifications or attainments, movements between industries and occupations, and data on pay and hours of work.

In addition, a study was made of the local labour market context of 20 travel-to-work areas, within which two thirds of the sample were located. This study involved analysis of secondary sources of information for the period 1971-81.

## 2. The local labour market background
The young unemployed people in the sample tended to be concentrated in areas of declining employment. Of the 20 travel-to-work areas

analysed, 17 had experienced employment contraction during 1971-81 at above the national rate.

Employment loss in these areas could be largely attributed to contraction in manufacturing, which in its turn could be accurately inferred from knowledge of the local industry structure and national trends by industry. Changes in service employment, however, were less predictable: some areas with considerable losses of manufacturing employment had substantially increased service employment, whereas in others the development of service employment had been greatly retarded.

Employment could also be accounted for in terms of occupations. Loss of employment, in the aggregate, was almost wholly confined to manual occupations; non-manual employment had grown or remained stable even in areas experiencing large overall contraction.

Many of the local labour markets had experienced relative increases in the size of the 16-24 age group during 1971-81, and this may have contributed to youth unemployment.

There was little sign of adaptation in the skill levels of local workforces to the changing labour markets of the 1971-81 period. Moreover, although qualifications attained by school leavers in each area were generally increasing over the period, the relative position of localities in terms of qualifications tended to persist. Hence many of these localities were characterised both by above-average proportions of less-skilled workers and by below-average proportions of qualified school leavers.

## 3. Where did this group fit into the labour market?
To establish where this group was located in the labour market, we examined the job most representative of their career to date, and their educational and vocational qualifications.

Excluding those who had yet to find their first job, we found that about nine tenths had come from the 'lower part' of the labour market; manual, personal service, and junior non-manual jobs. Even within this range, skilled manual and junior non-manual jobs were under-represented.

But, relative to the part of the job market in which they were competing, these young people were not under-qualified. The proportions without any qualification were in line with national statistics for this age group in these kinds of jobs.

Among those with qualifications, there was quite a wide variety by level and type, and the general qualification level was higher in the younger half of the sample (except for apprenticeships). It was only among those with two or more years of continuous unemployment that non-qualification approached the levels found in earlier studies of long-term unemployment.

The young long-term unemployed cannot therefore be regarded as a distinct 'low attainment' group within the lower part of the labour market, but rather as fairly typical of the prevalent low level of qualifications among young workers in manual and lower non-manual occupations.

## 4.  Social background and individual attainments

To an exceptional degree this group cam from large families, and more than one in six were from single-parent family backgrounds. Their housing was an unexceptional mix of council rented and owner occupied properties.

Housing, family size and (to a lesser extent) single-parent family upbringing were all found to be connected to individual attainments. (In this report we have assumed that the practical significance of social background, relative to employment, is its effect on individual attainments, and it is the latter which have been analysed in detail).

## 5.  Ethnic minority groups

Ethnic minority groups were considerably over-represented among the young long-term unemployed, and constituted seven per cent of the estimated population. Ethnic minority groups were found to have had particular difficulties in employment, but were not less qualified than the sample as a whole.

## 6.  Work patterns

From our analyses of the labour market histories of the respondents, three main 'patterns' have been identified.

First there were those who had spent most of their time in work, and whose longest job had lasted for two years or more. These can be regarded as relatively stable workers who have been displaced into unemployment. They were almost all from the 21-24 age range (who entered the labour market in 1975-79) and constituted nearly one half of this age group. We refer to these as the 'displaced' group.

In contrast, there was a group whose members had never held a job up to the time of interview. These were mostly, although not all, within the 18-20 age range, of which they comprised nearly 40 per cent. We refer to these as the 'excluded' group because of their difficulty in entering employment.

The contrasting experience of these two groups can most simply be accounted for by change in labour demand from the 1975-79 to the 1980-84 period. Not only did the young long-term unemployed get fewer jobs when entering the labour market after 1979, but they were much less able to get long-lasting jobs than had been the case with the older group in the sample, who had entered the labour market in the latter part of the 1970s.

The third group consisted of those who had held one or more jobs, but had not worked as much or as stably as the 'displaced' group. In fact many of these had had several different jobs of short duration, and were therefore similar to the 'recurrent unemployed' or 'young job changers' of much previous research.

## 7. Fragmentation of labour market experience

Experience in the labour market can be analysed in terms of the number of separate 'spells' or changes of status which the young people have passed through. An analysis of this type overlaps with that in section 6 above.

Although there were fewer jobs in 1980-84 than in the late 1970s, the degree of fragmentation among these young people actually increased. This was partly because such jobs as were available lasted for relatively short periods, and also because of increasing participation in government job creation and work experience schemes, notably the Youth Opportunities Programme.

## 8. Structure of past employment

Although lower labour demand (as reflected in the changes described in section 6) appeared to be the main influence after 1980, position in the industrial and occupational structure probably helps to explain why these young people had a high risk of becoming unemployed.

They were not evenly distributed through the employment structure. Rather, they were over-represented in occupational and industrial groups which have above average levels of unskilled, temporary, or seasonal jobs, and also in small firms. Conversely, they were under-represented in most 'white collar' occupations, in the engineering and related industries with their tradition of training for manual skills, and in the public sector.

## 9. New jobs

Between February and June 1984 16 per cent of this young unemployed group had found new jobs and were in them at the time of interview.

The characteristics of the new jobs seemed in part a continuation of past tendencies but there also appeared to be some new or emergent tendencies.

These latter included a shift towards self-employment among the men; a movement into part-time work among women, led by but by no means confined to those who were married; and a smaller move into part-time work among single men.

The follow-up survey in late 1985 showed that, by then, 40 per cent had obtained a job. Among those with one year or more of unemployment (at time of sampling), the proportion was 29 per cent, the same as was found in the 1980/81 DE/PSI survey. However, the jobs found in 1984-85 appeared to be more stable than the earlier survey, or the previous employment histories of the individuals, would have led one to expect.

## 10. The influence of qualifications

As noted, the young long-term unemployed were as a whole qualified to the expected extent for the mix of jobs from which they came.

It has sometimes been argued that qualifications have little influence on events in the lower part of the labour market. However, we found that qualifications had wide and important influences on the labour market outcomes within the young long-term unemployed group.

Broadly speaking, we found that qualifications:
increased the proportion of time spent in work;
reduced the duration of unemployment;
raised the chances of relatively long-lasting, stable jobs;
yielded better-paid jobs, especially jobs in the public sector;
improved the chances of getting a new job after long-term unemployment;

and became progressively more important as time in unemployment lengthened.

But there were differences in the importance of different kinds of qualification for men and women. For men, a combination of vocational with educational (school examination) qualifications was most advantageous. Educational qualifications on their own gave less consistent advantages, although this became increasingly important as time went on. For women, however, all qualifications whether vocational or educational were highly advantageous.

There were indications that educational qualifications below the level of CSE grade 1 passes were of some value in labour market competition.

Because various labour market outcomes tended to be affected by the type and level of qualification, it can be inferred that employers were to some extent responsive to gradations of qualification.

## 11. Car driving licence

Having a car driving licence considerably increased chances of getting back to work. The driving licence can be regarded as another kind of qualification or attainment, but it is distinct from educational or vocational qualifications.

The importance of having a driving licence increased as time went on in unemployment, as did the importance of other qualifications.

In addition, those with car driving licences had generally spent a larger proportion of time in work overall, and were less likely to experience very protracted unemployment.

It should be noted that, as well as being a form of qualification, the car driving licence may directly increase mobility in the job market, a topic discussed in section 14 below.

## 12. Government schemes

About half the men and 40 per cent of the women in this survey had attended a government training or work experience scheme. Most of these placements had been on the Youth Opportunities Programme (YOP), subsequently discontinued. The timing of the study means that it does not include any participants in the Youth Training Scheme. A small proportion had been on the Community Programme (CP), or were on placements at the time of the 1984 interview. CP placements became more important to the group during 1984-85.

Of those attending YOP, many had either entered relatively late after leaving school or had been placed on more than one scheme. These circumstances were associated with reduced chances of employment subsequently.

There appeared to be a substantial degree of selection into CP placements, although this conclusion is based on a small sample of participants. Earlier entrants into CP seemed better qualified than later entrants, a finding which may suggest a degree of queuing. Those becoming long-term unemployed again after CP placements appeared to have particularly low qualifications.

## 13. Training and experience

The majority of the group had had some formal training in their most representative job so far, but usually this was limited to on-the-job instruction by a supervisor or trainer. More elaborate forms of training - involving classroom instruction in the firm or attendance at external classes - had been received by only a small minority.

In new jobs, the amount of formal training provided was substantially less than in the most representative previous jobs. This accords with other research evidence in suggesting that (in lower-level jobs, at least) training is given soon after individuals enter the labour market, and is progressively less available thereafter.

Accordingly, those making changes of occupation or industry - as was usually the case with the present group - may receive relatively little training specifically relevant to their new jobs.

We looked for ways in which training in past employment might influence further employment - either by improving the chances of getting a new job, or by raising the quality (for example, the pay level) of new jobs. But there proved to be no clear influence of this type. In contrast to formal qualifications, job-related training seemed to count for little. The only exception was training received as part of a vocational qualification such as an apprenticeship.

Job experience also seemed to offer little advantage for this group of young people. Those entering the labour market in 1975-79 had accumulated far more work experience than those entering in 1980-83, but during 1984-85 this gave them no advantage in finding jobs. Among the young men, it was those entering the labour market in

1980-83 who had the better chances of returning to work despite their extremely limited work experience.

## 14. Job search

The great majority of young people (almost 90 per cent overall) regarded themselves as active job seekers. However, the proportion who had effectively ceased to look for employment, although small appeared to have increased by comparison with the 1980/81 DE/PSI survey of long-term unemployment.

In addition, about 20 per cent of those who regarded themselves as job seekers had made no job application the previous year.

Those making substantial numbers of job applications were distinguished from those making few job applications, or ceasing job search altogether, by the same characteristics as best predicted success in finding a new job. These were educational and vocational qualifications, possession of a car driving licence, and a period in unemployment which was not too long. Young women who had become mothers were particularly likely to drop out of the labour market. Otherwise, those dropping out of job search tended to be those without qualifications, without a car driving licence, and with a long period of unemployment already behind them.

The level of job search activity could be considerably influenced, however, by support received, in the form of information about possible jobs, either from Jobcentre staff or from family and friends. Both kinds of support appeared, in practice, to be given quite independently of young people's qualifications, and this increased the value of the support. Conversely, those lacking these types of support would be at a serious disadvantage.

The proportion of young people in long-term unemployment receiving support from Jobcentres, in the form of job information, appeared to have decreased since the 1980/81 DE/PSI survey, but this support was evenly distributed rather than (as in 1980/81) being concentrated on those with the best chances of being employed.

Job search was examined in the survey in terms of spatial mobility as well as frequency of job applications. However, the two aspects were strongly associated. Those prepared to consider jobs within a wide radius, or to visit areas outside their normal reach, were also likely to be those who made more frequent job applications.

Spatially extensive job search was influenced by the possession of qualifications and a car driving licence.

As noted previously, many of the young long-term unemployed (and not only women) had moved into part-time work in their new jobs. As expected, this was linked to search for part-time work, but the link was not as simple or clear as might be supposed. Whereas some of those getting part-time jobs were looking exclusively for full-time work up to that point, many more who were interested in part-time work (along with full-time work) ended in full-time work.

Search for or movement into part-time jobs was, for women, limited to localised job search, but for single men acceptance of part-time work was linked with spatially extensive job search.

## 15. Pay, and pay flexibility
In their most representative jobs to date, the young long-term unemployed as a whole had received pay at a level about 70-75 per cent of the average for their age group - or between the lower decile and lower quartile for their age group (within sex). This was broadly as would be expected, in view of their labour market position.

It appeared that pay levels had fallen considerably within the group between the 1975-79 and 1980-83 periods. In part this was the result of movement into lower level jobs rather than lower pay for comparable jobs.

In 1984, there was a strong tendency for those who had held relatively high-paid jobs in the past to have reduced their pay expectations. These were mainly in the over-20 age group. But those with relatively low-paid jobs in the past continued to expect increases in new jobs, and often expected substantial (greater than £10/week) increases. Those expecting increases outnumbered those expecting decreases.

These pay expectations, however, had little systematic influence on the chances of getting new jobs or on actual pay levels in new jobs.

Several factors blurred the relationship between expectations and outcomes. (i) The majority had minimum acceptable levels of pay far below their expectations. (ii) In practice the majority took new jobs at pay levels below their expectations. (iii) Conversely, those who expected substantial decreases often achieved higher pay than they had expected. More generally, one may point to imperfect information about pay expectations on the demand side and to the custom of employers making pay offers rather than ascertaining pay expectations.

It appeared that the range of pay in the available new jobs was narrower than in former jobs. Similarly, whereas in former jobs there was a tendency for public sector employers to pay the most, followed by large private sector firms and then small firms, in the new jobs these differences were much diminished.

Those who were 'trading down' from higher to lower pay levels appeared to achieve some competitive advantage over the remainder, but this advantage was slight.

Average wages in the new jobs were four per cent lower than corresponding previous jobs among the men, and 12 per cent lower in the case of women. However the figure for women was influenced by movement into part-time jobs. These results must also be contrasted with the customary increase in pay for young people moving from juvenile to adult rates.

## 16. Industrial and occupational flexibility

The work histories of the young long-term unemployed showed very high degrees of industrial and occupational flexibility. Only about one third had remained in the same industries, and one fifth in the same occupations, as those in which they began work. (This is based on the broad 10-industry, 16-occupation groupings of the OPCS 1980 classification).

In new jobs at the time of the study, this tendency to change industry and occupation continued. Only one third of the new jobs were in the same industry, and only one third in the same occupation, as in the job considered most representative up to the time of unemployment.

Those who had moved industry or changed occupation were not found to have different proportions of time in work, nor to be any more or less likely to get a new job, than those who remained in the same industry or occupation. For men only, there were some pay advantages for those who had been able to stay in the same industry in their new jobs.

Of those who had held two or more jobs prior to current unemployment, about one in three had experienced downward mobility. This movement into less advantageous jobs was associated with moves across industries.

# 1   Introduction

Youth unemployment has progressively emerged, since the 1970s, as one of the chief problems of labour markets in most of the countries of the industrialized world.  This has, for example, been identified as a priority area of social policy in the European Community[1]. In Britain, the particular problems of young people in the labour market has led to numerous measures both by the Labour administration of 1974-79 and in the subsequent Conservative governments, ranging from employment subsidies and special job creation schemes, to temporary schemes of work experience, and now to permanent schemes of work-based training[2].

Despite these measures, prolonged periods of unemployment have, during the early part of the 1980s, become considerably more prevalent among young people in the labour market.  Knowledge of the backgrounds, labour market experiences, and prospects of this group of young people has remained slight.  There have been two large studies of long-term unemployment, but neither was focused upon young people, and as both pre-dated the main growth in levels of long-term youth unemployment, the information which they provided about this group was limited[3].

The study reported here is intended to fill this gap in knowledge about the young people experiencing greatest difficulties in the labour market.  Its aim is to contribute towards a better understanding and interpretation of the labour market processes which lead up to, or are consequent upon, long-term unemployment among 18-24 year olds.

The basis for the study consisted in a national survey of people aged between 18 and 24, who had spent a continuous or nearly continuous[4] period of six months or more registered for benefit as unemployed, at the sampling date early in February 1984.

Taking six months as the qualifying period for inclusion in the survey departed from the customary definition of long-term unemployment as a period of one year or more. But there were strong practical reasons to include the group with between six and 12 months of unemployment: they were eligible for placement on the Community Programme scheme, at the time of the study the largest special programme designated for the long-term unemployed, and for a number of other special initiatives. The wider base for the survey not only makes it more relevant to these programmes, but also increases the range of comparisons which can be made with its results.

Much research into unemployment, in recent times, has been designed on the assumption that a current spell of unemployment cannot be fully understood except as part of a sequence of events experienced by the individual. This is also the assumption of the present study. The design of the 1984 survey placed particular emphasis upon obtaining a detailed 'labour market history' of each respondent from the age of 16 until the time of the interview. The study is able, as a result, not only to examine the current period of unemployment of those in the sample, but also the general position of the young people in the labour market over a period of years.

What happens after unemployment is, of course, at least equally important as what has gone before, especially from the viewpoint of understanding the practical consequences of prolonged unemployment. To obtain some information on this score, a small follow-up survey, covering a subsample of the original sample, was conducted in Autumn 1985, about 16 months after the initial interview. The findings from this follow-up survey permit us to assess both the prospects for the young long-term unemployed of finding new jobs, and the degree of stability in those jobs once obtained.

Unemployment is not only a national economic problem, it is also a problem which varies in form and severity from one area or locality to another. Inner city areas have come to be regarded as having special problems of unemployment, and of youth unemployment in particular - a perspective already clearly established in the writings (relating to the USA) of Myrdal 25 years ago[5]. The study of unemployment at local level has become a policy interest of local government[6] and of central government[7]. The analysis of employment data at the level of the locality or the local labour market has been advanced by the work of economic geographers[8] and of sociologists[9].

The design of the present study was in part intended to yield analysis at the level of local labour markets, but without sacrificing the goal of providing a nationally representative sample. This goal was pursued not only in the sampling design for the main survey, but also through supplementary analysis of secondary data for the 20 main local labour markets (excluding Greater London) covered by the national survey. Hence this report goes somewhat beyond the conventional presentation of survey research. It includes an extensive discussion of the contextual data on the 20 labour markets, and an analysis of the relationship between the contextual data and the survey data.

This introduction is intended to serve four purposes. First, the background to the study is briefly sketched in terms of overall changes of demand and supply in the labour market during the period 1975-84, and of the growth of long-term unemployment among 18-24 year olds during the early years of the 1980s. Second, we outline the main kinds of explanation which have so far been put forward by labour market theorists covering youth unemployment. Third, some further details are provided about the sources of information used in this study, including an outline of the scope, sampling, and response rates. (Further details of a technical nature are provided in Appendix 1.) Fourth, some of the conventions of presentation used in this report are introduced, in the hope of making it easier to read or refer to.

## The background of labour demand and supply

Before commencing upon the evidence of this study, it may be helpful to outline the main changes in labour supply and demand which took place during the period of 1975 to 1984 when the sample was entering the labour market. These changes can be thought of as the backcloth against which the actions and experiences of individuals in the labour market have taken place. However it is not our aim to embark on a searching review of the developments, but only to provide a few simple 'aide-memoires' for the period.

On conventional measures of demand, the period 1975-79 was one of slow recovery from the 1975 depression, but it was also one in which manufacturing industry continued to contract in terms of employment. Between the latter part of 1979 and 1982, however, this recovery was sharply reversed. Roughly speaking, unemployment doubled while officially notified vacancies decreased by approximately the same factor[10]. Hence, in terms of the index of labour demand provided by the unemployment-vacancies ratio, demand had declined by a factor of four within two years. (However we would stress that the unemployment-vacancies ratio has no absolute status as a measure of labour demand, especially as statistics of vacancies are themselves incomplete.) As was already occurring in the 1970s, there were substantial net losses of employment in manufacturing industries, with particularly large waves of redundancies in 1980 and 1981[11]. Moreover, employment in service industries, which had increased substantially in the 1970s and hence partially offset the employment losses in manufacturing, now flattened out and even fell back at the lowest point of the trough. Towards the end of the period under consideration, another gradual recovery of demand was under way, but manufacturing continued to shrink in terms of employment, while employment growth was once more concentrated in services[12].

While this thumbnail sketch of events on the demand side is probably both familiar and uncontroversial, the developments on the supply side were not brought together in a coherent form until the review of the labour force from 1971 with projections to 1991, published by the Department of Employment (*Employment Gazette*, July 1985). The period of particular concern to the present study (1975-84) was one in which the population of working age grew steadily - by a total of 1.8 million people - largely as a result of the 'baby boom' of the 1960s. This is evidently a point of particular relevance to the present study: the young people in our sample came precisely from that relatively large birth cohort which was raising the size of the working population in this period.

It appears, therefore, that the difficulties on the demand side may have been exacerbated by demographic growth in the labour supply.

However, closer examination of the labour force estimates shows that the growth in the labour force took place up to and including 1979 but not between 1980 and 1984. This was true both of the total labour force and of young workers in particular. So far as the total labour force was concerned, the larger population of working age was after 1979 offset by higher rates of early retirement and by a checking of growth in female participation (which was renewed only at the end of the period). Similarly, despite the growth in the size of the 16-24 age group in the population, its presence in the labour force did not increase after 1979, because it was offset by a reduction in participation rates. Here the role of government schemes may have been important in stabilizing what would otherwise have been an accumulating over-supply of young workers.

Although in aggregate terms the labour force did not change much during 1980-84, this does not necessarily mean that there were no supply effects. The withdrawal of many older workers into early retirement, and the retention of young people in government schemes, are themselves indications of supply-side pressures. More subtly, the effect of an increase in the population of working age relative to demand may be to give employers increased scope to recruit and retain workers from prime age groups and from among those with qualifications (where this term is used in the broadest sense). The aggregate labour force may remain static, but this is likely to be because of the withdrawal or 'holding back' of some of those with the least power to compete for jobs. Hence, despite the static aggregate picture, competition for jobs can intensify in a qualitative sense.

This outline of changes in aggregate demand and supply does not, of course, necessarily apply to particular regions or localities. On the contrary, studies have shown that there has been wide variation in the local experience of employment changes, economic activity changes, and inward and outward migration[13]. Particular inner city areas have become known for their concentrations of youth unemployment - parts of Liverpool provide a case in point[14]. Not only may particular areas undergo unusually large contractions of their established industries, but in addition such areas may be affected by an age structure which leaves them with many hard-to-employ young people relative to the total resources of skill in the community. This can happen, for example, because the best-qualified prime-age people move out, taking advantage of their position in national job markets to escape from local industrial decline, while school leavers or young adults from less mobile families are themselves less likely to be qualified and less able to move.

## Rising youth unemployment in the 1980s

In his review of the development of youth unemployment, Wells has shown that until around 1970 there was an excess demand for juvenile

5

and young adult workers, but that subsequently the position was progressively reversed, so that by the latter part of the 1970s the supply of young people to the labour market outran demand[15]. Even by the end of the 1970s, however, youth unemployment was only about one third of the level attained by the mid-1980s. Despite the long development of the problem of youth unemployment, its specially rapid acceleration during the 1980s requires particular attention because of the implications which it has for the present study.

A large component of the growth of long-term youth unemployment was simply the increase of total unemployment in the early 1980s, taking youth unemployment with it. Unemployment doubled in the course of little more than one year. In this period youth unemployment (that is, all unemployment in the 18-24 year old group) increased in line with total unemployment. From 1982 onwards, however, as total unemployment began to stabilize or to increase only relatively slowly, youth unemployment grew slightly more rapidly and so increased its share of total employment. This is shown in Figure 1.1(a) overleaf, which provides separate graphs for male and female unemployment.

But though the increase in youth unemployment as a percentage of total unemployment was slow, the increase of long-term youth unemployment as a proportion of all youth unemployment was much more rapid. This is shown in Figure 1.1(b), again with separate graphs for males and females. Among young unemployed men, at the beginning of 1981 about one third had been unemployed for six months or more, while by the end of 1984 the proportion was a little above one half. Among young women, the initial proportion was also about one third, and this grew to about 45 per cent.

The graphs also show that all the change in the distribution of unemployment durations among young people was concentrated in the group with one year or more of unemployment. The proportions in the group with 6-12 months of unemployment showed no consistent trend over the period, but the proportion with the longer periods of unemployment moved steadily upwards.

These analyses show the grounds for concern about the growth of long-term unemployment among 18-24 year olds. Not only was youth unemployment as a whole more than doubling over the period of the early 1980s, but there was a steady redistribution taking place into the more prolonged unemployment periods.

# Figure 1a

**Youth unemployment as a percentage of total unemployment (Male)**

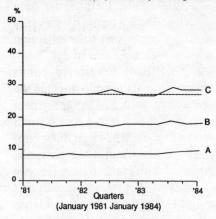

C = Nos. unemployed aged 18-24 as a
    percentage of total unemployment.

B = Nos. unemployed aged 20-24 as a
    percentage of total unemployment.

A = Nos. unemployed aged 18-19 as a
    percentage of total unemployment.

**Youth unemployment as a percentage of total unemployment (Female)**

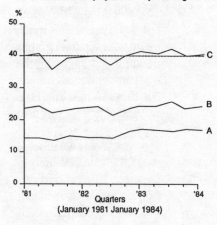

C = Nos. unemployed aged 18-24 as a
    percentage of total unemployment.

B = Nos. unemployed aged 20-24 as a
    percentage of total unemployment.

A = Nos. unemployed aged 18-19 as a
    percentage of total unemployment.

## Figure 1b

Youth Unemployment (for 26-52 and 52+ weeks) as a percentage of total youth unemployment (Male)

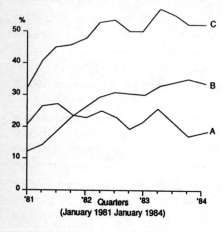

C = Youth unemployment (aged 18-24) for over 26 weeks as a percentage of total youth unemployment

B = Youth unemployment (aged 18-24) for 52+ weeks as a percentage of total youth unemployment

A = Youth unemployment (aged 18-24) for 26-52 weeks as a percentage of total youth unemployment

Youth Unemployment (for 26-52 and 52+ weeks) as a percentage of total youth unemployment (Female)

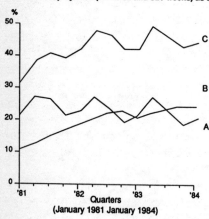

C = Youth unemployment (aged 18-24) for over 26 weeks as a percentage of total youth unemployment

B = Youth unemployment (aged 18-24) for 52+ weeks as a percentage of total youth unemployment

A = Youth unemployment (aged 18-24) for 26-52 weeks as a percentage of total youth unemployment

The developments just summarised refer to changes in the stocks of young people in unemployment: that is, the totals counted at particular points in time. These are the figures which nearly always receive the chief attention when unemployment is being discussed, whether in Parliament or in the press, radio and television. It cannot be stressed too strongly that this figure, the unemployment stock count is itself merely the outcome of two more basic processes: the rate of inflow and the rate of outflow, accumulated over a period. Hence the stock at the end of a given period is equal to the opening stock at the beginning of the period, plus entrants during the period, minus leavers during the period.

Any attempt to understand unemployment, rather than merely describing its course, must consider both the inflow to unemployment and the outflow. This becomes all the more important if we are concerned with long-term unemployment. Over the period under consideration, the general growth in unemployment resulted from a small increase in the inflow combined with a considerable decrease in the outflow[16]. In other words, the risk of becoming unemployed increased a little, but once unemployed, the difficulty of getting back into a job increased considerably. Hence long-term unemployment was a major component of rising unemployment: increasing numbers of the people entering unemployment were 'stuck' there.

It is also important to note that the inflows to unemployment can be not only from jobs but from other positions, and the outflows similarly are not only into jobs. In the case of youth unemployment, entry into unemployment may often be either directly from full-time education, or from participation in government training scheme or special employment scheme. Exits from unemployment may, similarly, often take place into government schemes or, particularly in the case of young women, into the domestic economy as housewife and mother.

The available government statistics do not permit a detailed analysis of the flows into and out of youth unemployment over the period 1975-1985[17]. However, the present survey, although based on a sample from the stock of long-term unemployed young people, gives some insight into both inflows and outflows, since we both have the previous work histories of those in the sample, and some follow-up information over a period of 16 months.

### Explanations of youth unemployment

Various explanations or theories have been advanced to account for the growth of youth unemployment in Britain or in other Western industrial nations. The academic literature on this topic, whether in economics, economic geography, or sociology, is indeed extensive. We will not attempt to review this literature systematically. Rather, we will confine ourselves to a brief outline of those ideas which have influenced the design and analysis of the present study, expressing those in the way which has seemed most helpful for our own objectives.

The most obvious line of explanation is to relate youth unemployment to changes in aggregate macroeconomic demand in product markets. The rise in unemployment in the early 1980s is then interpreted as a consequence of downswing in the business cycle, exacerbated by the 1979 oil shock into a serious economic depression. If this view of unemployment is correct, it accounts for youth unemployment to the extent that youth unemployment is proportionate to total unemployment. Because youth unemployment has risen more than total unemployment, some additional assumptions have to be introduced, but this is not difficult. Indeed, it has long been observed that cyclical unemployment tends to fall more heavily on young workers than on older workers, and there are common-sense reasons why this should be so. Most plausibly, employers tend to curtail recruitment during such periods, and there is no doubt whatever that young workers are most dependent on the existence of a flow of vacancies, both because many of them are entering the labour market for the first time, and because they are much more likely to leave jobs than are older workers.

One shortcoming of this explanation is that it would predict a more rapid reduction of youth unemployment than has actually taken place in the economic recovery since 1982. If it is the case that lack of vacancies affects the young disproportionately, should not an expansion of vacancies also disproportionately speed up the reemployment of young people? Equally, it does not cope with the gradually declining employment position of young people in the 1970s, even before the 1979 oil shock and 1980-81 recession. In other words, there is a longer-term persistence about the disadvantages of young workers, which a purely cyclical view of demand cannot cope with.

To explain these longer-term trends, it has been argued that the relative wages of young workers put them, during the 1970s, in a progressively more difficult position. That there has been such an effect seems very probable[18]. Young workers have, through much of the post-war period in Britain, enjoyed wages which (as a percentage of adults' wages) were considerably higher than in most European nations. This would, according to standard economic arguments, tend to depress employers' demand for workers of this age group, other things being equal. Until the end of the 60s the excess demand for juvenile and young adult workers (already referred to in the preceding section) masked the influence of high relative youth wages. But as the supply of young people increased and demand decreased, high relative wages became an obstacle to youth employment.

The next question to be posed, however, is whether young people in long-term unemployment have been prepared to take lower wages in order to get back into work. If they have not, then wages could be an important explanation of persistent long-term unemployment to this age group. If, on the other hand, they have, then other, possibly less simple, explanations would have to be considered.

Suppose, for the moment, that young people are not prepared to move to lower paid employment. That, in its turn, would require explanation. Two connected ideas, which have been advanced to explain individual wage rigidity concern the influence of state benefits and the value placed upon leisure. The existence of benefits might shift individuals' perceptions of acceptable wages upwards: the 'dole' may be subtracted from the pay on offer, and this difference, rather than the pay itself, used to judge whether the job is worth having. Similarly, if leisure is highly valued (and especially if the availability of state benefits makes more leisure accessible), then jobs would have to pay correspondingly better to attract young people. Put together, these ideas suggest the possible existence of a section of young people acclimatised to life in unemployment and willing to leave it only for reasonably well-paid jobs.

The kinds of explanations considered so far derive from long established lines of economic theory and conceptualization[19]. More recently, the human capital school of economics has drawn attention to the role of qualifications, training and experience in relation to pay and productivity; and these seem likely to be important for youth unemployment also.

Indeed, there is plenty of evidence that young unemployed people tend to have levels of qualification and experience much below the average for their society[20]. But one must take care to specify how human capital affects the chances of long-term unemployment. Let us assume, for example, that qualifications, training and experience mainly act as a means of competition between people seeking jobs. Broadly speaking, then, the more qualified get the better jobs, the less qualified the less attractive jobs or no job at all. In that case, human capital determines the distribution of unemployment, but not the amount of unemployment. Some quite separate explanation will still be needed to explain the unemployment level.

A purely distributive view of the role of human capital might, despite this limitation, be useful precisely for explaining youth unemployment. If a high or increasing level of unemployment is 'given' then as young people strive to join the labour force, the least qualified may be kept out as an unemployed residue. Also, depending on whether the quality of young entrants and workers is higher or lower, employers may decide either to favour them for their recruitment needs, or to take more experienced workers instead. The latter course may be more easily pursued at a time of high unemployment because more experienced workers will have lost their jobs and so be available on the market.

A stronger, or more extreme, view is that among labour market entrants there may be a section whose qualification level is too low for most jobs which need to be filled. In other words, this section of the youth labour force is virtually unemployable under present conditions. Such a view has some points of contact with the explanation based on relative wage levels, since 'unemployable' could mean, more precisely, 'unemployable at presently conceivable minimum wages'. On the other hand, the notion of qualification levels which are too low for existing jobs may also have something 'structural' about it: that is, the structure of jobs may have changed in a way which excludes more of the lower-qualified than hitherto.

There is however a variety of other structural explanations, and these form the final class to be considered here. One of the most important structural explanations of long term unemployment was put forward by Myrdal[21] 25 years ago, and particularly directed towards the inner city problems of the USA. Myrdal pointed to a persistent and widening gap between social investment (especially in education and training) on one hand, and on the other hand the needs of industry and society for better qualified and more productive workers. It was this gap, he argued, which both held back economic growth and created a permanent 'underclass' in the educationally disadvantaged inner cities.

The underlying structural change which Myrdal assumed concerned the distribution of occupations and the content of jobs; a shift from lower to higher occupations, and a change within jobs, still called by the same names, towards greater educational demands. There is, indeed, strong independent evidence that both types of change have been proceeding on a large scale in Britain[22, 23]. The shift towards greater proportions of higher occupations has been taking place on a long time scale, but has probably accelerated as a result of the great contraction of manufacturing industry since 1975, since manual occupations are heavily concentrated in manufacturing. Structural youth unemployment would then result if too many young people were attempting to locate themselves in the contracting layers of the occupational structure (most types of manual jobs), while too few were positioned in the expanding layers of salaried jobs[24]. It should be noted that low qualifications might not be the only reason for a structural imbalance of occupations. Young people might, for example, attempt to pursue the family's or locality's traditional occupations, even when qualified for entry to better placed jobs. Or the better placed jobs might not be available in the localities which most needed access to them.

If long-term youth unemployment has, in fact, a structural character, that also implies that there are some obstacles or barriers to successful adaptation. For example, once a young person has entered a particular occupational level (for example semi-skilled manual work) it may be difficult to change to a higher level (for example office or technical work) because the individual has 'missed out' on the vocational training required[25]. Here the tying of training to a particular career stage or age acts as an obstacle which keeps out some young people with the right capabilities, and hence reduces flexibility. In the present study, we can look directly at the issues of adaptation and flexibility only on the side of young workers: that is, we can consider how willing they are to move, to try new occupations, or to retrain. But we should not forget that a major source of inflexibility may lie in the institutions of the educational system and the labour market which constrain individual adaptation.

This brief review is sufficient to show that there is no lack of explanations for youth unemployment in all its aspects. There are almost too many plausible ideas available. We hope to achieve in this report a clarification of the relative contributions of the various kinds of explanation.

## Samples and other sources of information

The sample for the survey was based on a stratified design with 11 separate subsamples. These were drawn from each of six metropolitan counties including Greater London, from the City of Glasgow, from large industrial towns (those with more than 75,000 inhabitants), from other industrial towns, from rural areas, and from a cluster of 'prosperous' types of area (suburban localities, high-growth localities, and resort and retirement areas). Northern Ireland was excluded. The classification of localities for the stratification design was based on the work of Webber and Craig[26]. Further technical details are given in Appendix 1. The purpose of the design was to yield sufficient sample sizes in a number of metropolitan areas and large towns to permit separate study with linked contextual data, while at the same time yielding, in the aggregate, a national sample of adequate proportions and representativeness.

Sampling took place in two stages. First, from a list of all unemployment benefit offices in Britain a sample was chosen, within the strata described above, with probability proportional to numbers of 18-24 year olds in long-term unemployment. A random sample of individuals, meeting the criteria of selection, was then generated by the National Unemployment Benefit System computer for each unemployment benefit office in the sample. The samples were always divided in the ratio 2:3 between those 18-24 year olds who had been unemployed for 6-12 months, and those who had been unemployed for one year or more.

The method of data collection for the 1984 survey was personal interviews, using a structured interview schedule which was piloted in May 1984. The main survey fieldwork was carried out by Social and Community Planning Research in June and July 1984. The total sample achieved was of nearly 2500 respondents, with an approximate ratio of 2:1 between young men and young women - in line with the national picture for long-term youth unemployment. The response rate, at 73 per cent of the issued number, can be regarded as good for this type of social survey, although there had been a further seven per cent of loss of the initial sample as some individuals exercised their right to 'opt out' prior to the survey.

From the respondents to this survey, a further subsample was drawn for follow-up by means of a postal questionnaire in Autumn 1985, about 16 months after the initial interview. This subsample was stratified by period of unemployment at time of the original sample, so as to obtain approximately equal numbers of those in the groups with 6-12 months, 13-24 months, and 25 months or more of unemployment. A 'booster' sample was also included to increase representation of those who had held a new job at the time of the 1984 interview: we were anxious to establish how secure these new jobs were. The postal questionnaire, after piloting in September 1985, was sent out in late October 1985. A total of 584 usable replies was received from 971 questionnaires posted - slightly over 60 per cent. This is regarded as satisfactory for a postal questionnaire. Further details are contained in Appendix 1.

To develop the analysis of contextual data concerning local labour markets, the present writers were able to draw upon the expertise of the Centre for Urban and Regional Development Studies (CURDS) at the University of Newcastle. The main sets of data used were the Censuses of Production 1971 and 1981, and the Censuses of Population 1971 and 1981, both of which were analysed to local labour market level by means of the CURDS system of functional regions. This material has been reorganized as a computer 'spreadsheet' for the 20 local labour markets.

We also made use of a specially produced set of tables from the Department of Trade and Industry's Regional Office Information System (ROIS), so as to be able to examine the role of establishment size in employment change; and of educational statistics published by the Department of Education and Science. For more general background, as well as published literature sources we consulted the structure plans or other planning documents supplied by the metropolitan authorities; in several cases they provided additional documents concerning various aspects of employment or unemployment in their areas.

## Presentation of the report

The report begins with the contextual data on local labour markets, in Chapter 2. Chapters 3-9 present the findings from the 1984 interview survey and the 1985 postal follow-up survey. Within the chapters devoted to the survey material, there is a further division between the 'descriptive' (Chapters 3-6) and the 'explanatory' (Chapters 7-9). We apostrophize these terms, because the conventional distinction between them seems to us increasingly dubious. The descriptive material includes accounts of the changes experienced by young people over a period of years, and leads to interpretations of labour market processes which have at least as much value as the more standard explanatory factors considered at a later point.

It has been noted, above, that there were large changes in labour market demand taking place in 1975-84, the period when these young people were competing for jobs. Hence time is one of the main influences which has to be considered in this study.

The period 1980-83, when unemployment in general and long-term youth unemployment in particular were intensifying, was the period when those aged 18-20 in the survey sample were entering the labour market. Conversely, most of those aged 21-24 in our sample entered the labour market during 1975-79, under different conditions. Thus the age-related differences which young people would normally reflect within the 18-24 age group - differences of marital status and housing, of pay rates and job responsibility - were overlaid by the external changes in the economy and in the distribution of employment and income. The time variable in this study represents both age and economic period, inextricably combined.

We have chosen to present the time variables, throughout this report, in terms of 'period of entry to the labour market' for the members of the sample. For example, people who left school at age 18 and entered the labour market in 1980 are counted in our analyses in the same group as people leaving school and entering the labour market at age 16 in 1983. However, most of the sample left school at 16 or 17, so that the degree of blurring in terms of age-groups is slight. The advantage of maintaining clear distinctions in terms of periods of entry to labour markets with different circumstances appears of paramount importance.

The other main distinction which is consistently drawn, in presenting the findings of the surveys, is that between the young men and young women. There is so much evidence now available, for example from the DE/OPCS study of 'women and employment'[27], of gender divisions within the labour market, that the conventional practice of presenting results separately for men and women now takes on a greater necessity. In addition, the different treatment of married men and married women in the state benefit system introduces compositional differences in long-term unemployment, even in the 18-24 year old group. This provides a further reason for maintaining an awareness of gender differences throughout the report.

Finally, it would be wholly unrealistic to suppose that differences between the sexes in marital roles are no longer important. On the contrary, we must suppose that young women are relatively much more likely to leave unemployment and devote themselves to homecare and childcare.

Most of the statistics presented in this report and deriving from the survey have, because of the stratified sample design, been reweighted so as to be representative of all young people in the 18-24 age group with six or more months of unemployment, whether male or female, within Great Britain. For convenience of presentation, an arbitrary total base of 10,000 has been introduced. This can be read as 100.00 per cent, so that any number in any weighted table can be immediately interpreted as a percentage of the total base. For example, the number 761, which is the weighted number in the sample coming from the West Midlands region, can be read as 7.61 per cent of the total population of 18-24 year olds in long-term unemployment. It must of course be borne in mind that the actual sample size was approximately one quarter of the figure 10,000. Although nearly all tables from the surveys are presented in this weighted form, extensive analyses with unweighted tables have been performed to ensure that all the influences identified in this report were present in the data prior to weighting.

In addition, where the mutual influences or associations of sets of variables have needed to be considered together, we have conducted multivariate analyses. These have always been performed on unweighted data. The text presents the results of these multivariate analyses in a schematic way; further technical details can be referred to in Appendix 3.

Not all findings referred to in the text are supported by tables; moreover, some tables are presented in a condensed form so that, for example, they may lack sub-group sample size, standard errors of means, etc. The aim has been to make the statistical material less bulky and more readable. The full table for any finding referred to in the report is available on request from the authors.

The multivariate analyses presented in Appendix 3 incorporate test statistics and goodness of fit statistics of the customary types. However, we have not quoted test statistics in the main body of the text or in the tables. In general, large-sample surveys generate far more differences which would be considered 'significant' by a conventional statistical test, than one could find any practical use for. To illustrate this, let us consider differences under the binominal distribution with the present sample size of 2472. If there are two groups of equal size (n1=n2=1236), and in one the observed proportion of the particular characteristic is 0.50 while in the other it is 0.47, then this would (by conventional procedures) be regarded as statistically significant at the 95 per cent confidence level. Moreover, if the proportions were 0.50 and 0.45, the difference would be significant at the 99 per cent level. In other words, a three per cent difference in proportions would usually be adjudged significant, while a five per cent difference would almost always be adjudged significant.

In the present survey, it is true that one must also take account of the unequal stratified sampling design, which introduces a design effect reducing the significance of differences. The design effect must be calculated for each variable separately, and this is too costly to be pursued. However, an analysis for selected variables[28] suggests that in this study the design effect for means may have been of the order of 1.4. If, therefore, we double the confidence interval about a mean, we should be reasonably safe. This suggests that a difference of 10 per cent will be highly significant. Moreover, if we can predict the direction of the difference in advance (as we would normally expect), this increases the significance of the difference by as much as the design effect reduces it.

But there is usually little practical significance or interest in a difference of much less than 10 per cent, except perhaps where a small difference formed part of a larger pattern of findings. The differences which we point out in the report are generally of at least this magnitude, and usually considerably larger.

In the case of variables measured on a continuous scale (for example, wages), differences must of course be evaluated relative to dispersions and sample sizes. We have generally singled out differences of this sort for comment only if they are at least three times their standard error. In some instances, we draw attention to the fact that apparent differences do not satisfy such a statistical criterion.

In general, then, we have attempted to lighten the text by the omission of discussions of significance, preferring a more practical interpretation. Readers requiring more detailed information to permit them to examine aspects of significance should apply to the authors.

**Table 1.1   Composition of sample by area and sex (unweighted)**

*Absolutes/column percentages*

|  | Total | Male | Female |
|---|---|---|---|
| Greater London | 126 | 78 | 48 |
|  | 5.1 | 4.8 | 5.6 |
| West Midlands | 189 | 128 | 61 |
|  | 7.6 | 7.9 | 7.2 |
| Greater Manchester | 168 | 121 | 47 |
|  | 6.8 | 7.5 | 5.5 |
| Merseyside | 187 | 124 | 63 |
|  | 7.6 | 7.7 | 7.4 |
| West Yorks. | 172 | 104 | 68 |
|  | 7.0 | 6.4 | 8.0 |
| Tyne & Wear | 177 | 118 | 59 |
|  | 7.2 | 7.3 | 6.9 |
| Glasgow | 185 | 131 | 54 |
|  | 7.5 | 8.1 | 6.3 |
| Large industrial towns | 541 | 361 | 180 |
|  | 21.9 | 22.3 | 21.1 |
| Other industrial | 288 | 183 | 105 |
|  | 11.7 | 11.3 | 12.3 |
| Suburban/growth/resort/ retirement | 252 | 157 | 95 |
|  | 10.2 | 9.7 | 11.2 |
| Rural low-growth | 187 | 115 | 72 |
|  | 7.6 | 7.1 | 8.5 |
| *Total* | *2472* | *1620* | *852* |

Note:    For full explanation, see Appendix 1.

The original composition of the achieved sample, by the stratification areas, is shown in Table 1.1. The reweighted version of this table, which also serves as the basis for the reweighting of all other tables, is presented in Table 1.2.

**Table 1.2   Composition of sample reweighted to national basis (Great Britain)**

*Absolutes/column percentages*

|  | Total | Male | Female |
|---|---|---|---|
| Greater London | 812 | 501 | 311 |
|  | 8.1 | 7.7 | 8.9 |
| West Midlands | 761 | 517 | 244 |
|  | 7.6 | 8.0 | 7.0 |
| Greater Manchester | 393 | 283 | 110 |
|  | 3.9 | 4.4 | 3.1 |
| Merseyside | 468 | 311 | 157 |
|  | 4.7 | 4.8 | 4.5 |
| West Yorks. | 649 | 403 | 246 |
|  | 6.5 | 6.2 | 7.0 |
| Tyne & Wear | 409 | 274 | 135 |
|  | 4.1 | 4.2 | 3.8 |
| Glasgow | 389 | 280 | 109 |
|  | 3.9 | 4.3 | 3.1 |
| Large industrial towns | 1775 | 1187 | 588 |
|  | 17.8 | 18.3 | 16.8 |
| Other industrial | 2426 | 1556 | 870 |
|  | 24.3 | 24.0 | 24.8 |
| Suburban/growth/resort retirement | 1553 | 955 | 598 |
|  | 15.5 | 14.7 | 17.0 |
| Rural low-growth | 365 | 224 | 141 |
|  | 3.7 | 3.5 | 4.0 |
| *Total* | *10000* | *6492* | *3508* |

Note:   The total of 10,000 is arbitrary and can be thought of as equivalent to 100.00 per cent.

Finally, there is one general point of interpretation which should be emphasised at the outset, since it applies throughout. The survey cannot be regarded as representative of all youth unemployment, but only of the specific section of the young unemployed defined by the sample. For convenience we will often used the phrase 'young long-term unemployed', or may even on occasion lapse into 'young unemployed', when speaking of the survey, but these should always be regarded as shorthand for the full definition given in this introduction.

It should likewise be noted that the sample concerns the stock of all those who satisfied the definition at the sampling date early in February 1984. Such a stock sample will undoubtedly give a different perspective from that of a longitudinal study of those flowing into long-term unemployment within a particular period. The stock sample will contain, for example, a higher proportion of individuals with poor chances of moving into jobs than would a flow sample.

# 2 The Local Labour Market Context

It was explained in the Introduction that the design of the survey, discussed in the preceding chapters, was partly guided by the aim of setting its results in the context of aggregate data about local labour markets. A particular shortcoming of survey data concerning unemployment is that it provides an extremely limited and fragmentary view of the demand side of the local labour market. The respondents to such surveys can only provide information about their own experiences in the labour market, and however carefully the survey is designed to maintain the objectivity of that information, it cannot overcome the fact that the respondents are not a representative cross-section of all workers. In addition, individuals may tend to focus upon their current position and short-term changes, and have limited awareness of longer-term structural changes in the demand for their labour. The usefulness of local labour market data to complement surveys would be particularly great if the demand side could be better covered as a result.

The work on local labour markets and youth unemployment, has accordingly had as its chief aim an improved treatment of the demand side. The approach requires a synthesis of methods drawn from different disciplines, and involves the development of an interpretation using various forms of information together. In order to facilitate this development, the work has been carried forward cooperatively between the present writers and the Centre for Urban and Regional Development Studies, University of Newcastle

(CURDS). We begin by describing the data sources and methods used for this part of the study.

## Area definitions and sources of data

The first step in developing the present analysis was to decide upon the types of areas on which data would be obtained. For the purposes of analysing demand in the labour market, it is necessary that an area should have reasonably homogeneous conditions of competition between employers for recruitment of labour. For this condition to be satisfied there must be a high degree of closure, all the employers drawing their labour to a large extent from within the defined area. This condition is satisfied to a high degree by the system of functional regions developed by CURDS[1]. The local labour markets defined in the CURDS system are similar to the travel-to-work areas used in presenting national employment and unemployment data.

The chief demand-side data on which the present chapter is based consist of the Census of Employment for the years of 1971 and 1981, by CURDS local labour market areas. In addition, Census of Population data for the same years have been used to provide social indicators and to describe certain aspects of labour supply, and these too have been related to the CURDS local labour market areas.

While these are the chief sources of data used systematically to examine the local labour market background, some others have been introduced in a relatively *ad hoc* manner. Tables were provided by the Department of Trade and Industry to show changes in employment by size of manufacturing establishment, drawn from the DTI's Regional Office Information System (ROIS). For reasons of data quality, the years 1975 and 1981 were selected to make the comparisons, rather than 1971 and 1981. The areas used in the ROIS analysis also differed from the CURDS analyses, using 1970 travel-to-work areas; there is, however, a reasonable degree of similarity between the two definitions.

There was also interest, in view of the importance of qualifications in the survey analysis, in examining the output of qualified school-leavers by locality. Here the only source of information was the published statistical series of the Department of Education and Science, by local education authority areas. These administrative areas correspond rather poorly to local labour markets, but perhaps just sufficiently to make a comparison worthwhile.

The 1984 survey was sampled by unemployment benefit offices, since these provided the most convenient sampling points within the computer database from which the names of individuals were taken. Unemployment benefit offices (UBOs) do not in themselves constitute recognised labour market areas. In some instances there is a reasonable correspondence between the catchment areas of a UBO and the local labour market. This is most obviously the case, for example, when there is only one UBO within the labour market area. Where, as happens in many instances, there are two or more UBOs within the labour market area, the subsample drawn from a single UBO cannot be assumed to be representative of the whole area. The limitation with the design of the present survey is that we cannot, in general, make inferences from the survey data to the local labour market area as a whole. We can, however, use the local labour market data as a context within which the survey data (drawn from within that locality) can be reinterpreted. Our analysis and interpretation flows in one direction only, therefore - from the labour market background data, to the subsamples of survey information based on UBOs.

The survey was stratified by six metropolitan areas and four large industrial towns. In these areas, the survey yielded sufficient numbers of young long-term unemployed people for a separate analysis to be statistically sensible. In each metropolitan area, two or more distinct local labour markets were covered. It was decided, however, to exclude Greater London from the local labour market analysis: a proper analysis of London would require a complete study in its own right[2]. In total, with London excluded, there were 20 local labour markets to be analysed, details of which are given in Appendix 2.

*Accounting for change in employment*
The approach to analysis of the local labour market data is a hybrid of deterministic and statistical methods. The foundation consists of a simplified form of the 'shift-share' analysis which has been widely used by economic geographers[3]. From another point of view the method is similar to variance analysis in management accounting[4]. The underlying idea is to explain, as far as possible, the local or particular by the action of general processes of change. When this has been taken as far as possible, what remains is the genuinely distinctive local element in change, or local deviation from the general picture.

General changes in demand may be transmitted to a local labour market through its industrial structure. If, over a given period, the size of one industry increases by a certain proportion, while that of another decreases by some other proportion, then the simplest possible assumption to be made is that the local industry will be affected in the same proportions. If a locality initially has a large amount of employment in the growing industry, and a small amount in the shrinking industry, it will (other things being equal) tend to increase its available employment. If however the initial pattern is the opposite, then it will tend to have decreasing employment in the aggregate. In this way, from a knowledge of the initial industry structure in the locality, together with national data on employment change by industry, we can calculate the expected changes in employment at local level, and then compare them with the actual changes.

Of course, the changes in any industry are themselves the result of influences which are partly general or macroeconomic and partly specific to the industry. For present purposes, however, this is an issue which is not important. We are not concerned to explain the industrial changes, but only the locality changes.

With additional data organized along the same lines, we can perform a similar analysis for various types or groups of employment - by broad sector, male and female, manual and non-manual, full-time and part-time, and (most relevant for present purposes) for male and female under-25s. Hence for each group we can describe how much change has taken place locally, how far that change was to be expected from general trends taken in conjunction with local industrial structure, and how far the locality has deviated from expectations.

The accuracy with which changes are predicted by this method will of course differ from one locality to another. To assess the efficacy of the method, one should look not at any single example but across a range of cases. Here customary statistical methods can be applied to aid the assessment.

*Explaining local deviations from expectations*
Once the demand-side accounting has been completed, each locality may be described in terms of its deviation from expectations. In principle there are three ways in which such deviations might be explained. On one hand there may be supply-side characteristics of the local labour market which make it likely to do better or worse than

25

expectation. For example, if a locality has had an exceptionally high proportion of unskilled workers, this could lead employers to shun it as an area for investment, and this would result in a fall in employment greater than expectation.

The second type of explanation for local deviations consists in turning back to the demand side and studying it in more detail. The aggregate deviations have been built up from industry variances, and the pattern of these may provide clues to understanding a local labour market's exceptional position. Exceptionally high or exceptionally low employment in public services, for instance, might suggest that demand was being modified by political and fiscal processes at the local level.

Another detailed aspect of demand concerns the distribution of changes by establishment size or industry concentration. For example, it might be reasonable to expect that a labour market would have greater difficulty in assimilating the effects of plant closures, especially if large plants were involved, than in coping with a decline in manufacturing employment through progressive contraction of establishment size (without complete closure).

The third type of explanation of residual deviations of local employment from initial expectations, is through purely spatial influences upon the response to change. The capacity of an industry to grow may depend, for example, on its location relative to other industries (suppliers or customers), or to the motorway network. These locational aspects are beyond the resources of the present study to examine systematically, but they must of course be borne in mind.

**Employment change in 20 local labour markets, 1971-81**
Between 1971 and 1981, employment in Britain fell by about three per cent. As has been shown elsewhere[5], there have been great variations in local losses and gains of employment. Broadly speaking, metropolitan regions have lost most employment, proportionally, with large industrial cities next most adversely affected. The sampling design used in the present study therefore permits attention to be focused upon the areas most affected by loss of employment.

In fact, only two of the 20 local labour market areas had achieved a net increase in employment, while the average decrease in employment, across all 20, was nearly 11 per cent - more than three times the national average. The greatest falls were in Smethwick (on the south-western border of Birmingham) with 26 per cent, Liverpool with 21 per cent, Huddersfield with 20 per cent, Wolverhampton with 18 per cent, and Coventry and Sunderland with 17 per cent.

The concentration of the sample in areas of high unemployment, together with the decision to leave out London from the present analysis, left only one Southern town within its scope. This was Southampton, which had much the most buoyant economy (employment growth of 12 per cent over the decade). Yet variation in the pattern of change does not only exist between North and South. There are striking differences in the rates of change in employment even within a metropolitan region. Merseyside, to give a conspicuous example, encompassed not only Liverpool with its 21 per cent contraction of employment, but Birkenhead with only a five per cent reduction and the prosperous resort of Southport with seven per cent employment growth. Similarly Sunderland had twice the rate of employment loss to Newcastle. And in West Yorkshire, Huddersfield's 20 per cent job loss could be contrasted with Bradford's 11 per cent and Leeds' seven per cent.

Change in employment could be divided into a manufacturing part and a service part. Nationally, as is well known, while manufacturing employment contracted, that of services grew. This was also true of nearly all the 20 local labour markets included in the present sample. It is important to appreciate that, even in these most adversely affected of local labour markets, service employment was generally growing (Liverpool being the outstanding exception). But they were not in most cases growing fast enough to offset the contraction of manufacturing. The falls in manufacturing employment were usually very steep indeed, even if the increases in service employment were substantial.

The total loss of employment in a locality depended, at a simple descriptive level, not only on the rates of change in the two major sectors, but also on the initial sizes of those sectors. Coventry and Huddersfield, although realizing increases in service employment above the national average of 11 per cent, still experienced severe overall contraction of employment because they began the period with particularly large dependence upon manufacturing. The generally high level of dependence on manufacturing in the West Midlands provides an initial explanation for the fact that this area suffered the highest average loss of employment.

Table 2.1 summarizes the evidence concerning change in employment, not only by sector but also by category of employees - male and female, full-time and part-time. These latter results are, like those concerning industry sectors, consistent with what is known of national trends. The net loss of employment in the local labour markets was largely in jobs held by men, and to a much lesser extent in jobs held by women. Part-time jobs were also remaining at a stable level, or increasing somewhat, in these areas, so that most of the loss of employment was in full-time jobs.

**Table 2.1 Employment change 1971-81 in twenty local labour markets**

*Base: total employment in 1971*
*percentage differences*

| | All | Manu-facturing | Ser-vice | Male | Female | Full-time | Part-time |
|---|---|---|---|---|---|---|---|
| Coventry | -17.4 | -23.4 | 7.0 | -17.5 | 0.1 | -20.7 | 3.3 |
| Smethwick | -26.0 | -26.1 | 0.2 | -18.4 | -7.7 | -23.3 | -2.7 |
| Walsall | -12.4 | -22.8 | 8.6 | -11.8 | -0.5 | -14.6 | 2.2 |
| Wolverhampton | -17.7 | -16.2 | 0.5 | -15.5 | -2.2 | -19.0 | 1.3 |
| Bolton | -11.5 | -15.8 | 4.4 | -11.2 | -0.4 | -15.8 | 4.3 |
| Manchester | -10.9 | -12.8 | 2.4 | -10.2 | -0.7 | -14.1 | 3.2 |
| Birkenhead | -5.4 | -10.9 | 6.8 | -11.6 | 6.2 | -11.7 | 6.2 |
| Liverpool | -20.8 | -13.2 | -6.1 | -16.3 | -4.5 | -21.8 | 1.0 |
| Southport | 7.2 | -3.7 | 10.0 | -1.3 | 8.5 | -5.2 | 12.4 |
| Bradford | -10.6 | -18.2 | 7.2 | -9.5 | -1.1 | -13.4 | 2.8 |
| Huddersfield | -19.6 | -23.2 | 4.5 | -14.2 | -5.4 | -18.8 | -0.8 |
| Leeds | -7.1 | -12.7 | 6.0 | -7.1 | 0.0 | -10.1 | 3.0 |
| Newcastle | -8.4 | -8.8 | 4.2 | -9.7 | 1.2 | -12.4 | 4.0 |
| Sunderland | -17.2 | -14.0 | 4.0 | -16.1 | -1.1 | -21.9 | 4.7 |
| Glasgow | -13.4 | -13.8 | 0.7 | -12.1 | -1.4 | -17.1 | 3.6 |
| Motherwell | -11.9 | -15.3 | 7.1 | -12.7 | 0.8 | -16.7 | 4.8 |
| Newport | -13.2 | -13.3 | 0.4 | -15.6 | 2.4 | -16.6 | 3.4 |
| Nottingham | -1.8 | -11.2 | 10.8 | -4.5 | 2.7 | -6.1 | 4.3 |
| Sheffield | -10.7 | -16.6 | 6.9 | -11.4 | 0.6 | -13.4 | 2.6 |
| Southampton | 11.6 | -1.5 | 12.2 | 3.0 | 8.6 | 1.9 | 9.8 |

## Employment change for the 16-24 year old group
The decade of the 1970s was one of considerable demographic change. It could not therefore be assumed that the picture of employment

change in the aggregate, which has been summarized in Table 2.1, applied equally to the 18-24 year olds with which the present study is concerned. The Census of Employment, from which the data are drawn, does not cover the ages of employees, but does yield an analysis by industries[6] for each local labour market. From the Census of Population, the percentages of the 16-24 year old group in the various industries can be calculated, but on a national, not a local, basis. By applying these national percentages to the local industry totals, estimates of the change in employment of 16-24 year olds can be derived for each local labour market. It must be appreciated that this procedure involves an unknown degree of approximation.

Nevertheless, the results of the calculations, shown in Table 2.2, are both consistent and striking. In many cases, the percentage employment loss for the 16-24 year old group was considerably greater than the percentage loss of employment in the local labour market as a whole. There are two probable reasons for this, although they may apply with different force to different areas. One is that many industries were (nationally) reducing their proportionate employment of young people during the period. The other is that young people tend to be concentrated in some of the industries which have experienced severe contraction. Young men, particularly, tend to work in engineering and construction. Local labour markets with large contraction of such industries inevitably faced acute problems of youth employment.

At the same time, the supply of young people has also tended to be at its peak during this decade, and in many of the 20 local labour market areas, there were marked differences between the changes in overall population (mostly static or decreasing) and in the 16-24 population (always increasing substantially). These differences are also summarised in Table 2.2. The table gives an impression of those local labour markets where the problem of youth unemployment is likely to be most acute, as a result of both large decreases in potential employment and large increases in the numbers of young people relative to the local population trend.

## Accounting for loss of employment: the demand side

The descriptive summary of changes in employment to a large extent merely confirms, at a local level, what is known to have been taking place at the aggregate national level. The amount of variation between

29

local labour markets, however, has already been stressed, and this variation calls into question how far the local picture is purely a reflection of national aggregate demand.

**Table 2.2   Estimated employment change for 16-24 year olds, 1971-81**

Base: total 16-24 employment in 1971
percentage differences

| | Male | Female | Total | Total change for all employment |
|---|---|---|---|---|
| Coventry | -14.9 | -2.7 | -17.6 | -17.4 |
| Smethwick | -19.6 | -10.0 | -29.6 | -26.0 |
| Walsall | -13.1 | -4.7 | -17.8 | -12.4 |
| Wolverhampton | -15.6 | -6.5 | -22.1 | -17.7 |
| Bolton | -11.5 | -4.0 | -15.6 | -11.5 |
| Manchester | -12.2 | -6.5 | -18.7 | -10.9 |
| Birkenhead | -14.2 | 2.9 | -11.3 | -5.4 |
| Liverpool | -15.8 | -9.9 | -25.7 | -20.8 |
| Southport | -3.7 | 3.8 | 0.1 | 7.2 |
| Bradford | -11.7 | -5.7 | -17.4 | -10.6 |
| Huddersfield | -16.4 | -9.6 | -16.4 | -19.6 |
| Leeds | -9.0 | -4.9 | -13.9 | -7.1 |
| Newcastle | -11.5 | -2.3 | -13.9 | -8.4 |
| Sunderland | -14.9 | -5.0 | -19.8 | -17.2 |
| Glasgow | -13.4 | -6.5 | -19.9 | -13.4 |
| Motherwell | -14.1 | -4.9 | -19.0 | -11.9 |
| Newport | -15.7 | -1.6 | -17.3 | -13.2 |
| Nottingham | -7.2 | -2.5 | -9.6 | -1.8 |
| Sheffield | -12.9 | -2.9 | -15.8 | -10.7 |
| Southampton | -0.8 | 6.1 | 5.3 | 11.6 |

Using information about the distribution of employment by industry in each locality in 1971, and applying to that base the national changes in employment by industry between 1971 and 1981, we derived the local changes in employment which would be expected if they followed the national trends. These calculations were then separately summed for manufacturing, services, and total employment. Total employment is not simply the sum of manufacturing and services, since it also includes agriculture (very small in all the 20 local labour markets considered here), extractive industry (large in a few cases, such as Sunderland), construction (usually large), and utilities.

## Manufacturing sector

Beginning with manufacturing, we compared the expected change in employment with the actual change recorded over the period (Table 2.3). In general the actual changes were greater than those predicted by the national data, even though the method used takes full account of the actual numbers in the worst affected industries such as iron and steel or textiles. To find an appropriate weighting of the prediction from national data, a regression analysis was applied to the data, and this yielded the following equation:

change in manufacturing employment = 3.4 + (1.48 x expected change)

where the units are thousands employed. This equation resulted in an excellent fit to the actual changes in manufacturing employment, accounting for 89 per cent of the variation across the 20 local labour markets.

This result for the manufacturing sector as a whole does not of course necessarily apply to particular industries within local labour markets. In the case of industries of small size locally, one naturally encounters a great deal of variability over the decade, since a single closure or opening can make a big difference to the total employment in that industry. We have not had the resources to undertake a complete statistical analysis of all industries within local labour markets. We have however examined employment changes in the largest industry within each of the local labour markets. In general thse are quite well predicted by the estimation equation, although (as one might presume) less well than the total manufacturing employment for the area. But there was a tendency for the very largest industries to be affected by exceptionally large contractions.

Examples are the vehicles industry of Coventry where employment fell to 38 per cent of its 1971 level by 1981; the textiles industry of Bolton, where the fall was to 43 per cent of the initial level; and the shipbuilding industry of Birkenhead, where the fall was to 47 per cent of the initial level. Altogether, seven of the 20 local labour market areas saw their largest industries of 1971 shrink to less than half their initial size by 1981; and in 15 of the 20 labour markets, the fall in the largest industry was clearly greater than in that of manufacturing industry as a whole. However, it is not justifiable to regard this as an effect of industrial concentration in its own right. It is, just as reasonably, to be connected with the particular industries involved: textiles (in four cases), iron and steel (three cases), and mechanical engineering (three), all of which experienced particularly large declines on a national level.

**Table 2.3    Actual and predicted\* changes in manufacturing employment, 1971-81**

*000s employed*

|  | Actual | Predicted |
| --- | --- | --- |
| Coventry | -54.0 | -33.9 |
| Smethwick | -27.2 | -20.7 |
| Walsall | -31.3 | -25.4 |
| Wolverhampton | -26.7 | -21.8 |
| Bolton | -16.7 | -16.0 |
| Manchester | -76.9 | -50.4 |
| Birkenhead | -11.1 | -7.6 |
| Liverpool | -63.6 | -34.2 |
| Southport | -1.1 | -1.2 |
| Bradford | -33.0 | -23.7 |
| Huddersfield | -20.7 | -15.6 |
| Leeds | -41.2 | -35.8 |
| Newcastle | -33.3 | -28.8 |
| Sunderland | -15.7 | -9.2 |
| Glasgow | -78.2 | -48.5 |
| Motherwell | -16.4 | -14.1 |
| Newport | -10.0 | -10.2 |
| Nottingham | -32.6 | -35.2 |
| Sheffield | -47.6 | -41.2 |
| Southampton | -2.5 | -11.0 |

\*   Prior to weighting by regression method

## Size and manufacturing employment
There is, however, another sense in which industrial concentration may be significant in its effects on employment change. Very large

local industries may often take the form of many large establishments. If these large establishments are subject to closures or major contractions, this can flood the labour market with large numbers of workers that it is unable to absorb. This is one reason why the size structure of local labour markets may be important, as well as industry structure. Another aspect of size which has received recent attention is the apparent disadvantage of those who have only worked in large firms in taking to self-employment[8]. Again, therefore, it is the local labour market characterized by having many large establishments which is likely to be at a disadvantage in coping with industrial contraction.

The effect of the size of manufacturing establishments upon the course of changes in local employment could be pursued with information from the Department of Trade and Industry's ROIS databank. The proportion of all manufacturing employment in 1975 which was provided by plants with 500 or more employees, served as a convenient indicator of concentration, and revealed marked differences among the 18 localities covered (data being unavailable for Scotland).

There was no statistical relationship, however, between this indicator of size concentration and the amount of loss of manufacturing employment. While Coventry, Wolverhampton, Liverpool, and Wearside (Sunderland) all had both high proportions working in large plants, and high rates of contraction, Smethwick and Huddersfield, with much lower size concentration, also experienced particularly severe declines in employment. Moreover, some areas with very high size concentration fared much better than the average in their manufacturing employment: notably Birkenhead and Southampton.

Nor did large plants, across these 18 local labour markets, appear to be any more or less vulnerable to closure or contraction than were manufacturing establishments of smaller size. As shown in Table 2.4, the proportion of manufacturing job losses attributable to the large plants was closely in line with the share of manufacturing employment provided by those large plants at the start of the period. On average, the large plants accounted for 53 per cent of manufacturing employment, and for 54 per cent of job loss, and the common variation between the two measures was 92 per cent (a correlation coefficient of 0.96).

**Table 2.4   Losses of manufacturing employment from large establishments closures and contractions, 1975-81 (source: ROIS)**

*percentages*

|  | 1975: employment in plants of size 500+ | 1975-81: job loss from plants of size 500+ |
|---|---|---|
| Coventry | 78 | 81 |
| Smethwick | 42 | 49 |
| Walsall | 29 | 30 |
| Wolverhampton | 62 | 61 |
| Bolton | 50 | 44 |
| Manchester | 60 | 59 |
| Birkenhead | 74 | 65 |
| Liverpool | 76 | 79 |
| Southport | 0 | 0 |
| Bradford | 43 | 44 |
| Huddersfield | 44 | 32 |
| Leeds | 40 | 41 |
| Newcastle | 63 | 66 |
| Sunderland* | 58 | 63 |
| Glasgow | na | na |
| Motherwell | na | na |
| Newport | 65 | 74 |
| Nottingham | 52 | 59 |
| Sheffield | 57 | 51 |
| Southampton | 67 | 2 |

\*   average of North Tyne and South Tyne travel-to-work areas

Another way of looking at the effect of establishment size is by considering the average size of job loss per establishment experiencing closure or contraction. There was a strong overall relationship between this 'average size of job loss' measure and the initial degree of size concentration, as would be expected (with a correlation coefficient of 0.83), but there were some notable variations. Liverpool was particularly affected by large closures and contractions, even after allowing for its initially high concentration of large manufacturing establishments. Its average size of job loss was 222 jobs, which can be compared with 196 in neighbouring Birkenhead, the next highest, or with 167 in Coventry, which had a slightly higher size concentration. Wearside (Sunderland), with an average job loss of 158, also appears to have been particularly affected by large closures or contractions. But although the prevalence of large employment contractions through large establishments may be a factor of importance in some particular areas like these, no general statistical relationship with the extent of total job loss could be detected.

On the whole, then, we have come to the (perhaps surprising) conclusion that concentration of manufacturing industry in large plants had little effect on the rate of contraction. Of course, this conclusion does not gainsay the crucial role played by large plants in employment change. Simply because a small number of very large establishments can provide such a large proportion of all employment in a local labour market, they are likely to have an overwhelming influence on the trends in local employment.

## Service sector

The same method which was used to predict changes in employment in manufacturing was also applied to employment in services. The 'expected' local level of service employment in 1981 was estimated by means of national change data for each industry together with information about the distribution of service employment, locally, in 1971. The results were compared with actual changes in service employment over the period.

The initial set of results, summarized in Table 2.5, appeared to discourage the view that local service employment was controlled by national trends in combination with local service industry structure. Whereas the regression equation for manufacturing employment across the 20 local labour markets accounted for 89 per cent of the variation in employment, the corresponding regression equation for services accounted for less than one per cent of the variation.

Closer examination of the results suggested that there were particularly large discrepancies between the expected and actual change in employment in three local labour markets. These were Manchester, Liverpool, and Glasgow. These three 'outliers' were set aside, and the analysis repeated with the remaining 17 local labour markets. This led to more positive results, with 56 per cent of the variation in service employment changes being accounted for by the equation. This equation took the form:

actual employment change = 0.5 + 0.96(expected employment change)

where the units are thousands employed. Unlike the equation for manufacturing employment, discussed above, the weighting introduced by the regression equation was close to unity, so there was no 'North-South differential' required to explain the result. In essence, the equation says that (once Manchester, Liverpool and Glasgow have been taken out) national aggregate demand and the initial structure of services give quite a reasonable forecast of service employment change.

**Table 2.5   Actual and expected\* change in service employment, 1971-81**

*000s employed*

|  | Actual change | Expected change |
| --- | --- | --- |
| Coventry | 16.2 | 12.1 |
| Smethwick | -0.2 | 3.9 |
| Walsall | 11.8 | 5.6 |
| Wolverhampton | 0.8 | 9.9 |
| Bolton | 4.6 | 5.8 |
| Manchester | 14.5 | 49.6 |
| Birkenhead | 6.9 | 8.1 |
| Liverpool | -29.2 | 31.9 |
| Southport | 2.9 | 3.3 |
| Bradford | 11.5 | 10.5 |
| Huddersfield | 4.0 | 5.0 |
| Leeds | 19.3 | 24.9 |
| Newcastle | 15.9 | 23.9 |
| Sunderland | 4.5 | 6.7 |
| Glasgow | 3.8 | 42.4 |
| Motherwell | 7.6 | 5.1 |
| Newport | 0.3 | 3.8 |
| Nottingham | 31.5 | 17.3 |
| Sheffield | 19.9 | 18.6 |
| Southampton | 20.8 | 11.5 |

\*   Prior to weighting by regression method

The ability to account for more than half the variation in service employment change, by essentially simple means, further strengthens the case that local levels of employment change have been strongly driven by larger forces of demand. Nevertheless, this figure remains considerably below that obtained for change in manufacturing employment, and it is clear that (even setting aside the particular cases of Manchester, Liverpool and Glasgow) there has been a far less uniform pattern of change in services than in manufacturing. It is important to pursue this further.

It seems unlikely to be a coincidence that the three largest cities in our sample should experience the greatest shortfalls in service growth, compared with national trends. One plausible explanation of this shortfall is that Manchester, Liverpool and Glasgow were already mature, indeed historic, centres of service development, and hence did not have the scope for further increasing their service base which was available in areas of relatively recent development. In 1971, 58 per cent of Manchester's total employment was already in services, 60 per cent of Liverpool's, and 56 per cent of Glasgow's. With substantial contraction of manufacturing, by 1981 the place of services in these local economies had further increased - to 67 per cent in Manchester, 68 per cent in Liverpool, and 66 per cent in Glasgow. The 1981 service employment in these great cities remained higher, proportionately, than in centres of high service growth in our sample, such as Nottingham (moving from 46 per cent service employment in 1971 to 58 per cent in 1981) or Walsall (moving from 32 per cent to 46 per cent).

Hence a kind of 'ceiling' may be operating in these cases to limit the further growth of service employment. Of course, other interpretations may also be plausible (for example, an earlier history of manufacturing decline may have weakened the economic base for service growth); but our explanation seems worth further testing. To this end, the 20 local labour markets were divided into two groups, 11 which had less than 50 per cent of employment in services in 1971, and nine which had 50 per cent or more. There were some indications that, over the 1971-81 period, the level of service employment in the two groups was converging, as follows:

|  | Averages: per cent of all employment in services | |
|  | 1971 | 1981 |
| --- | --- | --- |
| Those with lower service employment in 1971 | 40 | 53 |
| Those with higher service employment in 1971 | 58 | 66 |

Whereas the group of local labour markets with lower initial service employment shifted 13 percentage points towards a higher proportion in service employment, the group with higher service employment shifted only eight percentage points in that direction. The lower rate of shift towards services was not peculiar to Manchester, Liverpool and Glasgow, but was common to all the members of their group.

Although this analysis contributes something towards an explanation of uneven service growth, there of course remains much to be added concerning particular cases. No simple, statistical approach can be expected to explain the large differences in service growth between neighbouring Wolverhampton and Walsall, for example, or can account for the tailing-off of service growth in the great provincial cities while the capital city itself continues to expand services without abatement. These contrasts would require a more intensive and historical study than can be addressed here. However, the present analysis, albeit limited, may have been of some value in drawing attention to the variability of service employment growth and contrasting this with the predictability of manufacturing employment contraction. Much of the discussion of employment in recent years has tended to assume that manufacturing is the driving force, with services in a secondary and dependent position[9]. That point of view seems difficult to sustain in the light of the present evidence. Service employment appears to have more scope for local development, independent of the path manufacturing is taking, than has usually been acknowledged.

*Occupational segments*
The preceding discussion has presented a view of the 20 local labour markets, which apparently accounts for the greater part of employment change in terms of national industrial trends and local structure of industry. However, the account would be incomplete without giving

parallel attention to the occupational aspects of industrial structure. Industries and occupational groups are interwoven and inseparable; each form of analysis is merely another perspective on the same structure. However, these perspectives give rise to rather different practical implications. In earlier chapters of this report we have given special emphasis to the occupational aspects of the young long-term unemployed. We accord the same importance to an occupational analysis of employment change in local labour markets.

The approach to occupational groups adopted here is a broad rather than a detailed one. The fundamental distinction is that between manual and nonmanual labour. Of course, this distinction is somewhat crude, by comparison with the information which would be contained in an analysis of labour segments by types of skill. However, the simple distinction between manual and nonmanual groups remains a powerful one. To illustrate this, we took the 27 industrial orders of the 1968 Standard Industrial Classification, and regressed percentage change in employment during 1971-81 on proportions of nonmanual workers (social classes I, II and IIIN) in 1981. The derived estimation equation accounted for 63 per cent of the variation in change of industry employment level, and was as follows:

employment change per cent = 49.4 + 0.95 (nonmanual employment)

In other words, industries with more than half their jobs in the nonmanual category (at the end of the period) had tended to grow between 1971-81, while those with less than half their jobs nonmanual had tended to shrink; and the rate of growth or shrinkage was roughly one-for-one with the numbers of nonmanual jobs above or below one half.

Although we did not have breakdowns by manual and nonmanual employment for the industries by local labour market area, we estimated these by applying national percentages (from the 1971 and 1981 Censuses of Population) to the local industry employment totals. This is a reasonable procedure, because the industries vary so widely in their manual-nonmanual composition; but a degree of local variation must be lost through the estimating process.

The results of calculations using these estimates are presented in Table 2.6. They are expressed in the same way as those for the manufacturing and service sectors in the preceding section: all percentages are to the base of total employment. Hence, for example, the figure of -17.7 per cent relating to manual employment in Coventry during 1971-81, does not mean that manual employment declined by 17.7 per cent, but that the fall in manual employment represented a 17.7 decrease in total employment.

**Table 2.6    Estimated contribution of manual and nonmanual occupations in total employment change, 1971-81**

*Base: total employment in 1971*
*Percentage differences*

|                | Manual | Nonmanual |
|----------------|--------|-----------|
| Coventry       | -17.7  | 0.3       |
| Smethwick      | -21.9  | -4.2      |
| Walsall        | -14.6  | 2.2       |
| Wolverhampton  | -15.6  | 2.1       |
| Bolton         | -13.1  | 1.6       |
| Manchester     | -10.9  | 0.0       |
| Birkenhead     | -10.3  | 4.9       |
| Liverpool      | -16.4  | -4.4      |
| Southport      | -0.2   | 7.4       |
| Bradford       | -13.5  | 2.9       |
| Huddersfield   | -18.9  | 0.7       |
| Leeds          | -10.8  | 3.7       |
| Newcastle      | -11.1  | 2.6       |
| Sunderland     | -18.0  | 0.8       |
| Glasgow        | -12.7  | 0.7       |
| Motherwell     | -13.5  | 1.6       |
| Newport        | -13.8  | 0.6       |
| Nottingham     | -8.0   | 5.0       |
| Sheffield      | -13.2  | 2.5       |
| Southampton    | 2.5    | 9.1       |

It can be seen from the table that most of the change in employment, in all 20 areas, was accounted for by the estimated falls in manual employment. Indeed, in most areas estimated nonmanual employment actually increased somewhat, so that loss of manual employment was greater than total (net) employment loss. Only in two local labour markets was there an appreciable estimated fall of nonmanual employment: Liverpool and Smethwick, both with a fall of about four per cent in nonmanual jobs. And in these cases, there was a fall in economic activity larger than four per cent, so that the loss of nonmanual jobs may not in practical terms be as considerable as it seems (the interpretation of changes in population and in economic activity rates will be discussed further in the next section). The local labour markets which, according to our estimates, may have had substantial increases in nonmanual employment included the three which were most successful in terms of overall employment: Southampton, with nine per cent growth; Southport (seven per cent); and Nottingham (five per cent). Runners-up were Birkenhead (with five per cent growth in nonmanual jobs) and Leeds (with four per cent). Even Walsall, Bradford and Sheffield, all with more than 10 per cent net employment loss over the decade, were increasing their nonmanual employment, over this period, by between two and three per cent.

These findings are remarkable. One would have expected that, in looking at a selection of the local labour markets worst affected by job loss, there would have been some impact on nonmanual as well as on manual occupations. Yet virtually everywhere the estimates suggest that nonmanual employment was maintained or even grew. Loss of employment was virtually synonymous with loss of manual employment.

The estimated change in manual employment between 1971 and 1981 itself had two elements:

(i)   the change in the local industrial structure;
(ii)  the changing national proportions of manual and nonmanual employment, within each industry.

Since these two elements are reflected within the estimating procedure for nonmanual jobs, and since the percentage of manual employment is equal to 100 minus the percentage of nonmanual employment, the two elements can be reconstituted from that estimating procedure. This is done by calculating what the manual employment in 1971 would have been, if the 1981 national proportions had then applied to the 1971 local industry structure, and conversely what the 1981 proportions would have been, if the 1971 national proportions had continued to apply to the 1981 local industry structure. These calculations can then be compared with the full 1981 estimates, in which both changes in national proportions and changes in local industry structure are brought together. The first of these comparisons estimates the effect of changes in the local structure of industrial employment between 1971-81; the second estimates the effect of changes in national proportions employed, by industry, over the same period.

We do not show these results in detail here, since they are presentationally somewhat cumbersome. In fact, the full analysis indicated that across all 20 local labour markets there was broad similarity in the split between the two elements of occupational change.

The chief feature of these results consists in an important difference between male and female manual employment. In the case of men, the fall in manual employment was virtually synonymous with the industry-linked changes in local male employment during 1971-81. There had been very little change in the national proportions of male manual workers across industries between 1971 and 1981. This was as true, in fact, for service employment as for manufacturing employment.

In the case of female manual workers, however, it was clear that there were two influences, both important, at work. One was the change in female local employment by industry - which generally meant fewer jobs in manufacturing, but more in services. The other was a national tendency for smaller proportions of women to be doing manual work, and higher proportions to be doing nonmanual work, by 1981; and this applied within both manufacturing and service industries. This national trend for women's employment to be shifted out of manual work by definition affected all the labour market areas, although to varying degrees which depended upon their different mixes of industry.

*Gender, part-time hours, and occupational change.* Early in this review of employment change in the 20 local labour markets, we presented summaries by male and female, and full-time and part-time, categories. It was noted there that changes at local labour market level generally followed well-known national trends, with large proportions of employment growth being provided by omen's jobs and by part-time jobs.

The discussion of the immediately preceding section suggests that the changes in employment by gender, and by hours of work, are in their turn linked to those by occupation. It is known that part-time working, although by no means confined to service industries, has been far less common in manufacturing. It is also known that the great majority of part-time jobs (almost 85 per cent nationally) are held by women[10]. Hence to a large, although not complete, degree, the various kinds of growth of employment can be seen as nested within one another: part-time working within female employment within growth of nonmanual occupations.

## Supply-side influences on local employment
Up to this point the discussion has stressed that local change in employment can, to a high degree, be accounted for on the 'demand side': through national aggregate demand by industry, and through local industry structure. But the preceding section with its occupational view of change in employment suggests a supply-side as well as a demand-side interpretation. And there are other supply-side aspects to be considered.

### *Population and economic activity rates*
The most obvious aspect of labour supply is its quantity, reflected in the population of working age and in the proportion of the population which is in employment or available for employment. These measures of supply, however, are affected by a complex set of factors which it is difficult to bring together systematically at the level of local labour markets. The factors include birth and death rates, which in turn reflect the age structure; flows to and from education; inward and outward migration from the area; rates of retirement or of discouraged withdrawal from activity; and rates of return to work among married women. It is important to stress, moreover, that each of these factors may be influenced itself by conditions of economic demand in the area. For example, it has been shown that rates of retirement are sensitive to levels of unemployment[11], and indeed, there were particularly large increases in early retirement in the late 1970s and early 1980s as unemployment rose in Britain[12].

It is only, therefore, in a pure book-keeping sense that one could 'adjust' changes in employment over the 1971-81 period to take account of changes in the economically active population. If employment has fallen by 10 per cent, but economic activity has also fallen at the same rate, this does not mean that there has been no 'real' job loss. To reach that conclusion, one would have to show that the change in economic activity was unconnected to the change in employment.

A further complication in assessing the relation between the quantity of demand and the quantity of labour supply lies in shifting commuting patterns. As employment in a local area falls or changes in its composition, more of the residents in that area may travel outside its boundaries to find employment. Conversely, growth in employment within an area may partly be captured by in-commuters from adjoining areas. Although the definition of local labour markets is intended to minimise these problems, the degree of closure achievable in practice - generally around 80-90 per cent - inevitably leaves a considerable margin of error in comparing employment change with change in economic activity.

From a statistical point of view, falling population and economic activity may partly offset the effects of employment contraction, leading to lower levels of unemployment than would otherwise have been registered. However, second-round effects of labour force contraction also have to be taken into account. Declining population may inhibit investment in business, both in the case of consumer services where a shrinking customer base would be a disincentive to firms, and more generally in the case of employers fearing that labour supply may be inadequate for future needs.

Despite these precautionary comments, the evidence concerning change in population and in economic activity for the 20 local labour market areas appears to offer some useful insights.

Nationally, population was virtually static over the period under consideration, rising by 0.55 per cent. In contrast, 16 of the 20 local labour markets recorded a decline in population during 1971-81, although in five of these cases of less than one per cent. Economic activity followed a similar pattern, with 15 of the 20 local labour market areas experiencing a decrease. Hence these areas of (generally speaking) severely contracting employment were also, for the most part, areas with a shrinking labour force. The only two labour markets with a net growth of employment over the period - Southport and Southampton - also had the most substantial growth of the labour force.

Most of the changes in population and economic activity were fairly small. There were, however, three cases where both population and economic activity fell markedly over the 1971-81 period. These consisted of Manchester, Liverpool, and Glasgow, whose deviant results have already been noted in the section on changes in service employment.

|  | 1981 as a percentage of 1971 | |
|  | Population | Economic activity |
| --- | --- | --- |
| Manchester | 89 | 88 |
| Liverpool | 88 | 90 |
| Glasgow | 88 | 92 |

This population contraction provides an additional partial explanation of the shortfall of service employment growth in these three major cities. Other things being equal, consumer services would be expected to be proportional to population. As population falls, not only is growth of consumer services curtailed, but also those business services which support consumer services are likely to be adversely affected. It should be stressed, however, that this is not necessarily the whole story.

The population contraction in these three cities may have been accelerated by employment contraction during the 1970s, but is unlikely to be wholly, or even largely, attributable to employment in itself. The depopulation of metropolitan inner city areas has been taking place over longer periods, and is generally regarded as being primarily shaped by housing, environment, and transport.

It is true that net outward migration rates from Manchester and Liverpool, immediately before the 1981 Census, were exceptionally high at 1.6 per cent of the economically active population base per annum (Glasgow's, at 0.8 per cent, was less unusual)[13]. But studies of migration also show (i) that housing rather than employment tends to be the dominant consideration; and (ii) that the rate of migration is lowest among older people of low occupational status, the group most affected by contraction of employment[14]. This is too large a topic to pursue within the confines of the present discussion. These brief points, however, suggest that population contraction in the three large inner city areas may be seen as much in terms of an exacerbating factor in employment contraction as in terms of an offsetting or balancing factor.

A rather different case is that of Smethwick, on the borders of Birmingham. There population fell by a little more than three per cent, but economic activity much more sharply by nine per cent. Smethwick had the highest dependence, of any of the 20 local labour markets, on manufacturing employment, and registered the largest net contraction in employment, of 26 per cent. It seems reasonable to interpret the large fall in economic activity, relative to population, in terms of a 'discouraged worker' effect. Consistent with this interpretation, Smethwick had much the largest fall in female employment, at nearly eight per cent, and in lower-skilled workers, of nearly 12 per cent.

Yet another pattern is illustrated by the case of Sunderland. In this local labour market, population fell by almost nine per cent over the period, but economic activity by only six per cent. Despite highly adverse local conditions for employment, the relative rate of participation increased. The same was true (though less markedly) of Liverpool and Glasgow (see above), and of Birkenhead, Newcastle, Newport, and Motherwell. The regional clustering of these cases (Liverpool-Birkenhead, Sunderland-Newcastle, Glasgow-Motherwell) may be connected with high regional fertility rates, leading to particularly large demographic shifts in the direction of a younger work-force, and hence rising rates of labour force participation contrary to the economic trend of the market. This age effect clearly seems to have been present in Sunderland, Liverpool, Glasgow and Motherwell, at least, where Census of Population data show that the under-25s formed a specially high proportion of the total labour force.

Our review of this complex aspect of the local labour market data has, we must emphasize, been somewhat cursory, and based on qualitative interpretation in the light of the background literature, rather than (as in the case of the demand side) on a systematic quantitative method. But the broad conclusion seems sufficiently clear. There are little grounds for supposing that changes in population and economic activity were, in these areas, generally acting to mitigate the effects of employment contraction, especially for the under-25 age group. Only in one of the 20 areas - Smethwick - did the evidence suggest a substantial 'discouraged worker' effect in part diverting the impact of employment contraction away from unemployment.

## Indicators of labour 'quality'

It has long been argued that among the reasons for differences in employment growth and contraction among local labour markets or regions, is the different composition of local labour forces in terms of skills or adaptability. In practice, our ability to assess the quality of local labour forces is severely limited, and a complex notion has to be reduced to a few simple indicators in order to examine it statistically.

One such indicator is the proportion of unskilled and semi-skilled manual workers in the economically active population. It might be thought that where these lower-skilled workers form a large part of the labour force, there is less encouragement for firms to invest and expand in the area, because of anxiety about the availability of skilled workers in sufficient numbers. But it is known that the greater part of lower-skilled jobs exist in manufacturing, and wherever manufacturing is highly prevalent, there are also large concentrations of the lower-skilled. It would seem, then, that areas of manufacturing concentration will inevitably be at a disadvantage in a period when employment growth depends on an increased use of skills by employers.

Because occupations are so intertwined with industries, it is difficult if not impossible to devise any statistical test of this argument. Areas with high concentrations of manufacturing industry have (as we have already seen) been particularly adversely affected since 1971, but this cannot be attributed to the higher concentrations of lower-skilled workers in these areas on a statistical basis. The correlation between the local proportions of lower-skilled workers and subsequent decline of manufacturing employment was substantial ($r=0.69$), but even larger was the initial correlation of the lower-skilled proportion with the relative size of manufacturing industry in 1971 ($r=0.76$). Thus, when the influence of this initial structural fact is controlled, the link between skill-composition and employment change disappears. Similarly, there is a weak negative corrrelation between the proportion of lower-skilled workers and the rate of growth of local service employment ($r=-0.27$), but this can be attributed to the correlation between manufacturing and service employment - severe contraction of manufacturing holds back services to some extent ($r=0.39$). The role of skill-levels in these aggregate changes may be assumed with some plausibility, but cannot be demonstrated with this type of data.

Another way of considering the issue, which may be more productive, is to consider how the proportion of lower-skilled workers in the local labour market *changes* with altered economic circumstances. Given that manufacturing is contracting, given that so many lower-skilled jobs have been in manufacturing, and given that growing service industries offer so many more job opportunities at intermediate and higher occupational levels, it would be expected that there would be a shift out of the lower levels. Such a shift could come about, over a decade or so, in a variety of ways: through processes of qualification and occupational choice of new entrants to the labour force, and through training or occupational mobility among existing members of the labour force. To the extent that it does *not* come about in response to pressures of change, it can be reasonably argued that there must be obstacles either inherent in existing skill structures or associated with them.

As a standard towards which local labour markets might be expected to evolve, one might point to Southampton, a successful local economy which started the period under consideration with a substantial manufacturing base (33 per cent of total employment), and experienced only slow contraction in this base, but rapid expansion of service employment. In fact, throughout the period Southampton's proportion of lower-skilled workers hardly changed - 21.4 per cent in 1971, 21.1 per cent in 1981. Indeed, this proportion is extremely close to the average for total employment in Britain. It might be argued, then, that something of this order represents an 'appropriate' level of lower-skilled workers for the period 1971-81.

With the marginal exception of Southport, which is primarily a resort town with service employment, only Birkenhead (with 20.9 per cent in the lower-skilled group in 1971) was similar to Southampton, and this was with a substantially smaller manufacturing base (24 per cent of total employment, compared with Southampton's 33 per cent). The remaining 17 local labour markets all had (in 1971) proportions of lower-skilled workers ranging upwards from Leeds (with 23.8 per cent) to Smethwick with 30.9 per cent. Complete figures are shown in Table 2.7.

More relevant to the argument, however, is the change in those proportions between 1971 and 1981, which are also shown in the table. In fact, only four of the 16 local labour markets which had experienced significant contraction had clearly reduced their proportions of lower-skilled workers: these were Smethwick, Newport, Glasgow and Motherwell. Moreover, five of the local labour markets had experienced clear shifts in the opposite direction: Bolton, Birkenhead, Liverpool, Bradford, and Sunderland. In the remaining cases, the proportion had remained within one percentage point of its initial value. On balance, then, there had not been the expected shift away from lower-skilled occupations which economic circumstances appeared to require.

**Table 2.7   The prevalence of lower-skilled workers in 1971 and 1981**

| | lower-skilled as a percentage of economically active | |
| --- | --- | --- |
| | 1971 | 1981 |
| Coventry | 27.0 | 26.8 |
| Smethwick | 30.9 | 27.3 |
| Walsall | 26.5 | 26.8 |
| Wolverhampton | 24.7 | 25.6 |
| Bolton | 26.8 | 28.6 |
| Manchester | 25.9 | 25.4 |
| Birkenhead | 20.9 | 23.7 |
| Liverpool | 26.3 | 27.8 |
| Southport | 16.3 | 16.8 |
| Bradford | 26.8 | 28.9 |
| Huddersfield | 27.3 | 26.9 |
| Leeds | 23.8 | 23.3 |
| Newcastle | 24.5 | 24.5 |
| Sunderland | 25.1 | 26.4 |
| Glasgow | 25.8 | 24.4 |
| Motherwell | 29.0 | 26.1 |
| Newport | 26.8 | 24.5 |
| Nottingham | 25.6 | 25.0 |
| Sheffield | 25.6 | 26.5 |
| Southampton | 21.4 | 21.1 |

It should be stressed, again, that these results do not demonstrate any causal relationship between labour supply 'quality' (as indicated by the proportion of lower-skilled workers) and employment contraction. The difficulty apparently experienced in most of these localities of adapting their skill supply in the required direction could as much result from, as lead to, employment contraction. It is when growth is taking place that, for example, more apprenticed places are available or upward mobility is easier to achieve.

Nevertheless, there is one category of supply which should be relatively free of these constraints, and therefore able in principle to respond to the shifts in labour market demand. This is the school system and its associated system of qualification, which influences the entry-points and career possibilities of new entrants to the labour market.

### The supply of school leavers
In turning to the evidence about school leavers, we are faced with a lack of correspondence between educational statistics and the labour market information which has been used in this chapter. The published statistics of education are analysed, at the local level, only by local education authority areas, which correspond, in the metropolitan regions, with administrative districts and not with labour markets. In many cases districts are somewhat larger than local labour markets, but in others they are smaller; in many, also, their boundaries do not correspond to travel-to-work patterns. In one case - that of Smethwick - two education authorities, Dudley and Sandwell, share the territory. In general, then, information about school leavers can only be related to the labour market data in a rough-and-ready way. Furthermore, local information in comparable form is available only for English local authority areas, and hence the two Scottish and one Welsh local labour market have been omitted from this part of the review. As a final limitation, it seemed prudent to avoid the complications caused by change in the school leaving age in 1974, so the data we consider concern 1976/77 and 1981/82 rather than the full 10-year period used for the labour market statistics.

Two measures of 'educational output' which were extracted from the published statistics are reviewed here. These are:
(i)   the proportion who left school without any examination pass - not even an ungraded CSE;
(ii)  those who left school for further full-time education.

The wholly unqualified can be assumed to be particularly likely to enter lower-skilled occupations and to be vulnerable to unemployment. Those entering full-time further education constitute a particularly interesting indication of the attempts of young people with some educational attainments to adapt to changing labour market conditions.

Nationally, in fact, significant changes in the qualifications and destinations of school leavers were taking place in the late 1970s. The proportion leaving school totally without qualification was being rapidly reduced, largely because of increased success in the CSE examinations. Also, between 1976 and 1981 there were large increases in the proportions leaving school for further full-time education. This however did not reflect any substantial increase in A-level qualifications, which remained relatively static over the period. Rather, it seems that increasing proportions with some school qualifications chose to enhance them rather than enter an increasingly difficult job market.

In the 17 local labour market areas which we can examine, the national patterns were generally followed, with all but one reducing their proportion of wholly unqualified school leavers, and all but one increasing their proportion of school leavers going to further education.

We found that the proportions leaving school wholly unqualified in 1981/82 were significantly related to the change in employment over the 1971-81 period: the higher the proportion of unqualified school leavers, the lower the level of employment in 1981 relative to 1971. In the case of the manufacturing sector, this could partly be attributed to the links between school qualification rates and social class composition on one hand, and between social class composition and the prevalence of manufacturing industry on the other. However, this confounding factor was much less important in the case of service sector employment change, yet the relationship between local levels of school qualification and local levels of service employment persisted. In fact, the correlations were the same between on-qualification rates and manufacturing employment change, and between non-qualification rates and service employment ($r=-0.54$). The correlation seems particularly high when the lack of correspondence between spatial definitions for the educational and employment series is taken into account.

Furthermore, the likelihood that this is a genuine rather than a spurious link is enhanced by the contrast between the findings for non-qualification and those for entry to further education. In the latter case the relationship with both change in manufacturing employment and change in service employment was small and non-significant (r=0.07 and r=0.06 respectively). It is difficult to attribute the link between non-qualification levels and employment change to general social background influences, when on that argument the same social background influences should have similarly linked entry to further education with employment change.

If therefore the reality of the link between non-qualification levels and employment change is provisionally accepted, how is it to be interpreted? It is possible that there are causal effects in both directions.

While it is improbable that the flow of unqualified young people into the labour market at the end of the 1970s would in itself have influenced the employment or investment decisions of employers, and so have affected aggregate employment change, it is possible that the relative rate of non-qualification could be persistent over long periods and so progressively down-grade the quality of the labour force. Comparison of the 1981/82 educational statistics with those for 1976/77 gives some support to this notion. The correlation for the local non-qualification rates in the two years was 0.84, which points to a high degree of relative stability in non-qualification even in a period when the average level of non-qualification was falling sharply.

This means that localities with raditionally high rates of non-qualification tend to remain behind the average even when they are improving their performance in absolute terms. So, for example, Manchester, Liverpool and Bradford, despite considerable reductions in their non-qualification rates between 1976 and 1981, still in 1981/82 had getting on for twice the proportions of unqualified school leavers as the average for England. Although by the end of the 1970s the absolute proportions were not large, earlier in that decade the non-qualified in these areas of low educational attainment constituted a substantial group which may have been capable of having a marked effect on the perceived quality of the labour force as a whole.

But it is also possible that the educational achievement of young people is itself affected by local employment opportunities. Those young people who perceive their prospects entirely in terms of a job on leaving school may be particularly demotivated as unemployment rises and this may then be reflected in educational performance. Those young people, however, who redefine their plans by making use of further educational opportunities may be better able to maintain their motivation in the face of uncertain local conditions, especially as further qualifications would tend to increase their mobility beyond the local labour market.

## Summary and concluding comments

Because of the length and range of this chapter, it may be helpful to precede the brief concluding comments, which discuss the salient points from this review, with a summary of the chapter's larger findings.

*Demand explains change in employment* Information about national change in demand by industry, and about local industry structure in 1971, was sufficient to account for 89 per cent of change in manufacturing employment across all 20 local labour markets, and 56 per cent of change in service employment across 17 of the 20 local labour markets, between 1971 and 1981.

*Service employment appears more affected by local variations* There was far more unexplained variation in change of service employment, across the 20 local labour markets, than was the case with manufacturing employment. Change in service employment was only weakly associated with change in manufacturing employment.

*Lack of influence of establishment size* There was no evidence to suggest that areas characterized by large manufacturing establishments had experienced particularly severe contractions of employment.

*Pressure on the 18-24 year old group* Estimates suggested that, in 19 of the 20 local labour markets, change in employment opportunities would be less favourable for the 18-24 year old group than for the working population as a whole. In most cases the pressure on this age group was compounded by its relative population growth.

*Employment loss is in manual jobs* In even the local labour markets with most adverse changes in total employment, net job loss was (on the basis of the estimation method used) essentially confined to manual occupations, and did not spread into nonmanual occupations.

*Occupational shifts are different by gender* In most of the local labour markets, male manual job loss tended to follow directly from the aggregate changes in industries. In the case of women, however, manual employment contraction in part took the form of a shift from manual to non-manual occupations, and this tended to reduce the overall effect on jobs.

*Complex changes in economic activity* While population was tending to fall across the labour markets, changes in economic activity did not closely parallel population changes. Economic activity appeared resilient in the face of employment contraction, with only a single clear exception.

*Population decline in the great cities, and service stagnation* The great cities of Manchester, Liverpool and Glasgow exhibited a distinctive pattern of rapid population decline, and slow growth of service employment from an initially high base.

*Persistence of low skill levels* Compared with national levels, most of the local labour markets had high proportions of low-skilled workers. There was no consistent reduction of these proportions during 1971-81 despite large-scale contraction of manufacturing employment.

*Non-qualified school leavers, and employment loss* In local education authorities associated with local labour markets, there was generally a reduction in the numbers leaving school without any qualification, over the period 1975-82. Despite this, many of the localities continued to have relatively high levels of non-qualified school leavers. These levels were correlated with employment change both in manufacturing and in services.

## Concluding comments
The study of the 20 local labour markets has been most obviously useful in clarifying the relative role of demand and supply in employment change over the period 1971-81. In these local labour markets, demand clearly played the dominant role. By this term, however, we mean not only aggregate demand as it is usually conceived, but also the local occupational and industry structure of employment. These together gave a statistically satisfactory account of employment change.

But the same approach also gave rise to a notable contrast, between manufacturing and service employment. Service employment was much less satisfactorily accounted for, and it is natural to see in this a greater dependence of services on purely local features, such as locational advantages or disadvantages. The established view, that services are generally dependent upon manufacturing, is difficult to sustain in relation to this set of results. It is particularly notable that a local labour market such as Liverpool, known for its severe employment problems, was characterized by our analysis as an area of 'normal' manufacturing employment contraction but of deficient service growth. Improved understanding of local variations in service employment emerges as an important objective for future study.

While we have pointed out the strength of the demand-side explanation of this set of employment data, we would not wish to suggest that there is a direct opposition between demand-side and supply-side explanations. On the contrary, since our point of view is essentially structuralist, we see see demand and supply as being interwoven in the structure of production. On one side, employment change can be represented as a changing pattern of demand upon the structure of industries. On the other side, it can be represented as a changing pattern of supply to the structure of occupations. And in fact the occupational changes across the 20 labour markets were even clearer and more consistent than those expressed in terms of industrial sectors, with manual employment everywhere declining and nonmanual employment maintaining its position or growing.

# 3 The Composition of the Young Long-Term Unemployed

We now begin our account of the survey of 18-24 year olds in long term unemployment. The purpose of this chapter is to report the findings of the survey concerning the labour market position, individual attainments, and social characteristics of the young people, and wherever possible to place these findings in a comparative perspective. This assessment of the composition of the young long-term unemployed is necessary in order later to interpret their experience and behaviour in the labour market.

Apart from its descriptive purpose, the chapter is relevant to a fundamental issue of interpretation. Are the young long-term unemployed a distinctive group, segregated from the remainder of the youth labour market by their particular characteristics? Specifically, are they a residue or underclass of socially deprived, unqualified, or unemployable young people? Or are they, rather, indistinguishable from some larger group, so that their experience reflects the workings of some wider section of the labour market? The answer to this question not only shapes the nature of the present inquiry, but will also be of significance for the determination of policy concerning long-term youth unemployment.

## Occupational level and type

Occupations are generally regarded, along with age and sex, as providing the basic framework of social description. In the case of the present study, with its focus upon the labour market, it is doubly necessary to begin the analysis with a description of the occupational positions of the young long-term unemployed. Our initial aim is not to describe the occupations in any detail (that will follow in Chapter 4), but simply to assess whether the young long-term unemployed are located in a particular section or sections of the occupational strata, which could in their turn serve as a guide to their position in the labour market.

The young people in the survey were asked for details of up to three previous jobs, sufficient to classify the occupations and industries where they had had experience. These details are available for the first job after leaving school, the most recent job (which in some cases is a current job at the time of the interview), and the 'main or most important job' as the individual saw it. Of course, these jobs can only differ from one another where the person has had more than one job.

The first point to consider, however, is whether the person has had any job experience at all. In fact, substantial proportions in the survey had never held a job - 23 per cent of men and 28 per cent of women - and these proportions were much greater among those who had entered the market in the period 1980-83. From those entering the labour market earlier, in 1975-79, the proportions were 8 per cent of men and 12 per cent of women, but for the later entrants it was in excess of 40 per cent. The simplest explanation for this difference would be the more difficult labour market conditions after 1979, as discussed in Chapter 1. The complete absence of an employment record is a special disadvantage faced by these young people.

To gauge the occupational level of those who had held jobs previously, it is perhaps most useful to look at those jobs which they themselves put forward as the 'main' employment. Roughly four out of five of those who had had more than one job were prepared to make this distinction. Where no 'main' job could be pointed out, we take instead the most recent job before the latest unemployment, or the only job where there was not more than one. By these means, we can identify a representative occupation for 71 per cent of the men and some 65 per cent of women in the sample. The full results are shown in Table 3.1.

A convenient comparison is with the General Household Survey, where occupations are broadly grouped into seven chief categories. The most relevant[1] available results from the GHS are for 1979, for

**Table 3.1    Occupational levels in 'main' or latest job**

*percentages*

|  | Men | Women |
|---|---|---|
| Professional | 0.4 | 0.0 |
| Employers, managers | 2.0 | 1.4 |
| Intermediate non-manual | 2.6 | 5.3 |
| Junior non-manual | 6.9 | 36.8 |
| Skilled manual; own account workers | 35.8 | 9.9 |
| Semi-skilled; personal service | 30.7 | 42.2 |
| Unskilled | 21.6 | 4.4 |
| *Weighted base: excluding those never employed, unclassified or lacking information* | *4614* | *2286* |

Note:    Occupational groupings are defined in accordance with the General
Household Survey socio-economic groups

those aged 20-29. Several important points emerged from the analysis and comparison:

(i)    The young men in long-term unemployment consisted predominantly of manual and personal service workers: 87 per cent in all, by comparison with 63 per cent in the male 20-29 employed group from the 1979 General Household Survey.

(ii)   Similarly, the young women in long-term unemployment consisted chiefly of manual, personal service and junior non-manual workers. These groups constituted 92 per cent of the weighted female sample, to be compared with 78 per cent from the General Household Survey 1979.

(iii)  It follows that, compared with young people in employment, the young long-term unemployed included much smaller proportions from the upper non-manual occupations. For example, only 5 per cent of the male sample came from the top three occupational categories by comparison with 25 per cent of 20-29 year olds in the 1979 General Household Survey.

(iv)   Among young unemployed men with former manual occupations, there was a lower proportion who had attained skilled jobs than among the 20-29 group in the General Household Survey sample: the figures being 41 per cent and 66 per cent respectively. However, as the unemployed survey covers a somewhat younger age-range, it would be likely that with time more of the unemployed sample would - under normal circumstances - move up into skilled manual jobs. This point does not alter the real disadvantage, since it is those who are in continuous work who have the readiest opportunity to raise their skill-level. (It should be noted that the category of skilled manual occupations derived from the OPCS 1980 classification does not correspond to apprenticed craft occupations, although it includes these. A substantial proportion of skilled manual jobs, in this broader sense, can be attained without passing through an apprenticeship, for example by obtaining partial qualifications or by training and experience within the employer's job structure).

(v) Similarly, among the young unemployed women, manual jobs (few of which were skilled) were more numerous than junior non-manual jobs, whereas among the corresponding group in the General Household Survey the reverse was true.

In brief, almost all the young long-term unemployed were located in what might be called the lower part of the occupational structure. (The term 'lower part' is not meant to be precise, but rather to serve a convenient shorthand for 'skilled semi-skilled or unskilled manual or personal service employment'. Some junior non-manual jobs lacking career ladders might also be included within this concept.) Moreover, almost half of those with previous jobs had only worked at the lower skilled levels within this lower segment, probably because of a combination of low starting level and the disruption of progress resulting from unemployment.

## Qualifications

Among the explanations put forward to account for youth unemployment, those involving lack of qualifications are particularly prominent (see Chapter 1). However, there are considerable complications involved in interpreting information about qualifications and, in particular, in making comparisons which help to assess the role of qualifications or of underqualification.

It seems reasonable to assume that the supposed importance of qualifications, in relation to youth unemployment, is because of its role in selection processes. If so, then we must bear in mind that several different kinds of selection are involved.

(i) When leaving school (or a period of post-school training), qualifications may affect the chances of going into employment as opposed to going into unemployment.

(ii) Qualifications may influence the type of employment entered; and different types of employment may be prone to different risks of unemployment.

(iii) Within all or most types of employment, those young people with less qualifications may be more at risk of becoming unemployed than those with more qualifications.

(iv) Within unemployment, those with qualifications may have higher chances of being selected into new jobs than those without qualifications.

It is particularly necessary, from a practical viewpoint, to distinguish the last of these four types of influence from the first three. The first three concern the inflow into unemployment, while the last concerns the outflow from unemployment.

In later chapters we discuss how the outflow is influenced by qualifications, at some length. We can get a quicker, preliminary view of its possible importance by considering the proportions of qualified and non-qualified young people within our sample, by different periods of unemployment. If qualifications improve chances of leaving unemployment and getting a job, then there will tend to be higher proportions of the non-qualified among the groups which have spent longer in unemployment. This is what we find, as Table 3.2 shows. (The questions used to establish qualifications were closely modelled on those in the General Household Survey; non-qualification means total absence of certificated educational or vocational qualifications).

Clearly, since a stock sample is used for the present study, the overall qualification level is considerably reduced, by comparison with the qualification level of the inflow to unemployment, because of the selective removal of the qualified young people as time goes on. The first column of figures in Table 3.2 shows those in the sample who had been unemployed for between six and nine months. This provides our most reasonable view of the level of non-qualification among 18-24 year olds entering unemployment and at risk of a prolonged stay, and suggests that the proportion of this group entirely without qualifications was around one third.

**Table 3.2   Non-qualification by period of unemployment (weighted basis)**

*per cent with no qualification*

| Months | 6-9 | 10-12 | 13-24 | 25 or more |
|--------|-----|-------|-------|------------|
| Male   | 36  | 45    | 47    | 63         |
| Female | 31  | 29    | 46    | 51         |

It is natural to compare this figure of non-qualification among the inflow to long-term youth unemployment with non-qualification among school leavers over the period in question (1975-83). Strictly comparable figures are not available, but the information published in annual Statistics of Education suffices to show that the general level of non-qualification has been much lower than among the inflow to our sample. At the beginning of the period, about 17 per cent of school leavers in England and Wales had no examination pass, and this fell to about 10 per cent by the end of the period. Moreover, some of these will certainly have obtained vocational qualifications subsequently. In broad terms, one could say that non-qualification among the inflow to long-term youth unemployment was two to three times as high as non-qualification in the outflow from school.

However, the outflow from school includes the substantial proportion going to further and higher education and, eventually, into the administrative, technical, professional and other higher occupations. The young long-term unemployed, as already shown, rarely come from such higher occupations but have had jobs largely concentrated in the manual or routine non-manual strata. It is therefore essential to bring occupations into the comparison. The data examined so far show that the young long-term unemployed comprise a relatively low-qualified stream among school leavers as a whole, but do not establish whether they are low-qualified relative to those entering the range of occupations which they themselves enter.

Information about qualifications by occupational level of those entering employment is not available in a form which would permit comparison with the present survey. However, as we have used questions about qualification which are closely similar to those used in the General Household Survey, and are also able to classify occupations in accordance with the GHS, comparisons can be made with that source.

These comparisons are rather rough, for a number of reasons. The GHS reports provide a variety of analyses across different years, rather than a standard series across years, so that the influence of trends in qualification over the period cannot be directly estimated. Moreover, the age breakdowns provided by the GHS do not match our age group: the nearest is an analysis of 20-29 years olds for the years 1978 and 1979 combined. Finally, it must be borne in mind that, with this type of comparison, we cannot separate the influence of selection at different moves between education, employment and unemployment. Rather, the GHS data reflect the joint effects of qualification upon entry into occupations and upon retention in occupations, just as our own survey data reflect the joint effects of qualifications upon entry into unemployment and upon retention in unemployment. Despite these limitations, the features of the data are sufficiently strongly marked to let us reach some conclusions.

**Table 3.3   Non-qualification among young employed and unemployed, by occupational groupings**

| | Male 1984 survey age 20-24 | Male GHS 79 age 20-29 | Female 1984 survey age 20-24 | Female GHS 79 age 20-29 |
|---|---|---|---|---|
| Professional | 0 | 0 | - | - |
| Employers & managers | 27 | 17 | 38 | 11 |
| Intermediate non-manual | 16 | 0 | 26 | 0 |
| Junior non-manual | 39 | 14 | 25 | 24 |
| Skilled manual & own account non-professional | 54 | 33 | 49 | 58 |
| Semi- and unskilled manual & personal service | 65 | 62 | 57 | 61 |
| Never worked | 62 | na | 44 | na |

Notes:   All figures are percentages; GHS = General Household Survey 1979; - = sample size too small in GHS; qualification criterion includes both education and vocational certification; GHS occupations refer to current employment; 1984 survey occupations refer to either most recent employment or to 'main' occupation defined by respondent.

In Table 3.3 we have taken results from the General Household Survey 1979 as our best available comparison[2]. This provides us with a picture of the relationship between qualifications and the occupational level of young workers in a year which is in the middle of the period we are considering. In order to lessen the impact of differing age bands, and also of the different labour market conditions after 1979, we exclude those in our sample entering the labour market during 1980-83: that is, we include only 20-24 year olds entering the labour market before 1980.

The first point to be made about this table is, simply, that qualifications do make a great difference to occupational level. This of course is already well known, but it is worth dwelling on the strength of the influence. Among 20-29 year old men in employment at the end of the 1970s, the proportion without any qualifications in the white-collar occupations was less than 10 per cent, but this rose to 33 per cent in skilled and unskilled categories. Among the corresponding group of women, the proportions without any qualifications rose from around 20 per cent in the non-manual occupations to around 60 per cent in the manual occupational groups.

We have already shown, in the preceding section, that the young long-term unemployed were substantially over-represented in the manual occupations, where nonqualification is most prevalent, and under-represented in the non-manual occupations, where non-qualification is least prevalent. In other words, the risk of becoming unemployed was much higher for young people in the lower, and lower-qualified, occupations. This appears to be a major element in the apparent link between non-qualification and long-term youth unemployment. Qualifications greatly influence selection into occupations, and then occupational level greatly influences selection into unemployment: it is a two-stage process with qualification exerting its force at one remove.

But does lack of qualification have a further effect on risk of entering unemployment, even after taking occupational level into account? This could be the case if the proportions of non-qualification were higher for the young unemployed within each occupational level. Here Table 3.3 must be used with caution, however, for reasons already indicated but worth re-emphasising. During the late 1970s and early 80s, few school leavers were entering the labour market without qualifications, largely because of the growing impact of the

Certificate of School Education. If the age bands for the GHS data were matched with our 20-24 year olds, this would undoubtedly reduce the tabulated levels of non-qualification, perhaps by as much as 7-8 percentage points. Similarly, if we could separately quantify and remove the effect of qualification upon returning to work from unemployment, the figures we would be left with (purer indications of the effect of qualification upon entering unemployment) would obviously be lower than those presented in the table. The most that we can reasonably assume is that any adjustments of this kind would be proportionately spread across occupational levels. If so, we may be able to interpret the overall pattern in broad, relative terms despite uncertainty about the precise comparative figures.

Young people in our sample, like those in employment, were more likely to lack qualifications if they came from manual, and especially lower manual, occupations. This is consistent with the view that risks of entering unemployment depend on occupational level rather than directly upon qualification, for it were the latter, we would expect to find high levels of non-qualification among the unemployed, whatever their occupational level.

Moreover, in the largest single occupational group of the young long-term unemployed - the semi-skilled, unskilled and personal service workers - the proportions of non-qualified were broadly similar to those in employment.

At the same time, differences in non-qualification across occupations were less marked for the young unemployed group than for the group in employment. Relative to the semi-skilled and unskilled, among the employed non-qualification decreases steeply across the skilled manual and the non-manual occupations. Among the young unemployed, it still falls away, but less steeply. This is particularly true of the young men in our survey. There appeared to be many more non-qualified young men, now unemployed, in the skilled manual group, than would be predicted on the basis of the figures for the employed young men. This was a large group, and the finding is correspondingly important. A similar finding applied to young unemployed men in non-manual occupations, but these groups were relatively small. In the case of the unemployed young women, an over-prevalence of the non-qualified was only apparent in the small groups from higher occupations (employers, managers, technical and intermediate non-manual).

These observations suggest that non-qualification may play some part in bringing young people into unemployment, over and above its effect of allocating them to occupational levels; but such an additional effect would be a small one, and of practical importance only in the skilled manual (chiefly male) category. Because so much of the variation in qualifications is 'used up' in the process of occupational selection and segregation, there is correspondingly less scope for qualification to exert an influence within occupational levels.

Again, if qualification and non-qualification were of crucial importance in separating those who entered unemployment from those who entered the lower occupations, then one would expect to find particularly high levels of non-qualification among those who had never worked. As Table 3.3. shows (see bottom row), this was not the case. The young people in our sample who had never worked were, in the case of men, about as likely to be non-qualified as those who had previously entered lower manual occupations; and in the case of women, considerably less likely to be non-qualified than those in the manual occupations as a whole.

This entire comparative analysis does not support the notion that the young long-term unemployed are an underqualified residue in the labour market. Their qualification level appears to be broadly in line with that of the occupational levels where they are concentrated, with the probable exception of skilled male manual occupations. One might say that it was the lower qualified occupations, rather than the lower qualified individuals, which were particularly at risk of unemployment.

The picture so far brings us to the end of the 1970s. The position of young people in the labour market became more unfavourable in the early 1980s, as already described in Chapter 1. How did this affect the relationship between qualifications and unemployment? A study by Payne and Payne[3], based on further analysis of GHS data, has shown that the risks of unemployment for the non-qualified grew progressively higher, and the association between qualification and employment progressively stronger. In 1977, for example, among 16-19 year olds without any qualifications some 31 per cent were unemployed, but by 1981 this figure had risen to 63 per cent. Other things being equal, this would have resulted in the young long-term unemployed becoming progressively a pool of the non-qualified. But other things were not equal: large changes were taking place in the structure of the youth labour market. The proportion of non-qualified school-leavers entering the labour market was being reduced, largely because of the increasing success rate in CSE examinations. The number of job vacancies was being halved, while the rate of flow into unemployment was somewhat increasing. And the average period of spells of unemployment was considerably increasing.

As the volume of youth unemployment grew, while the inflow of the unqualified to the labour market diminished, the arithmetically inevitable result was that more of the group with some qualifications were drawn into unemployment. Moreover, a general lengthening of durations of unemployment meant that more of these somewhat-qualified young people were remaining in unemployment for long periods. As a result, while the non-qualified had the worst chances of reemployment, their prominence in the long-term unemployed stock did not increase as much as might have been expected. And, equally, while the qualified were gaining in relative terms over the non-qualified in the competition for jobs, this did not compensate for the circumstances that there were increasing numbers of qualified competing for a smaller number of vacancies.

The result can be seen clearly in our 1984 survey sample. The young women entering the labour market in 1980-83 had a closely similar level of qualification to those entering the labour market in 1975-79, while among the young men the more recent entrants were considerably better qualified, on average, than the earlier entrants. This is summarized in Table 3.4 below:

**Table 3.4  Non-qualification by period of entry to labour market**

*per cent without qualification*

|        | 1975-79 | 1980-83 |
|--------|---------|---------|
| Male   | 54      | 41      |
| Female | 40      | 40      |

Another way of showing the change is through comparison with the 1980 DE/PSI survey of long-term unemployment. Since that survey covered only those with one year or more of current unemployment, it is necessary to exclude from the comparison those in the present survey who had been unemployed for less than one year. The 1980 survey estimated that no less than 72 per cent of 17-25 year olds in long-term unemployment were devoid of qualifications. Referring back to Table 3.2, we see that in the present sample those with between one and two years of unemployment had far lower proportions of non-qualification (47 and 46 per cent for men and women, respectively); and even for those with more than two years of current unemployment, the proportion rose only to 63 and 51 per cent respectively. This clearly confirms that, despite worsening relative chances for the non-qualified since 1980, the young long-term unemployed have been becoming a more qualified group during this period.

These findings suggest that the aggregate level of non-qualification or qualification cannot predict levels of youth unemployment except in conjunction with levels of demand. Moreover, demand has to be considered in relation to occupational level when assessing the aggregate influence of qualification levels.

**Table 3.5   School examinations passed**

*percentages*

| | By sex | | By period of entry to labour market | |
|---|---|---|---|---|
| | Male | Female | 1975-79 | 1980-83 |
| None | 51 | 42 | 52 | 42 |
| Only CSE below grade 1 | 20 | 21 | 18 | 23 |
| (following are non-exclusive) | | | | |
| CSE grade 1 | 13 | 20 | 14 | 17 |
| GCE O-level, A-E | 19 | 25 | 18 | 24 |
| GCE A-level, A-E | 5 | 5 | 3 | 8 |
| SCE Ordinary | 5 | 4 | 4 | 5 |
| SCE Higher* | 1 | 2 | 1 | 2 |
| *Weighted base: total survey* | *6492* | *3508* | *5526* | *4474* |

\* Includes other Scottish higher examination passes

We can now fill out the picture of qualifications among the young long-term unemployed. Table 3.5 presents further details of the types of school educational qualifications held by them.

As expected, A-levels were under-represented among those with school examination passes. However it is notable that the proportion with A-levels rose from three per cent among 1975-79 labour market entrants to almost eight per cent among 1980-83 entrants. The mix of O-level and CSE qualifications, within those having any school qualification, was not greatly different from that found among all school-leavers with examination passes. For example, in 1981-82 89 per cent of leavers from English schools had some examination pass, and this included 37 per cent with one or more O-level or CSE grade 1 pass (but no A-levels) and 36 per cent with one or more lower CSE grade passes only. Thus, of all school-leavers with qualifications below A-levels, roughly equal numbers obtained O-level or equivalent, and passes at a lower standard. And among the present sample, 25 per cent had O-level or equivalent as their highest attainment, while 20 per cent had CSE passes only below grade 1.

Comparative figures are not available for the various vocational and higher qualifications shown in Table 3.6, but impressionistically it can be said that apprenticeships and the linked City and Guilds examinations are less prominent than might have been expected in a

**Table 3.6    Vocational and higher qualifications**

*percentages*

|  | By sex | | By period of entry to labour market | |
|---|---|---|---|---|
|  | Male | Female | 1975-79 | 1980-83 |
| None | 86 | 77 | 82 | 84 |
| (following are non-exclusive) | | | | |
| Trade apprenticehip | 3.1 | 1.4 | 4.3 | 0.3 |
| City & Guilds 1 | 7.4 | 3.5 | 7.3 | 4.6 |
| City & Guilds 2-3 | 3.0 | 0.7 | 3.2 | 0.9 |
| City & Guilds Tech. | 0.6 | 0.3 | 0.6 | 0.4 |
| BTEC-ONC/OND | 1.7 | 1.2 | 1.5 | 1.5 |
| BTEC-HNC-HND | 0.9 | 0.8 | 0.9 | 0.8 |
| Clerical, commercial | 0.7 | 13.7 | 4.3 | 6.5 |
| Nursing | 0.1 | 0.5 | 0.4 | 0.0 |
| Diploma, degree | 2.7 | 3.7 | 3.0 | 3.3 |
| *Weighted base:* | | | | |
| *total survey* | *6492* | *3508* | *5526* | *4474* |

group highly concentrated in manual occupations. There was a sharp drop in the proportion with apprentice type qualifications in the 1980-83 labour market intake, which probably reflects the known national decline in the apprenticeship intake during the period. However, the proportions with clerical or commercial qualifications increased slightly in 1980-83.

The descriptive details concerning qualifications therefore do not indicate that our previous conclusions based on broader indicators were misleading. Rather, they confirm that while the young long-term unemployed lack the further or higher qualifications which confer entry to higher occupations, their spread of lower qualifications is quite wide. In particular, if those with the lowest level of school qualifications are considered separately, they are not more prominent among the young long-term unemployed than among school-leavers generally.

## Local educational attainments and the qualifications of the young long-term unemployed

We noted in Chapter 2 the surprisingly strong relationship between the output of schools, in terms of educational attainments, and the employment contraction or growth in their localities. (Surprising, that is, because of the rough-and-ready nature of the information available, which would have reduced the observed relationships below their true level.) Does the output of the educational system show through in qualification levels among the young long-term unemployed in the localities, permitting us to link the educational context with current youth unemployment?

The apparent answer is that it does. The measures selected for the analysis were the proportion leaving school in 1981/82 with no qualification whatever, and the proportion of the survey sample who, likewise, lacked any qualification. It is necessary to omit Glasgow, Motherwell, and Newport from the analysis, because of lack of comparable information. The analysis showed common variation of about 20 per cent between the two measures ($r=0.45$). Once again, in interpreting this result one should take account of the considerable limitations of the available data - notably, the different areas covered by the educational statistics and the sampling units in the 1984 survey. This is likely to lead to an understatement of the true strength of the relationship.

The result, then, supports the view that it is possible for the characteristics of the young long-term unemployed to reflect the objective conditions of their locality. The larger the numbers of unqualified leaving the school system, the greater will be the proportions of unqualified among the long-term unemployed. The difficulty of placing this unqualified, long-term unemployed group into employment can therefore be traced back, in part, to the achievement level in local schools. However, in interpreting this one should take account of possible adverse motivational effects on young people's attainments resulting from deteriorating prospects of employment on leaving school: the direction of the relationship is not necessarily one-way.

An obvious comparative point, which should nonetheless not be passed by, is that the levels of nonqualification in the local sub-samples of young long-term unemployed are always very much higher than the annual rates of nonqualification from the local schools. Because the young long-term unemployed are highly selected by occupational level so too they are highly selected by qualification level - as we have already stressed.

## Driving licences

It may seem strange to move from educational and vocational qualifications to possession of driving licences. However, the attainment of driving a car, and the access given by that skill to use of personal transport, may have been unduly neglected in labour market studies. The skill of driving is directly used in many jobs, and is therefore an attainment of direct relevance to employment. Moreover, where ability to drive is linked to access to a vehicle for personal use, the individual may have an advantage in being able to search more widely and more flexibly for jobs than another who is limited to the lines of search provided by public transport. Unlike educational qualifications, possession of a driving licence is unlikely to influence entry to an occupation when leaving school, but it may become progressively important in the subsequent years, in aiding movement between jobs and changes of occupation, and in competing for jobs from unemployment.

Among the young long-term unemployed, the proportions with driving licences can be briefly summarized as follows:

percentages

|                                    | Men | Women |
|------------------------------------|-----|-------|
| Entering the labour market in 1975-79 | 37  | 26    |
| Entering the labour market in 1980-83 | 34  | 20    |

This can be compared, in a rather approximate manner, with national figures from the General Household Survey 1980 (data from National Travel Surveys of earlier years show that for the age-group in question, the national proportions with driving licences change very slowly).

percentages

|              | Men | Women |
|--------------|-----|-------|
| Aged 17-20   | 30  | 15    |
| Aged 21-29   | 69  | 42    |

The proportions acquiring driving licences rise quickly with age from 17 through to 29, and to make use of the national statistics, with different age bands to those available in our survey, requires assumptions about the shape of the underlying curve. Study of the complete published statistics suggests that the majority of people learn to drive early on, with a progressively more gradual rate thereafter. On this basis, the proportions of the younger age group of young unemployed with driving licences was close to the expected value derived from the national figure. However, for women aged 21-24 the proportion with driving licences nationally would be about 35 per cent (somewhat higher than the young unemployed figure of about 30 per cent), while nationally for men the proportion would be about 60 per cent - very much higher than that for the young male unemployed in the 21-24 age group.

A further factor to bear in mind, however, is social class or occupational composition. Although no national statistics by age within social class are available, there are marked differences by social

71

class (for all ages combined) in the proportions holding driving licences. For example, in 1980, 88 per cent of employers and managers, 67 per cent of intermediate non-manual workers, 64 per cent of skilled manual workers, but only 30 per cent of semi-skilled manual workers, held driving licences. It could be that there is a tendency for such differences to be reduced among younger age groups, but it seems unlikely that they vanish completely.

If this additional point is borne in mind, it seems likely that the young long-term unemployed did not have a lower level of attainment in regard to driving licences than comparable employed groups, with the possible exception of the young men in the 21-24 age range.

## Social characteristics

Educational and vocational qualifications, and possession of a driving licence, can be regarded as individual attainments. Such attainments are likely to be influenced by the social background in which learning and development take place. There is a substantial body of research relating educational attainments and educational deficits to advantages and disadvantages in social background[4]. Because the young long-term unemployed included substantial proportions without qualifications, the analysis of social backgrounds is of relevance to the interpretation of their competitive position in the labour market. There is the additional possibility that the same social characteristics which influence low educational attainments may carry over into employment and continue to retard the transition to working life for young people.

The study of social background influences on attainments has to some extent suffered from an undue dependence on the concept of social class. Through more recent work, however, such as that of the National Child Development Study[5] the social background influences upon attainment have started to be unpacked, and this is yielding a more detailed understanding. For example, it has been shown that upbringing in single-parent households is strongly related not only to attainments but also to lower levels of occupational aspiration when entering the labour market.

The present survey did not obtain information on the social class of respondents' parents (the nearest proxy was the type of housing tenure), but with this exception it has been possible to follow through the earlier analysis with data from the survey. In addition we begin by reviewing the marital status of respondents.

## Marital status

Marital status is of potential importance to unemployment because of its relationship to benefit entitlements, to female participation in the labour market, and to the motivational implications of being a 'breadwinner'.

In the survey sample 22 per cent of men, and 24 per cent of women were married. Our chief interest at this stage is simply to assess whether this differs from the comparable economically active population. A reasonably close comparison is available from the Census of Population 1981. The relevant Census tabulation however gives results for the 16-19 and 20-24 age groups. To get correspondence with our 18-24 range, we assumed (a) that those in ages 18 and 19 in the Census constituted half of the 16-19 group, (b) that none of the 16 and 17 year olds were married. The second assumption obviously leads to some overestimation, but this is unlikely to be greater than one per cent in the case of men and three per cent in the case of women.

The outcome is an estimate, for the economically active population aged 18-24, of 22 per cent of men married, and 29 per cent of women. Taking the overestimation factor into account, we conclude that the proportions married in the present sample are closely in line with the economically active population.

Although we have no national figures to compare them with, it is of relevance to consider how many of the young unemployed had dependant children. The proportion was the same for both men and women, at 18 per cent. So it can be seen that the great majority, if married, also had a child to care for. In the case of 11 per cent of men, and of four per cent of women, there were two or more dependent children.

*Gender, marital status, and period of unemployment* The sample for the 1984 survey was not stratified by gender: young men and young women had chances of selection for the sample which were proportional to their actual prevalence in long-term unemployment. This resulted in a sample containing 35 per cent of women and 65 per cent of men. But examination of the gender distributions by length of time in unemployment showed that women tended to be more concentrated at the shorter periods and less prevalent at the longer periods. Thus in the group with between 6 and 12 months of unemployment, women constituted about 40 per cent, but in the remainder with more than 12 months of unemployment, only about 25 per cent. It is important to explore this difference further, since it clarifies some of the most important distinctions between men and women in the present sample.

Marital status, and the link between marital status and eligibility for benefits, provides the key to understanding this difference. Among the young men in the sample, marital status was linked in a straightforward way with age. The proportion married (or living as married) increased steadily with duration of unemployment, which in turn was connected with age. It was 15 per cent for men unemployed for 6-12 months, rising to 36 per cent for those unemployed for three years or more. And among men unemployed for 6-12 months, 36 per cent were aged 18-20, the remainder 21-24; but among those unemployed for three years or more, only four per cent were aged 18-20, and 95 per cent over 20. Thus the increase in the proportion of married men in each unemployment duration reflects the increasing age of the respondents.

**Table 3.7    Proportion of women married, by period of unemployment**

| Period of unemployment | Percentage married |
|---|---|
| 6-12 months | 39 |
| 13-24 months | 15 |
| 25-36 months | 7 |
| more than 36 months | 10 |

A very different pattern exists among the women however. In particular, the women show no similarity to the relationship found among the men between age and marital status; nor between marital status and duration of employment. Instead, women who were unemployed for 6-12 months were more than twice as likely to be married as other women, or as men in this duration of unemployment.

In fact, the proportions married work out roughly inversely to period of unemployment, as shown in Table 3.7.

Furthermore, the differences between women and men in this respect cannot be accounted for simply by age distribution. For, in fact, the proportion of women unemployed 6-12 months and aged 18-20 varies only a little from that of men in the same category (31 per cent in the case of women; 36 per cent in the case of men). And although there are proportionally somewhat fewer women than men aged 21-24 in the longest duration of unemployment (81 per cent against 95 per cent), this difference is insufficient to account for the fact that nearly four times as many men as women in this category are married.

Rather, the disproportionate representation of married women in the shortest duration of unemployment probably reflects the inclusion, among the young unemployed, of women registered for benefits following childbirth. This group inflates the figures of female unemployment in the 6-12 month category, but many or most of these will cease to be registered, and hence will fall out from the unemployed count, once that they complete 12 months in unemployment and lose eligibility for benefits.

This explanation is supported by the pattern of employment found among the spouses or partners of these young men and women. Among the married men, the proportions with wives or partners not in paid employment varied only slightly across the spectrum of unemployment durations, from 86 per cent of men unemployed 6-12 months to 92 per cent of men unemployed more than two years. In short, nearly all the wives or partners of these unemployed men were themselves not in employment[6]. In the 6-12 month period of unemployment, the proportion of women with employed husbands is the mirror image of that for men: 84 per cent of these women have employed partners. But beyond 12 months' unemployment, there is little reason for women to remain on the register if they have a working husband: hence not only were there fewer married women in these categories, but smaller proportions of these reported that their husbands or partners were working.

These differences, then, reflect the different family and childcare responsibilities of men and women in our society, and the different recognition given to their position by the system of state benefits. One result is that married women become progressively less visible in registered unemployment at longer durations. Another result is that, while single unemployed people of both sexes are comparable in terms of their social characteristics, married unemployed people tend to be in different social circumstances, depending upon their sex. This is also likely to have repercussions on job search in unemployment. The findings of this survey show that these conclusions are as applicable to 18-24 year olds as to older groups in unemployment[7].

## *Housing*

The majority of the young long-term unemployed, if not married, were living with their parents and were not heads of households. Type of housing is, in the present survey, the closest proxy to social class. It is also relevant to the issue of overcrowding, which is known to result most often with large families in Council rented accommodation.

**Table 3.8    Housing type by marital status**

percentages

|  | Male | | | Female | | |
|---|---|---|---|---|---|---|
|  | All | Married | Not married | All | Married | Not married |
| Owner occupied | 28 | 9 | 33 | 39 | 50 | 35 |
| Council rented | 58 | 77 | 53 | 46 | 33 | 50 |
| Private rented | 8 | 11 | 8 | 9 | 8 | 9 |
| Hostel/other | 5 | 3 | 5 | 7 | 9 | 6 |
| Not stated | 1 | 0 | 1 | * | 0 | * |
| *Weighted base: total survey* | 6492 | 1437 | 5055 | 3508 | 822 | 2686 |

* less than 0.5 per cent

Table 3.8 shows the types of housing in which the young long-term unemployed were living. The largest category in the case of men was rented Council housing (58 per cent), with 28 per cent being in owner occupied properties (whether purchased outright or on a mortgage). Privately rented accommodation accounted for nine per cent of housing for men. However there was a marked contrast in the case of young unemployed women, 39 per cent of whom were living in owner-occupied properties and 46 per cent in Council rented properties. This however is affected by the differential effect of marriage on housing, which is also clearly shown in Table 3.8. Young married men were extremely likely to go into Council rented accommodation. Young married women, however, were more likely to go into owner occupied housing (50 per cent) than into Council rented housing (33 per cent). The explanation of this is that the great majority of the young married women had husbands in employment, while the great majority of the young married men's wives were not in employment. The financial positions of the two kinds of households were, accordingly, likely to be quite different.

In confirmation of this, it can be seen from Table 3.9 that the greatest differences between the men and women were in the 21-24 age group. In the younger (18-20) age group, who give the most accurate impression of parents' social class because nearly all are still living at home, the proportions (for both men and women) were about half in Council housing, and about 35 per cent in owner-occupied property.

**Table 3.9    Housing type by period of entry to labour market**

*column percentages*

|  | 1975-79 | | 1980-83 | |
|---|---|---|---|---|
|  | Male | Female | Male | Female |
| Owner occupied | 23 | 43 | 35 | 36 |
| Council rented | 64 | 40 | 51 | 51 |
| Private rented | 9 | 10 | 8 | 7 |
| Hostel/other | 4 | 7 | 7 | 6 |
| Not stated | 1 | * | * | 0 |
| Weighted base: total survey | 3808 | 1718 | 2684 | 1790 |

* less than 0.5 per cent

There is a marked difference between the housing of the present sample and that of the long-term unemployed sample, of all ages, in the 1980-81 DE/PSI study. In this latter sample, which was drawn at a time immediately before the steepest rise in long-term unemployment, two-thirds were in Council rented accommodation. From this point of view it seems possible that the young long-term unemployed come from a less 'traditional working class' background than did the earlier sample.

### Family size

Family size coupled with overcrowding have been identified by the National Child Development Study as having important effects on educational attainment and development[8]. The nearest measure in the present survey is the number of brothers and sisters of the respondents, data for which are shown in Table 3.10.

**Table 3.10  Number of siblings**

*column percentages*

|  | Sex | | Entry period to labour market | |
|---|---|---|---|---|
|  | Male | Female | 1975-79 | 1980-83 |
| None | 4 | 7 | 6 | 4 |
| One | 18 | 21 | 18 | 19 |
| Two | 23 | 24 | 22 | 25 |
| Three | 17 | 20 | 17 | 20 |
| Four or more | 38 | 28 | 37 | 31 |
| Not stated | 1 | 1 | 1 | * |
| Weighted base: total survey | 6492 | 3508 | 5526 | 4474 |

*  less than 0.5 per cent

There were moderate differences in family size between the male and female parts of the sample, and between the 18020 and 21-24 age groups. Men, and the older age group, were slightly more likely to have large numbers of brothers ror sisters. However, these differences were not so large as to complicate comparisons with the national picture. Quite a good comparison is provided by statistics from the National Child Development Study. These however were based on the numbers of children aged under 21 who were in the household when each child on which that study focusses was aged 11. The NCDS therefore slightly underestimates the size of completed families. We select from the NCDS results those relating to families with four or more children (equivalent to three or more siblings in our Table 3.10):

|  | Families with four or more children in NCDS |
| --- | --- |
| Non-manual heads of household: | 60 per cent |
| Manual heads of household: | 36 per cent |
| All households in NCDS: | 32 per cent |

In the present study, the equivalent proportion (averaged across male and female, as are the NCDS results) was 53 per cent with three or more siblings. Even after allowing for a degree of underestimation in the NCDS findings, it seems very probable that the young long-term unemployed were concentrated to an exceptional degree in large families.

## Upbringing in single-parent families

We asked the young people how they had been brought up when at secondary school - whether by both parents, or by one parent only. The youngest group of women came somewhat more often from single parent families than did the remainder. Overall, 18 per cent of young men and 20 per cent of young women came from single-parent families, but the latter proportion rose to 24 per cent for young women aged 18-20.

Although a variety of sources of information about single-parent families is available, comparisons are fraught with difficulties of definition. The question asked in our survey must be regarded as simplistic by comparison with the detailed analysis in the National Child Development Study[9] which illustrates the difficulties. If a single-parent upbringing is taken to mean 'being cared for by one natural parent living alone', then at age 16 8.4 per cent of the NCDS fell into this category - less than half the figure encountered with the young long-term unemployed. If however it is taken to include a single natural parent living with a step-parent, co-habitee, adoptive parent, or relative, then the total rises to 14.4 per cent. Furthermore, the NCDS data relate to 1975, and it is believed that there has been a considerable increase in the prevalence of single-parent families since then.

It therefore seems to be imprudent to draw any firm conclusion as to whether single-parent upbringing was a more common feature of the background of young long-term unemployed people than of others of their age group.

## *Ethnic groups*

Although ethnic minority groups constitute only a small fraction of all those in unemployment, they are known to be over-represented relative to their population, and it seems that they face distinctive problems in the labour market resulting from employment discrimination - a problem which has been extensively documented in studies of racial disadvantage[10].

Our analysis of ethnic groups is based on visual classification by interviewers. The results are shown in Table 3.11. Overall, 8.0 per cent of men and 7.5 per cent of women were classified as Asian, West Indian or African by their appearance. In the case of men, there was little difference in the proportions between the two age groups of 18-20 and 21-24. In the case of women, however, there appeared to be a marked increase between those entering the labour market in 1975-79 (5.6 per cent in the ethnic minority groups) and those entering in 1980-83 (10.5 per cent in ethnic minority groups).

**Table 3.11  Ethnic group by sex and period of entry to labour market**

*column percentages*

|  | Male | | | Female | | |
| --- | --- | --- | --- | --- | --- | --- |
|  | All | 75-79 | 80-83 | All | 75-79 | 80-83 |
| White | 90.9 | 91.5 | 90.0 | 91.0 | 93.5 | 88.7 |
| Asian | 3.1 | 2.9 | 3.3 | 3.2 | 3.3 | 3.2 |
| West Indian or African | 4.9 | 4.7 | 5.2 | 4.3 | 1.9 | 6.7 |
| Other | 0.5 | 0.5 | 0.4 | 0.4 | 0.3 | 0.5 |
| No information | 0.6 | 0.4 | 1.0 | 1.0 | 1.0 | 1.0 |
| *Weighted base: total survey* | *6492* | *3808* | *2684* | *3508* | *1718* | *1790* |

The most recent information up to 1984 concerning the proportions of ethnic minority group members in unemployment relates to August 1982 and was published in the *Employment Gazette*. The proportion for Great Britain as a whole was 4.2 per cent, although there were large regional variations - an important complication in making estimates concerning ethnicity. It is apparent, therefore, that young people from ethnic minority groups were over-represented in our sample relative to the levels of ethnic minority unemployment - which in their turn are known to constitute exceptionally high levels relative to the ethnic minority population[11].

The ethnic minority groups formed only a small proportion of the total 1984 survey, but a much higher proportion of the young long-term unemployed in some localities. This is because ethnic minorities tend to be concentrated in a few areas rather than spread evenly over many areas. Six of the areas in the study, which provided 31 per cent of the whole sample (unweighted), had 82 per cent of the ethnic minority members. While many of the areas had not a single member of an ethnic minority in their samples, in others - such as Wolverhampton or Bradford - ethnic minority group members constituted up to one third of the sample, and are likely to have been an important influence upon conditions in the local labour market.

## Social characteristics, individual attainments, and labour market outcomes

We have speculated that the social background of young people may exert an influence on levels of youth unemployment indirectly, through educational attainment or educational deficit and hence through occupational selection. We have been able to test the hypothesis in this survey by examining the relationships between the social background measures described above, and measures of individual attainment - educational and vocational qualifications, and possession of a driving licence.

A full account of these analyses is not presented in this chapter because to do so would delay the main subject matter. However, because the individual attainments (or their lack) will occupy such a large part of the account given in this report, it is worthwhile to sketch in outline the main outcome of our analyses in this respect, and the resulting assumptions with which the main part of the report has been approached.

Housing type, family size, and upbringing in single-parent families were all significantly related, in our sample, to all the measures of individual attainment. However, the association of single-parent upbringing with attainment measures was considerably weaker than that of the other two factors. Ethnicity was unrelated to individual attainment: in common with a number of other studies, we found that young people in ethnic minority groups had similar levels of attainment to the average for all the young long-term unemployed. We did, however, find a complex interaction between qualifications, ethnic group, sex and period of unemployment, which will be discussed in Chapter 7.

The analyses therefore confirmed our hypothesis that a group of social background variables was acting on individual levels of attainment, which in turn were likely to be influencing the propensity to unemployment among young people.

The further question posed by this set of findings is whether youth unemployment is best depicted as influenced by individual attainments such as qualifications, or by the social background characteristics which could arguably be regarded as more fundamental. Although this is a matter which can be examined by statistical methods, we have considered that a practical rather than a technical answer can be given. The social background of young people is largely beyond alteration except in the long term; but it is possible to modify attainments by further training and development in the short to medium term. This practical consideration in our view greatly outweighs the calls of conceptual elegance. For this reason alone, we have chosen to focus our further discussion in this report upon individual attainments rather than on social background factors. However, at certain points in the argument, we introduce a statistical control for social background so as to be able to provide some assessment of how this may affect the interpretation.

Also, our analyses usually keep separate the results for men and for women in our sample. As has been shown, several difference in social background exist between the sexes in long-term youth unemployed, so that keeping their results separate tends to reduce any influence from social background.

## Concluding comments

The large question was posed at the outset of this chapter, as to whether the young people in long-term unemployment should be regarded as a distinct group within the labour market, or whether they were merely an indistinguishable part of some larger section.

The evidence of the survey showed that the young long-term unemployed were almost wholly located in the lower part of the labour market - which consists of manual, personal service and lower non-manual jobs. It also showed, however, that relative to that location in the labour market, their educational and vocational qualifications were fairly typical of all their age group in employment. In terms of individual attainments, they could not reasonably be regarded as a 'lowest stream' within the lower half of the labour market. Their qualifications reflected the occupations from which they came.

In terms of social background, the evidence was more varied. They were as likely to be married as the economically active population of their age. Their housing, a good indicator of the social class of their parents, indicated a more varied social mix than that found in the long-term unemployed as a whole. However, there was clear evidence that they came to an exceptional degree from large families, and it is possible (although reliable comparisons are lacking) that single-parent upbringing was also over-represented in their background. Finally, young people from ethnic minority groups were clearly over-represented among them, as was expected; these however still constituted only a small proportion of the total.

Although social background influences are possibly important in developing a full explanation of long-term youth unemployment, we have argued that for practical purposes these influences (with the exception of ethnicity) are likely to be embodied in individual attainments. Because of what has been found concerning the attainments of the young long-term unemployed, relative to their broad location in the lower part of the labour market, we consider that their entry into unemployment chiefly resulted from the vulnerability of the occupational levels where they worked to structural change and to altered economic conditions. At the same time, we assume that within the young long-term unemployed variations in the ability to find jobs exist between individuals because of variations in attainments and in labour market behaviour. These notions provide the programme for the remainder of this report.

# 4 Patterns of Work

A large section of the survey interview was devoted to obtaining a labour market history for each individual from the age of 16 to the present. Getting such personal histories completed is one of the more difficult tasks facing survey research. In the present case, there were several helpful circumstances to make the aim more attainable. In the first place, the use of labour market histories has been increasing in recent years so that there was a variety of experience to build upon. Then, the importance attached to this aspect of the inquiry led to it receiving a high priority in the design and piloting stages. Finally, the fact that the oldest respondents had no more than nine years in the labour market - while the average was five - meant that the problem of recall was kept within reasonable bounds.

In view of the effort devoted to this aspect of the study, and the various procedures applied to enhance detail and coherence[1], we feel confident that a high quality of information about the labour market background of these young people has been achieved.

In addition to the labour market histories, we obtained occupational and industrial details about up to four previous jobs: the latest before unemployment, the penultimate, the first job after leaving school, and the job considered to be the 'main' or most important one held. (Some aspects of this information have already been used in the previous chapter.) In many cases, however, only one or two jobs had been held, or the 'main' job was identical with one of the others referred to, so that fewer than four jobs were covered in this way.

The 'main' job - that is, the one which the respondent considered the most important he or she had held - was then the focus of further questioning, covering such matters as training, pay, hours of work, type of employer and travel costs. About four fifths of those with two or more previous jobs identified one of them as the 'main' job. In other cases, the most recent job prior to unemployment was considered instead.

## Three labour market patterns

In appraising the labour market histories of young people, two questions appear particularly appropriate. How much of their time in the labour market have the young people spent in jobs? How stable have their jobs been? The answer to the first question will indicate how successful they have been in competing in the labour market. The answer to the second question will indicate how successful they have been in establishing themselves within a job and in making the transition to stable employment which typifies most adult workers.

**Table 4.1 Proportion of time in employment, by duration of longest job**

| | | | Longest job (in months) | | | |
| --- | --- | --- | --- | --- | --- | --- |
| | All | No job | 1-12 | 13-24 | 25-36 | 37+ |
| **Those entering the labour market in 1975-79** | | | | | | |
| *Total (weighted)* | *5526* | *528* | *1475* | *1223* | *954* | *1346* |
| Row % of total | | 10 | 27 | 22 | 17 | 24 |
| Mean % time in employment* | 44 | 0 | 19 | 47 | 59 | 73 |
| **Those entering the labour market in 1980-83** | | | | | | |
| *Total (weighted)* | *4474* | *1959* | *2060* | *359* | *94* | *2* |
| Row % of total | | 44 | 46 | 8 | 2 | — |
| Mean % time in employment* | 15 | 0 | 20 | 53 | 67 | 73 |

\*      The total time to which employment is percentaged excludes periods of
       non-registered education, but includes periods on government schemes.
       Standard errors of the non-zero means were in the range 0.7-2.3 per cent
       — Less than 0.1 per cent.

Table 4.1 brings together information which is relevant to both these questions. It covers both males and females so as to give a first overall view of employment histories, dividing the sample into those who entered the labour market in 1975-79 and those entering in

1980-83. The table measures the average proportion of time in the labour market spent in work[2], and this is cross-tabulated by various lengths of time in the longest job held. The table also shows the total number who never held a job up to the time of the interview: this has an important bearing on the main measure of proportion of time in work, since when many fail to obtain any job, this average is sharply reduced.

Several important points emerged from this analysis.

(i)    A substantial part of the 1975-79 entrants to the labour market had spent more than two years, in many cases more than three years, in their longest job; and these on average had spent about two-thirds of their time in the labour market in work. On either criterion it would be reasonable to regard these as having had a normal or stable position in the labour market prior to the long-term unemployment. It appears, then, that approaching half (42 per cent) of the sample who entered the labour market in 1975-79 had been displaced from a relatively stable or normal employment pattern.

(ii)    Applying the same criteria of normal or stable employment to those who entered the labour market in 1980-83, one finds that only 2 per cent had achieved this.

(iii)    At the other extreme were those who had had no jobs since entering the labour market. Among the 1975-79 entrants these constituted 10 per cent of the sample, while among the 1980-83 entrants they comprised 44 per cent.

(iv)    The third and residual group consisted of those who had not held a job for as long as two years and who had spent a lower proportion of their time in work than the group described in (a) above. The size of this group did not differ so much between the 1975-79 entrants and the 1980-83 entrants. It was 49 per cent in the former group and 54 per cent in the latter.

The fact that more than 40 per cent of the 1975-79 entrants to the labour market had achieved reasonably stable employment at one stage appears to be consistent with the suggestion made in Chapter 2 that the young long-term unemployed consist of a fairly broad cross-section of young workers from manual and lower non-manual occupations. Since 1980, however, it appears that it has been more difficult for young workers in this stratum of the labour market to achieve settled employment. Within the young unemployed there are sharply contrasting histories, of displacement from settled employment on one hand, and of failure to gain entry to employment on the other. Much of the difference between the 1975-79 and 1980-83 entrants can be reduced to a change from the former to the latter pattern of labour market experience.

It might be, though, that the differences between the 1975-79 entrants and the 1980-83 group reflect in part their different lengths of time in the labour market, as well as different labour market conditions. To gain a more balanced comparison with the 1980-83 entrants, we have separately analysed the labour market experience of the 1975-78 intake (omitting those who joined the labour market in 1979 to avoid overlap with the later period) up to the end of 1979 only. The key results are shown in Table 4.2.

**Table 4.2 Proportion of time in work for 1975-78 entrants, up to 1979**

|  | All | No job | Longest job (in months) | | | |
|---|---|---|---|---|---|---|
|  |  |  | 1-12 | 13-24 | 25-36 | 37+ |
| Row % of total |  | 13 | 21 | 20 | 15 | 30 |
| Mean % of time in employment* | 67 | 0 | 46 | 78 | 87 | 95 |
| *Total (weighted)* | *4144* | *547* | *884* | *843* | *642* | *1229* |

\*       Calculated as in Table 4.1. Standard errors for non-zero items were in the range 0.5-2.3 per cent.

When attention is confined to the first period, the contrast between the 1975-78 and 1980-83 entrants is sharply accentuated. Within the 1975-79 period, the majority of young people in this group spent most of their time in work. This applied not only to most of those with jobs of two years' duration and longer, but even to the numerous young people whose longest job was between one and two years' long. It was only those who had never had a job of more than one year who had spent appreciably lower proportions of time in work. So it is clear that the decrease in proportions of time in work, and of attainment of relatively stable jobs, which were illustrated in Table 4.1, reflect changing demand for young people in the job market, relative to supply and are not the result of differences in age or length of experience between the entrants in 1975-79 and 1980-83.

### Recurrent unemployment or unstable employment

Although a substantial proportion of the young long-term unemployed had initially achieved a reasonable degree of stability in employment, many others passed through numerous distinct periods of work, unemployment, or participation in government training and work experience schemes. This is not of course a new phenomenon. On the contrary, it has often been remarked that the tendency to make many moves in the labour market is characteristic of young people in Britain, especially those in manual jobs. In the DE/PSI 1980 survey of long-term unemployment it was found that about half the respondents aged 35 or under had a history of 'recurrent unemployment', where the repeated spells of unemployment separated jobs which were often short-lived. Since 1980 the analysis has been somewhat complicated by the increasingly wide involvement of young people in government training and work experience schemes, so that it is no longer sufficient merely to consider spells in work and in unemployment.

**Table 4.3   Number of distinct 'spells', by period of entry and sex**

*percentages*

|  | Entry to labour market | | | |
|  | 1975-79 | | 1980-83 | |
|  | Male | Female | Male | Female |
|---|---|---|---|---|
| 1-3 spells | 22 | 34 | 48 | 56 |
| 4-6 spells | 46 | 42 | 42 | 34 |
| 7+ spells | 32 | 23 | 10 | 10 |
| *Base (weighted)* | *3808* | *1718* | *2684* | *1790* |

Note:   A spell means any distinct period of employment, unemployment, or economic inactivity (including attendance on government schemes).

Table 4.3 shows the number of separate labour market 'spells' for those entering the labour market in 1975-79 and 1980-03. The results are also tabulated separately for young men and young women. The women had fewer separate spells on average than the men, especially among 1975-79 entrants. Among 1975-79 entrants, almost half the men had had six or more dinstinct spells, while almost half the women had had five or more spells. Among 1980-83 entrants, who had spent on average less than half the time in the labour market compared with the 1975-79 group, there were still half who had had four or more separate spells - and this applied to both the men and the women. Thus the degree of instablility or fragmentation was still high in the second period. Whereas the spells for 1975-79 entrants were most influenced by frequency of unemployment, for 1980-83 entrants the additional new factor was growth of participation in government schemes.

To put this feature of labour market histories in context, it is necessary to sketch briefly the development of government youth schemes during the period. In 1975-76 the Job Creation scheme was in being, but operated on a small scale with just over 7,000 participants. In the following year however the Work Experience Programme commenced and by 1977-78 there were 53,000 participants in both WEP and Job Creation schemes. WEP was then absorbed into the larger and more varied Youth Opportunities Programme, while Job Creation was discontinued. By 1979/80 - the final year relating to the group in our survey whom we have called the 1975-79 entrants - there were 216,000 YOP participants. YOP continued to grow, to a peak of 553,000 in 1981/82. Thereafter the places tapered down to 230,000 in the final year with which we are concerned, 1983/84, but this had been partly compensated by the growth of the Young Workers Scheme, with 110,000 subsidised jobs, and the Community Programme with 57,000 participants in the 18-24 age group.

Participants do not necessarily equate with individuals - a person may take part in the same scheme more than once, or in different schemes at different times. If this is ignored, however, it can be calculated that the total scheme placements, as a proportion of total school-leavers, was about 12-13 per cent in the period from 1975/76 to 1979/80, and about 57-58 per cent in the period from 1980/81 to 1983/84. (These calculations have been based on Manpower Services Commission annual reports and on the Statistics of Education published by the Department of Education and Science.)

For the young long-term unemployed, 38 per cent of the men entering the labour market in 1975-79 attended one or more schemes, and 28 per cent of the women. Of the 1980-83 entrants to the labour market, 63 per cent of men and 56 per cent of women had been on one or more schemes. So it is clear that, overall, the young long-term unemployed had attended schemes more frequently than the average of all school-leavers in the period 1975-84. In fact the national average appears to be about one-third of school-leavers going on schemes over the period; for the young men in our sample, the corresponding figure was almost one half, and for women in our sample over 40 per cent.

The declining frequency of unemployment, and the rising frequency of schemes, are shown in Table 4.4. In particular, the proportions going on schemes roughly doubled for entrants in the second period - a little less than a doubling for men (who were more prominent than women on the schemes attended by the first period's entrants), and a full doubling for women. It is also notable that the proportions of young people going on more than one scheme placement rose considerably for 1980-83 entrants. For men in this younger age-group, it was almost as common to go on more than one scheme as to go once only.

**Table 4.4.   Spells of unemployment and on government schemes**

*percentages*

|  | Entry to labour market | | | |
|  | 1975-79 | | 1980-83 | |
|  | Male | Female | Male | Female |
|---|---|---|---|---|
| **Unemployment:** | | | | |
| 1 spell | 25 | 39 | 42 | 51 |
| 2 spells | 33 | 35 | 32 | 29 |
| 3 spells | 23 | 12 | 22 | 17 |
| 4+ spells | 19 | 14 | 5 | 3 |
| **Government schemes:** | | | | |
| None | 63 | 71 | 37 | 44 |
| 1 | 26 | 20 | 34 | 35 |
| 2+ | 12 | 9 | 29 | 21 |
| *Base (weighted)* | *3808* | *1718* | *2684* | *1790* |

Does a fragmented labour market history, with numerous distinct spells of one kind or another, have adverse implications for the proportion of time spent in work? Tabulating the proportion of time in work by the number of spells, separately for 1975-79 and 1980-83 entrants, we found no consistent relationship emerging. (Of course, it is desirable to have more than one spell, since in the context of this survey one spell means that the whole time has been spent in unemployment.) Indeed, it is notable that among the 1980-83 entrants it was those with the most fragmented history - the 10 per cent with seven or more separate spells- who had the highest proportion of time in work.

If however data are drawn only from what took place in 1975-79 (for those who entered the labour market in 1975-78) then a clear relationship emerges (Table 4.5). In this earlier period, a more fragmented work history was strongly associated with a reduced proportion of time spent in jobs. The lack of overall relationship between number of spells and time in work must therefore result from disruption of that relationship after 1980, overlaying the picture from the earlier period and so obscuring it.

**Table 4.5    Proportion of time in work, and number of spells, up to 1979**

|  | Number of spells | | | | | | | |
|---|---|---|---|---|---|---|---|---|
|  | All | 1 | 2 | 3 | 4 | 5 | 6 | 7+ |
| Mean % time in employment* | 67 | 74 | 79 | 66 | 62 | 62 | 60 | 51 |
| Total (weighted) | 4144 | 305 | 1054 | 889 | 547 | 316 | 221 | 225 |

* See Table 4.1 for definition.

The explanation of the change probably lies in the near-disappearance of stable or long-lasting jobs for these young people, in the 1980-83 period, as already illustrated in Table 4.1. Whereas many young people during 1975-79 were able to find their way into jobs that continued for two or three years, this happened to only two per cent of the 1980-83 entrants. To look at this in terms of the young person's job strategy, in 1975-79 the best approach to maximizing time in work was clearly to find a job and stick to it. In 1980-83, however, it is as if this option is foreclosed: the only possibility is to chase a succession of short-lived jobs.

That picture, however, would not necessarily apply to young people in the more secure sections of the labour market, especially those with access to jobs on career ladders. Some indications of a growing gap in labour market experience, between those in stable and those in unstable jobs, comes from a comparison of the present survey with the results of the study by Ashton and Maguire of young people in the labour market[3]. That study covered young people in employment as well as those currently unemployed; however, it excluded those who had gone on to higher eduction, a group which could be expected to enter the higher-level occupational strata. For their sample as a whole, Ashton and Maguire have reported (i) a declining degree of job mobility, and (ii) an increased tendency to remain in the first job obtained after leaving school. Moreover, there were considerable differences by occupational level in the length of time for which young people remained in their first jobs, with those in higher white-collar, clerical and skilled manual occupations much more likely to remain for a substantial period. Conversely, the highest tendency to move within the first year was among those in unskilled jobs. Ashton and Maguire also note that the pattern for second jobs was similar to that for first jobs, and that this was unaffected by the individual's previous job - those getting into higher level jobs were just as likely to remain in them if their first job had been at a lower level. Hence stability appears to be specific to the occupation rather than the individual.

It seems possible, then, that since 1980 the job market for 18-24 year olds has been increasingly polarized between relatively stable and relatively unstable segments. The young people in the more secure white-collar or skilled manual jobs have themselves perhaps become more intent on job security. Those in long-term unemployment, however, including many who have lost formerly stable jobs, seem to have very little access to longer-lasting jobs within the lower part of the job market where they are largely confined. The practical problem for these young people is not merely one of finding a job, but of being able to hold on to the job once they have it. Whether or not this pattern shows any signs of changing is considered further in Chapter 6, which deals with new jobs after unemployment.

## Industries, occupations and mobility

So far we have spoken of the employment background of the young unemployed people in our survey only in broad terms. A somewhat greater degree of detail should help to develop a more vivid or realistic picture of their position in the job market. It is of particular interest to examine whether in their previous employment they tended to be over-represented in certain industrial and occupational categories. We would expect that relatively high concentrations of this sort might help to suggest the circumstances leading to declining stability of employment.

A further question of interest is whether there had been substantial movement of the sample across occupations and industries. On one hand, a high degree of movement might be part of the pattern of instability to which we have referred, preventing cumulative experience and the formation of skills. On the other hand, it could indicate flexibility within the labour market and a rational response to highly competitive conditions. Without attempting to judge these complex issues at the present stage, it is important to establish what changes had taken place.

Table 4.6 relates to the 'main' job of the respondent, as he or she perceived it, or if there was no such job, to the most recent before the current unemployment. This job can, one way or another, be regarded as the most representative of the individual's work history. The table shows in which occupations these main or most recent jobs were held. For purposes of comparison, the occupations of all economically active 18-24 year olds at the 1981 Census of Population are displayed alongside.

It has already been shown, in Chapter 3, that the young long-term unemployed were predominantly found in the manual occupations and, in the case of young women, in lower non-manual occupations. Table 4.6 to a large extent merely confirms that finding, but in some respects it also amplifies it. The young unemployed men were under-represented in all the white-collar occupations except the small 'literary, artistic and sports' group and the more significant 'selling' group. They were over-represented in all the other occupational groups, except the small 'miscellaneous' category and the large and important category of occupations concerned with the processing, making and repairing of metal and electrical goods. These latter are the manual occupations of the engineering, electronics and vehicles industries and contain a large proportion of the apprenticed jobs. Whereas in the 1981 Census these accounted for 22 per cent of all jobs for 18-24 year old males, they accounted for 18 per cent of the main

**Table 4.6    Occupation by sex and period of entry to the labour market with 1981 Census comparisons**

*column percentages*

| Occupation order | Male | | | Female | | |
|---|---|---|---|---|---|---|
| | 1975-79 | 1980-83 | Census* | 1975-79 | 1980-83 | Census* |
| (All) | (100) | (100) | (100) | (100) | (100) | (100) |
| 1 | 1 | – | 3 | 4 | 3 | 2 |
| 2 | | | 1 | | | 11 |
| 3 | 1 | 4 | 1 | 0 | 2 | 1 |
| 4 | 2 | 1 | 5 | 0 | 0 | 1 |
| 5 | 1 | 2 | 5 | 1 | 1 | 3 |
| 6 | 3 | 4 | 9 | 24 | 19 | 41 |
| 7 | 5 | 6 | 4 | 14 | 22 | 9 |
| 8 | 2 | 2 | 5 | 0 | 0 | 1 |
| 9 | 9 | 10 | 4 | 21 | 23 | 11 |
| 10 | 4 | 3 | 3 | 2 | 2 | 1 |
| 11 | 14 | 14 | 10 | 16 | 13 | 7 |
| 12 | 18 | 15 | 21 | 3 | 3 | 1 |
| 13 | 7 | 7 | 4 | 14 | 11 | 4 |
| 14 | 14 | 13 | 6 | 0 | 0 | – |
| 15 | 14 | 15 | 8 | 1 | 0 | 1 |
| 16 | 3 | 2 | 4 | – | 0 | 1 |
| 17 | 3 | 2 | 7 | 0 | 2 | 7 |

\*        Census 1981 10 per cent sample aged 18-24
–        Less than 0.5 per cent

Key to occupation order:
1        Professional supporting management
2        Professional in education, welfare and health
3        Literary, artistic and sports
4        Professional in science, engineering and technology
5        Managerial
6        Clinical
7        Selling
8        Security protective service
9        Catering, cleaning, hairdressing and personal service
10      Farming, fishing
11      Materials processing (excluding metal and electrical)
12      Processing (metal and electrical)
13      Painting, assembling, inspecting, packaging
14      Construction, mining
15      Transport
16      Miscellaneous
17      Inadequately described

jobs of the young long-term unemployed who entered the labour market in 1975-79, and for only 15 per cent of the main jobs of 1980-83 entrants. Indeed, whereas these occupations in the engineering industries accounted for one third of all 18-24 manual occupations, they accounted for only 20 per cent of the manual jobs obtained by young men in the long-term unemployed sample.

Thus one specific factor about the young long-term unemployed men seems to be their lack of success in entering the manual occupations in engineering. By comparison with the levels in other manual occupations, there are less than half the expected number in this grouping. Conversely, the numbers in catering, cleaning and personal service occupations, in construction, and in transport operating (which includes warehouse jobs), are substantially higher than expected.

Among the young unemployed women, it is again the case that the higher white-collar occupations are under-represented, as was expected. It is interesting to note in passing that in the economically active population aged 18-24 no less than 12 per cent of women are in professional groups, largely because of their careers in health and education. But only four per cent of the young unemployed women in our sample had come from jobs such as these. Moreover, although clerical work was one of the largest groupings for the young unemployed women, their representation in these occupations was still far below the population level for 18-24 year olds: 22 per cent as against 41 per cent. Also, the proportion had fallen from 23 per cent among the 1975-79 intake to the labour market, to only 18 per cent among the 1980-83 intake. So relative failure to gain entry to clerical occupations is one of the distinguishing characteristics of the young long-term unemployed women as a whole.

Conversely, the young long-term unemployed women had been over-represented in 'selling' (largely as retail sales assistants), in catering, cleaning and personal service occupations, and in those manual manufacturing occupations where women are generally found in large numbers.

The industry of the main or latest job is, in Table 4.7, analysed and compared along similar lines. The findings here are both more striking and more unexpected than in the case of occupations, and there is a greater degree of commonality between the results for men and women.

**Table 4.7    Industrial employment by sex and period of entry
to labour market, with 1981 Census comparisons**

| Industrial division | Male | | | Female | | |
|---|---|---|---|---|---|---|
| | 1975-79 | 1980-83 | Census* | 1975-79 | 1980-83 | Census* |
| Agriculture etc | 2 | 2 | 3 | 1 | 1 | 1 |
| Energy & water etc | 2 | — | 4 | 1 | 0 | 1 |
| Metals & chemicals | 6 | 3 | 5 | 5 | 1 | 3 |
| Engineering | 13 | 11 | 16 | 9 | 6 | 7 |
| Other manufacture | 14 | 18 | 11 | 25 | 23 | 12 |
| Construction | 18 | 19 | 12 | 0 | 1 | 1 |
| Distribution, hotels, catering etc | 24 | 28 | 19 | 34 | 42 | 23 |
| Transport & communications | 4 | 3 | 7 | 1 | 0 | 4 |
| Banking, finance & business services | 4 | 2 | 7 | 3 | 6 | 15 |
| Other services | 13 | 15 | 16 | 21 | 18 | 32 |
| Other/not stated | 1 | 1 | 2 | 0 | 1 | 1 |

*       1981 Census 10 per cent sample aged 18-24
—       Less than 0.5 per cent

In the case of the young men, it can be seen that three of the 10 industry groupings account for the greater part of main or most recent jobs. These are 'other manufacturing', 'construction', and 'distribution, hotels and catering and repair services' - a set which straddles the manufacturing and service sectors. At the 1981 Census these industries had 41 per cent of 18-24 year old men who were in employment, but they accounted for 56 per cent of the young long-term unemployed men who entered the labour market in 1975-79, and for 65 per cent of the 1980-83 entrants.

Just two of these industries - 'other manufacturing', and 'distribution, hotels and catering and repair services' - had an even greater proportion of the young long-term unemployed women. At the 1981 Census, 35 per cent of 18-24 year old females were in these two industry groupings, but they covered 58 per cent of the main jobs of our 1975-79 intake and 66 per cent of the main jobs of the 1980-83 intake.

Evidently the industrial concentration of the young long-term unemployed cannot be characterized in terms of a simple contrast between manufacturing and services, since the dominant industries come from both these sectors. Instead, we have to consider whether there are common characteristics which could account for their prominence despite the difference in sectors.

'Other manufacturing' includes food drink and tobacco, textiles, clothing, footwear, timber and furniture, paper printing and publishing, and rubber and plastics. Food and drink, textiles, clothing and footwear all employ many women in manual jobs. They also provide many part-time, temporary or seasonal jobs. Food and drink has large numbers of unskilled and semi-skilled jobs, and textiles clothing and footwear - while requiring many skilled workers - involve skills which are not readily transferable elsewhere.

It may be speculated, therefore, that what these industries share with distribution, hotels and catering and repair services (and, in the case of male workers, with construction) is a tendency to generate relatively impermanent or marginal jobs to a greater degree than most other manufacturing industries. A particularly high concentration of part-time and temporary jobs is in distribution and in hotels and catering, where job security is also reduced because of the high closure rate of the smaller establishments. Work in construction, as is well known, is governed to a large extent by the contract system, hence particularly unstable, and that industry also contains many small firms with a high rate of bankruptcies.

To summarize, it can be said that the main jobs (or latest jobs) of the young long-term unemployed had been under-represented in those occupations which would be expected to provide greatest stability - not only the higher nonmanual occupations, but the manual occupations in engineering and related industries which lead to skilled status, and the clerical occupations. At the same time they had been over-represented in those industries which, because of their market conditions and employment traditions, might be expected to generate large numbers of lower-skilled or insecure jobs.

## Local industry structure and employment by sector
In Chapter 2 we showed both that many of the local labour markets with high rates of youth unemployment had industrial structures biassed towards manufacturing. We also showed that local change in

employment during 1971-81 could, to a large degree, be accounted for in terms of local industrial structure in 1971 together with national trends in demand by industry. It seems plausible that young people in our sample will tend to have come from the local industries affected by contraction.

The limitations of the sub-sample sizes for the separate labour markets made it impossible to examine their distribution by industry in fine detail: at the level of particular industries, there would usually be too few people in each locality sample for any reliable analysis to be performed. What the local labour market data permit us to add is the context of sectoral change. We can look at the survey data in the light of the broad shifts between manufacturing and services which were taking place. Were the young people in long-term unemployment representative of both sectors, or were they concentrated in the declining manufacturing sectors of their local economies?

In order to compare employment by sector between the local labour market aggregate data and the survey sub-samples, we first had to make some allowance for the fact that young women are under-represented among the young long-term unemployed. We therefore reweighted the aggregate data to accord with male and female proportions in the sample, before carrying out the comparison. Sectoral employment was divided into three groups: manufacturing, services and 'other'. This last consisted of agriculture, mining, public utilities, and construction. The sectoral origin of young people in the sample was as usual taken to be their 'main' or most recent job. The analysis was limited to young people in the sample within the 20 local labour markets studied in Chapter 2.

In view of the various sources of approximation in the data (not least, the small sample size and imperfect spatial coverage of the survey data), the degree of accord found in the sectoral comparison proved to be remarkably high. For the proportions in or from manufacturing employment, the common variation between the (reweighted) aggregate data and the survey data was almost 60 per cent ($r=0.77$). For the service sector, the correspondence was somewhat lower, but still subtantial, with a common variation of 43 per cent ($r=0.66$). In general, then, it appears that the sectoral background of the sub-samples of young long-term unemployed people was to a degree predictable from knowledge of the sectoral structure of the local labour markets.

There were however some significant deviations from the overall pattern, among the 20 local labour markets, and these are of considerable interest in their own right. In Bolton, Liverpool, Southport and Nottingham, the service sector was under-represented among the young long-term unemployed (relative to the local aggregate level in each case). In each of these cases, close examination of the survey data revealed that there was a large excess of young men from a background of work in the construction industry, and this was particularly marked in Liverpool, where the effect was so strong that the manufacturing sector was also somewhat under-represented in the survey sample. The over-representation in construction was, on a lesser scale, also present in several of the other local labour markets. It does appear, therefore, that among the young long-term unemployed there are substantial pockets of young men with some past experience of construction work, but unable to obtain a permanent foothold in it at present, and these may constitute a focus of special disadvantages in the local labour markets concerned.

In two local labour markets - Leeds and Walsall - there was again an under-representation of former service workers among the young long-term unemployed sample, but in these cases the displacement was chiefly in the direction of manufacturing, which was correspondingly over-reseprented. Both Leeds and Walsall enjoyed considerable growth of services over the period, so the low level of experience in the service industries among the young long-term unemployed in these areas was doubly surprising.

The overall conclusion, despite these partial exceptions, remains that the sectoral origins of the young long-term unemployed follow from the sectoral structure of their local labour markets. There is no clear evidence of a systematic bias either towards manufacturing or towards services.

## Changes of industry and occupation

As the interview did not obtain occupational and industry information for every job in the labour market history, it is not possible for us to state the total degree of inter-occupation or inter-industry movement across all jobs. However we are able to examine movement between key junctures in the young person's labour market history. Two comparisons appear potentially most important. First, there is the comparison of occupation and industry between the first job held after leaving school or full-time education, and the most recent job of all. For the purpose of this comparison, we include any jobs held at the time of the survey interview, although for most respondents the latest job was the one immediately prior to long-term unemployment. Such a comparison gives an indication of what movement there had been over the whole period in the labour market. The second comparison on which we focus takes the 'main' job as the starting point and asks whether there had been a change between that and the most recent job. Since the main job can be regarded as the nearest that individuals have got to what they wanted, subsequent change might give an indication of 'drifting off target' in career terms. Where the main job and the latest job are one and the same, it is included on both sides of the comparison, since otherwise career progress might be understated.

**Table 4.8    Industry and occupational mobility, for those having two or more jobs**

*percentages*

| | Male | | Female | |
| --- | --- | --- | --- | --- |
| | | entry to labour market | | |
| | 1975-79 | 1980-83 | 1975-79 | 1980-83 |
| --- | --- | --- | --- | --- |
| Moved industry between first and latest job | 70 | 66 | 61 | 60 |
| Moved occupation between first and latest job | 82 | 83 | 77 | 67 |

Table 4.8 shows change of industry and of occupation between the first and the latest job. The results for men and women are given separately, as are those for 1975-79 and 1980-83 entrants to the labour market. It can be seen that:

(i)    there was a very considerable degree of movement between both industries and occupations - indeed the great majority had changed industries and occupations;

(ii)   there was a somewhat greater degree of occupational movement than of inter-industry movement - which implies intra-industry changes of occupation;

(iii) the amount of change, both occupationally and by industry, was less for women than for men;

(iv) the amount of change was almost as great for those entering the labour market in 1980-83 as for those entering in 1975-79, despite the shorter period involved.

In interpreting these findings, it should be borne in mind that the comparisons have been made in terms of the broadest groupings of the occupational and industrial classifications (published by the Office of Population Censuses and Surveys). There are 16 occupational groups and 10 industrial groups. Hence it can be seen that the changes involved are large, and that relatively few of those with two or more jobs have experienced continuity from their initial job.

Next we consider changes of industry and occupation between the main job and most recent job. Since in some cases these are one and the same, and since even when not so the time between main jobs and subsequent jobs will on average be shorter than the time between first and most recent jobs, it is certain that the amount of change will be less than in the preceding tables. Change, however, continues to be substantial. Overall, more than one third had moved industry after their main job, and more than 40 per cent had changed occupation. There was very little difference between the men and women on this indicator, but there was a consistent tendency for the 1980-83 intake to have moved away from the industries and occupations of their main jobs to a greater degree than the 1975-79 intake. In one way this is unexpected because the earlier intake, having spent longer in the labour market and having experienced a greater change of labour market conditions, might well have had both more opportunity and more need to change. But on the other hand, the finding ties in with the generally greater instability in the labour market experienced by the 1980-83 entrants.

It might be thought that the young people who had moved industry or changed occupation, especially after finding a job which they were ready to regard as their 'main' one, would tend to be the less well-established or successful competitors in the labour market. And conversely, one might expect those who had stayed in a job for two or three years to be better 'anchored' in the labour market and less likely to change thereafter. However, neither of these assumptions holds true. Through further analyses (not shown here) we have explored the possibility of relationships between occupational and inter-industry movement on one hand, and proportion of time in work, duration of longest job, and tendency to a fragmented labour history pattern. In general the relationships are quite small or nonsignificant; the only clear positive finding was that the young women who had changed industry or occupation were more likely to have a fragmented labour market history. Those with fairly long-lasting jobs behind them still had a very high probability of having moved industry or occupation.

In one way these findings may be regarded as reassuring, since they suggest that a high degree of movement across industries and occupations does not, at least within the present group, in itself point to additional difficulties in finding or keeping work. This section's results also show that a high degree of flexibility and mobility exists at the occupational and industrial level, a factor which may be important in achieving growth in the labour market. At the same time, the lack of continuity in career terms among this group of young people points to the potential problems of realizing a return on investment in training and job experience.

## Characteristics of the 'main' or most recent job

The 'main' job should also have been the individual's best chance of getting established in work. As such it also provides us with the best indications of the 'quality' of previous employment and of the formation of skill.

It is common in classifications of employers for purposes of labour market analysis to distinguish between the small-firm sector, the large-firm private sector, and the public sector, since it is believed that there are systematic differences in the employment practices and in the product-market circumstances of these groups. It is important, however, to distinguish between size of establishment and size of organization. Many small establishments form part of large organizations - for example, the branches of a retail chain or a building society - and the conditions of employment and the recruitment practices of such establishments may be determined or influenced by organizational policy. In our questioning on this topic this distinction was made clear, and it is on the organizational level that we focus.

Table 4.9 shows the kinds of organizations giving the young people in our survey their main or most recent jobs. The original more detailed question posed has been condensed to the three conventional categories of small firms, large private firms, and public sector; self-employed jobs have been amalgamated with jobs in small firms.

The large and medium-sized private sector firms formed the largest category, with just half of all the jobs for men and women. The small-firm group covered 38 per cent in the case of men and 34 per cent of women's. The balance, 13 per cent in the case of men and 15 per cent in the case of women, were in the public sector.

**Table 4.9    Type of employer in main or latest job**

*column percentages*

|  | Male | | Female | |
|---|---|---|---|---|
|  | entry to labour market | | | |
|  | 1975-79 | 1980-83 | 1975-79 | 1980-83 |
| Small firm, or self-employed | 33 | 49 | 32 | 43 |
| Large or medium-sized firm | 52 | 45 | 51 | 48 |
| Public sector | 15 | 5 | 16 | 7 |
| *Total (weighted basis)* | *3435* | *1316* | *1471* | *838* |

However, as can also be seen from Table 4.9, there was a marked change between those entering the labour market in 1975-79 and those entering in 1980-83. The shift was towards employment by small firms and away from medium-sized private firms. Judged by the main jobs, public sector employment dropped to less than half its 1975-79 level for these young people. Among the men, the percentage with main jobs in small firms rose from 33 per cent for the 1975-79 intake to 49 per cent for the 1980-83 intake; and the corresponding increase among women was from 32 per cent to 47 per cent. It is interesting that contrary to stereotypes the women were no more frequently found in small firms than were the men.

While there is no national statistical source with which to compare these results, an adequate comparison is available from a survey by Daniel and Hogarth based on a probability sample of 1050 working people in Great Britain[4]. Exactly the same question was used in that survey to elicit the type of current employer. The findings are that, nationally, less than 25 per cent of working people are in small firms, 44 per cent are in large firms, and 33 per cent are in the public sector. Hence the young long-term unemployed were heavily over-represented in the small firms, heavily under-represented in the public sector, and slightly over-represented (though probably not to a significant degree) in the large and medium sized category of private firms.

**Pay in the 'main 'job**
While we have already, in the previous chapter, provided some indications of the skill-level of the young long-term unemployed in their previous occupations, that analysis was based on conventional socio-economic groupings which are known not to be highly precise. There is widespread distrust of such classification methods among economists, who generally prefer to assess the quality or level of an employment by the price which it commands. In our view this approach to assessing the quality of jobs is also open to serious criticisms, but this is not the place to embark on a discussion of methodological issues. We will simply assume that while information about pay does help to assess employment, it cannot be interpreted fully without relating it to other information of a more qualitative type.

In this section, as in all parts of the report, pay data are reported adjusted for inflation, via the Retail Price Index, to May 1984 values. It might be argued that the index of earnings should have been used as the deflator, since this would give better comparability with current earnings of those in employment. But a particular objection to doing so is that in the years prior to the study there was an increase in pay differentials, with higher-paid jobs moving ahead relatively rapidly and lower-paid jobs moving relatively slowly. Since it can be expected that the young long-term unemployed generally come from lower-paid jobs, using the earnings index which is averaged across all levels of job would tend to exaggerate the value of jobs held in earlier years. Use of the RPI as a deflator avoids this problem and yields a measure of job value which is independent of the current bargaining power of different groups.

We calculated the average pay levels in the main job, or latest job before unemployment, for the 1975-79 entrants and 1980-83 entrants to the labour market, and for men and women in the sample. We then sought to compare these with figures taken from the New Earnings Survey 1984[5]. The results are summarised in Table 4.10.

**Table 4.10  Net (take-home) earnings in main or most recent job, with comparisons to New Earnings Survey Data**

|  |  | Mean £/week |
| --- | --- | --- |
| **Male** |  |  |
| entry to labour market: | 1975-79 | 76.5 |
|  | 1980-83 | 54.2 |
| NES comparison, age: | 18-20 | 78.8 |
|  | 21-24 | 104.4 |
| **Female** |  |  |
| entry to labour market: | 1975-79 | 58.3 |
|  | 1980-83 | 43.5 |
| NES comparison, age: | 18-20 | 64.2 |
|  | 21-24 | 80.7 |

Note:    New Earnings Survey (1984) gross earnings data for all occupations (full-time workers only) have been multiplied by 0.78 to estimate net earnings.

The main points from this global view of young unemployed people's former pay can be briefly stated.

(a)    The young unemployed had on average been earning about 70-75 per cent of the average level of their corresponding age group. This level falls between the lowest decile and the lowest quartile of the earnings distribution.

(b)    The relationship between male and female average earnings was about in line with the national figures, except that young unemployed females entering in 1980-83 earned at an exceptionally low level. We will shortly show that this is a distortion brought about by part-time working.

Turning next to hourly wage rates, we show in Table 4.11 that in these terms the young women in the 1980-83 intake had actually drawn level with the young men. The reason was that the members of this group were much the most likely to refer to a part-time job (less than 30 hours a week) as their main or most recent job. Male entrants in 1975-79 did so in only three per cent of cases; this rose to five per cent for male 1980-83 entrants. Female 1975-79 entrants referred to part-time work in six per cent of cases, but this rose to no less than 15

105

per cent among the 1980-83 entrants. These findings do not indicate in themselves that there has been a growing tendency to take part-time work among this group. It could equally well be a tendency among the more recent entrants, because of the more adverse labour market conditions which they have experienced, to be willing to consider even a part-time job as their 'main' job.

**Table 4.11  Hourly wage rates in main or most recent job**

|  | Male | | Female | |
|---|---|---|---|---|
|  | entry to labour market | | | |
|  | 1975-79 | 1980-83 | 1975-79 | 1980-83 |
| Mean £/hour | 1.8 | 1.3 | 1.5 | 1.3 |
| Standard error | 0.04 | 0.03 | 0.04 | 0.04 |
| *Sample (weighted)* | *2991* | *1152* | *321* | *742* |

## Variations in pay of main jobs

There were of course considerable variations in the pay of the young people in our sample. One of the most important of these was the variation of the pay of the young long-term unemployed over time. The main jobs were analysed by the year in which they ended, and Table 4.12 presents an analysis with average pay in groups of two or three years, for those entering the labour market in 1975-79 only. (The analysis for those entering in 1980-83 will merely reflect differences in age, since pay tends to rise quite rapidly in the 16-19 age range.) It can be seen from the table that both men and women whose main job ended in the 1980s had substantially lower pay than those whose main job ended in the latter half of the 1970s. This is despite two factors which might have been expected to lead to the opposite result: (a) those with main jobs ending in the latter 1970s will have been younger at that time than those with main jobs ending in 1980-83; (b) we have deflated only by the RPI and not by the index of earnings, so that the value of the earlier jobs is if anything estimated conservatively.

Put simply, the pay of jobs to which this group of young people had access, and which they regarded as of sufficient quality to be their 'main' jobs, fell by something like £7-10 per week in the transition from the 1970s to the 1980s. This is not proposed as a precise figure, nor is it suggested that there is a consistent downward trend over the

**Table 4.12  Net pay in the main or most recent job, at different times (excluding those entering the labour market in 1980-83)**

|  | Year in which main job ended | | | |
|---|---|---|---|---|
|  | 1975-77 | 1978-79 | 1980-81 | 1982-83 |
| **Male** | | | | |
| Mean £/week | 79.7 | 83.7 | 75.0 | 73.5 |
| Sample size (weighted) | 130 | 691 | 1324 | 1010 |
| **Female** | | | | |
| Mean £/week | 60.9 | 64.9 | 56.6 | 57.9 |
| Sample size (weighted) | 49 | 193 | 408 | 686 |

period. But it is a servicable way of summarizing the change. For men, the main jobs of the late 70s were paying £80 plus, while the main jobs of the early 80s were paying £70 plus. Similarly, the young women's main jobs of the late 70s were paying £60 plus, while those of the early 80s were paying £55 plus.

**Table 4.13  Pay in main or most recent job, by duration of job**

|  | Duration of job (months) | | | | |
|---|---|---|---|---|---|
|  | All | 1-6 | 7-12 | 13-24 | 25+ |
| **Male** | | | | | |
| Mean £/week | 70.3 | 65.8 | 72.3 | 68.7 | 76.5 |
| **Female** | | | | | |
| Mean £/week | 52.9 | 48.4 | 50.6 | 48.7 | 61.3 |

We asked our respondents to report their pay as it was at the end of the main job, so the length of jobs could have had an influence on our findings. Table 4.13 analyses this, but shows that there was no neat trend of pay on length of time in job. There was however a clear pay advantage for jobs which had lasted longer than two years, which enjoyed pay more than £6 above the average for men, and more than £8 above the average in the case of women. Since the groups with these longer jobs account for almost one quarter of the men and one third of the women, the shorter duration of jobs in the 1980s (as discussed earlier in the chapter) seems to be part of the explanation for lower pay, though not sufficient to account for the whole of the observed change.

## Training and experience

We have seen that even the 'main' jobs of the young long-term unemployed, those which would tend to show their job attainments in the best light, were low in the pay league for their own age groups, and hence could be regarded as of somewhat low quality. It has often been noted by labour market researchers that the characteristics of jobs tend to be positively correlated: well-paid jobs tend to have good working conditions and prospects, for instance, while poorly paid jobs tend to have poor working conditions and prospects. By the same token, low-paid jobs are also likely to offer relatively little training or marketable experience.

Our chief question about training was based on one used in the study of young people in the labour market by Ashton and Maguire[6]. They directed the question to the first job upon entering the labour market, while we preferred to focus upon the 'main' or most recent job in the belief that that would give a better indication of future prospects. The question took the form of a list of different forms of training: on-the-job training from a trainer or supervisor, full-time attendance at an internal training centre, part-time attendance at the same, a day release course, a course with evening classes, and any other external course.

This question can also be thought of in broader terms as distinguishing three types of jobs. First, there are the jobs with no formal training at all - either the skills required are rudimentary, or learning is acquired by 'watching Nellie'. Such jobs are identified when none of the categories in our question are answered positively. Then, there are the jobs where only on-the-job training (by a qualified person, not 'Nellie') is given; we would expect this to be a substantial group. Finally, there are jobs involving a greater degree of formal classroom training, inside the firm, outside it, or both, as might be the case with apprenticeships or traineeships.

In Table 4.14, the results from this question are summarized as a simple 'item score' with a possible range from nought to six. About 30 per cent of the young men, and 20 per cent of the young women, reported no training or instruction in the course of their main or most recent job. A little more than half the men, and almost two-thirds of the women, had received one type of training only, and this was in most instances on-the-job training by a trainer or instructor. The remaining 17 per cent of men, and 13 per cent of women, had had more than one type of training, implying some classroom element.

**Table 4.14 Training in main or most recent job**

*column percentages*

|  | Male | | Female | |
|  | entry to labour market | | | |
|  | 1975-79 | 1980-83 | 1975-79 | 1980-83 |
| --- | --- | --- | --- | --- |
| No training | 29 | 32 | 19 | 24 |
| One type of training (usually on-the-job) | 53 | 57 | 64 | 69 |
| Two or more types (includes off-job elements) | 19 | 12 | 17 | 7 |
| *Total (weighted)* | *3333* | *1245* | *1460* | *820* |

 The proportions entering an apprenticeship or traineeship were established by a separate question. Only 12 per cent of the young men, and just four per cent of young women, had done so. There was also a decline in access to apprenticeships and traineeships for those entering the labour market in 1980-83. For male and female together, 14 per cent of the 1975-79 intake went at some stage into such vocational schemes, but this fell to four per cent for the later intake.

 The proportions entering an apprenticeship or traineeship were established by a separate question. Only 12 per cent of the young men, and just four per cent of young women, had done so. There was also a decline in access to apprenticeships and traineeships for those entering the labour market in 1980-83. For male and female together, 14 per cent of the 1975-79 intake went at some stage into such vocational schemes, but this fell to four per cent for the later intake.

 Comparisons with the Ashton and Maguire study are made difficult partly because our notion of the 'main' job is not used in their study, but also because the findings for their four local labour market areas varied to a great extent. Impressionistically, it appears that the amount of training for the young long-term unemployed was generally somewhat less than found in the Ashton and Maguire study, with the possible exception of their findings relating to the Leicester area. It is also notable that in their study, the amount of training tended to be greatest in the first job after leaving school, and to decrease progressively in later jobs. As the information in our study concerns the most representative job of the individual's work history to date, and not the first job, it may be that the apparently low levels of formal training which we see merely reflect normal practice. Further information about training, this time in new jobs held at the time of interview, will be discussed in the next chapter; and to anticipate that discussion, it seems to confirm that training tends to diminish in successive jobs.

## Concluding comments on patterns of work

The dominant impression from the labour market histories and job information of the young long-term unemployed is the way in which the world they faced changed from the late 1970s to the early 1980s. The period saw a great decrease in the proportion of time spent in work, a virtual disappearance of reasonably long-lasting jobs, a great increase in the proportions never becoming employed, a great increase in the role of government schemes of job creation or work experience, and a marked increase in what we have called 'fragmentation' - that is, the frequency with which individuals change their labour market status. There were also large shifts in the types of jobs obtained and a reduction in levels of pay received. Finally, the availability of apprenticehsips and traineeships declined.

We have suggested that it may be helpful to think of the young long-term unemployed as falling into three groups - two mutually exclusive, the third overlapping. First, there is a sizable group of those who at one stage appeared established in a stable working life, since they had spent most of their time since leaving school in work and had held jobs of two or three years.

At the other extreme, among the younger, newer entrants to the labour market, is another substantial group - one which, in contrast with the first, has never established any foothold in employment. The problems of this group are much easier to visualize, perhaps, then those of the formerly stable young workers in our first group. Losing the initial competition to get into work, they are at obvious risk of protracted exclusion from employment.

The largest group, though, consists of those with intermediate work patterns: those whose histories, since entering the labour merket, were a mixture of short-lived jobs, unemployment spells, and, perhaps, attendance on government schemes. These look very much like the young people encountered in previous studies of unemployment, often characterised as 'recurrent unemployed', 'job changers', or simply as passing through a normal transitional phase towards settled employment. The present survey in part shows what many commentators of recent years have pointed out: that the tendency of young people at the lower end of the job market to shift in and out of work places them at serious risk of long-term unemployment when labour demand is reduced. In part, also, the present survey shows the pattern of fragmented labour market experience becoming more pervasive for the young people with whom the study is concerned.

In stressing the magnitude of the changes between the 1975-79 and 1980-83 periods, it might appear that long-term youth unemployment is being wholly attributed to reduction of demand, but this does not follow. Different positions in the economy may be differentially affected by economic developments, and those occupying the most exposed positions will have varying degrees of difficulty in finding alternative positions.

The information about the previous jobs of the young long-term unemployed shows that they were, indeed, distributed in a far from random manner through the economy. Relative to the employed population, they were under-represented in the public sector, over-represented in small firms; they were under-represented in the skilled manual occupations associated with the engineering and electronics industries, and over-represented in the food and drink, clothing and footwear, hotel and catering, and distributive and personal service industries and occupations. Most importantly, they were under-represented in higher non-manual and lower clerical occupations, and over-represented in unskilled and semi-skilled work. In short, they tended to come more from the employers, industries and occupations offering (on the whole) relatively vulnerable employment and less from the employers, industries and occupations offering (on the whole) relatively stable careers. However powerful the effects of changes in demand during this period, those effects were mediated - and may even have been amplified - by structural factors in the labour market of the kinds destribed in Chapters 2 and 3.

When an economy is faced with change, adaptation depends partly on individuals' willingness to be mobile and flexible in the labour market. The work histories show, indeed, a very high degree of industrial and occupational mobility on the part of the young unemployed: it would be hard to imagine how these aspects of flexibility could be increased further. In addition, there was fairly clear evidence of lower pay being accepted in the 1980s than in the late 1970s, by young people at comparable ages or stages of development.

As we turn to mobility, flexibility, and pay, however, we begin to anticipate the subjects of later chapters. In this chapter and the next, the task is to describe rather than to explain or predict. Subsequently some of the characteristics of work histories which have been described here will receive further consideration.

# 5 Government Schemes in the Employment Process

In Chapter 4 we briefly pointed to the development, since the mid-1970s, of government schemes of work experience and job creation, and to the substantial part which these schemes had played in the labour market experience of the young long-term unemployed. About half the young men in our sample, and about 40 per cent of the young women, had taken part in our one or more of these schemes, and multiple schemes participation was common. The great majority of the placements were on the Youth Opportunities Programme (YOP), which ceased to operate in 1983. The timing of the survey, and the definition of the group which it covered, were such that it contained no participants in the Youth Training Scheme which replaced YOP. In addition, however, there were some within the survey who had taken part in the Community Enterprise Programme and its successor, the Community Programme (CP). CP was being expanded towards the end of the period which the survey was considering, and was accordingly becoming more important for the group under consideration, to which it was particularly though not exclusively directed. By the time of the interview in 1984, and even more so by the time of the 1985 follow-up survey, there was an increased rate of movement among the sample into CP schemes.

This chapter will consider the relationship between participation in schemes and the experience of employment and unemployment among the 18-24 group in long-term unemployment. Although we will consider schemes in their totality, the great majority of placements for this group were on YOP and so the available information from the survey chiefly relates to this group. In the latter part of the chapter, however, we will separately consider the characteristics of those who had been placed on CEP or CP schemes, which shed some interpretive light upon the processes involved in selection into schemes and from schemes back into unemployment.

## The nature of YOP

Since YOP has ceased to operate, it may seem academic to evaluate its position in labour market experience, all the more so since a considerable body of research evidence concerning the characteristics of YOP participants, and their labour market destinations, has been compiled[1]. Nevertheless, because YOP formed such a substantial part of the experience of the survey group, especially during the period from 1980 onwards, it is essential to analyse its role in order to obtain a full picture of the influences on these young people's development. In addition, the type of evidence provided by the survey is different to that obtained by the various follow-up studies of YOP which are already available.

The advantage of the present study is that YOP is being seen within a longer period of time than has been the case with the various follow-up studies concerning this scheme. Its limitation, on the other hand, is its confinement to the young long-term unemployed. Those within the present survey who had participated in YOP cannot be regarded as a representative cross-section of all YOP participants.

Before presenting our findings concerning government schemes, it may be helpful to consider how participation in YOP, the main provision of the period, can best be conceptualized. In human capital theory, qualifications, training and on-the-job experience are seen as a continuum. Each contributes to the value of individuals for employers. In YOP, a variety of forms of scheme was encompassed, but one of the main themes was certainly to provide periods of work experience. It would therefore be inferred that YOP contributed to the creation of human capital, and hence that those who participated gained some tradeable advantage.

However, it should be noted that YOP (and analogous schemes) were introduced in part as measures to counter the effects on the youngest section of the labour force of rising unemployment. YOP was also partly targeted on groups of young people having special disadvantages in the labour market. Nor did YOP claim to provide a substantial amount of vocational training during placements, although training was supplied by some employers. For these reasons, YOP can be considered in part as a remedial measure.

## Comparative characteristics of scheme participants

It was found that those who had been on schemes (as already noted, mainly YOP but also including a minority from other schemes such as CEP, CP and TOPS) differed little in their personal characteristics from the remainder of the sample. In terms of the main social background influences which the survey examined - notably marital status, type of housing, family size, upbringing in one-parent households, and ethnic group - there were only minor differences in the composition of those who had been on schemes and the remainder. To this extent, the scheme participants seem to have been subject to a similar set of social conditions as applied to all the young people in long-term unemployment.

Differences of school and vocational qualifications were present, however, between the scheme participants and others. In order to examine these, we look separately at the young men and the young women in the sample, and at those entering the labour market in 1975-79 and in 1980-83 (corresponding roughly to the 21-24 and 18-20 age groups). The results of this analysis are shown in Table 5.1.

Among men, looking first at the 1975-79 entrants to the labour market, we see that those who were qualified and those who had no qualification were about equally likely to go on schemes. However, because in this group those without qualifications constituted the majority, the unqualified also predominated among the scheme participants. Although in global terms the qualified and non-qualified were about equally likely to join schemes, there were some finer differences. Those with the lowest level of school qualifications - CSE passes below grade 1 - were particularly likely to have taken part in more than one scheme.

Comparing these findings with those for the younger group of men, who entered the labour market in 1980-83, we face a set of shifts in the composition of qualified and non-qualified which is rather complex.

(i) Everyone, whatever their level of qualification, was now more likely to be going on a scheme, because by this time scheme provision for school leavers had become much more extensive.

**Table 5.1    Participation in schemes for those with different qualifications**

*percentages*

| | Number of schemes attended | | |
| --- | --- | --- | --- |
| | None | One | Two |
| **Male: entry to labour market in 1975-79** | | | |
| No qualification | 55 | 55 | 49 |
| Any qualification | 45 | 45 | 51 |
| -CSE below grade 1 only | 15 | 16 | 25 |
| *Total (weighted)* | *2384* | *978* | *446* |
| **Male: entry to labour market in 1980-83** | | | |
| No qualification | 30 | 43 | 49 |
| Any qualification | 70 | 57 | 51 |
| -CSE below grade 1 only | 15 | 26 | 34 |
| *Total (weighted)* | *998* | *899* | *788* |
| **Female: entry to labour market in 1975-79** | | | |
| No qualification | 39 | 39 | 48 |
| Any qualification | 61 | 61 | 52 |
| -CSE below grade 1 only | 21 | 21 | 25 |
| *Total (weighted)* | *1224* | *340* | *154* |
| **Female: entry to labour market in 1980-83** | | | |
| No qualification | 27 | 46 | 59 |
| Any qualification | 73 | 54 | 41 |
| -CSE below grade 1 only | 17 | 22 | 23 |
| *Total (weighted)* | *789* | *628* | *373* |

(ii)  Relatively speaking, the unqualified were by this time more likely to go on a scheme while the qualified (compared with the unqualified) were becoming less likely to go. The probability of someone going on a scheme, given that he or she was qualified, was lower than the probability of someone going on a scheme given that he or she was unqualified.

(iii) But, as is known from published statistics of education, the unqualified males were becoming a smaller proportion of all entrants to the labour market, while the proportion of qualified entrants was correspondingly increasing. The composition of the present sample followed this national trend. So, despite the relative shift described in (b) above, the total share of scheme participation taken by qualified entrants was actually growing. (This is consistent with trends identified in YOP surveys in the early 1980s[2].) An accentuating factor was the smaller intake of qualified school-leavers to apprenticeships; this meant that a greater proportion was available for YOP.

For the young women in the long-term unemployed sample, the picture is a much simpler one, partly because among these the proportions with various levels of qualification remained more or less the same across the two entry-periods (1975-79 and 1980-83). Among the older group the chances of going on a scheme were little affected by qualification or nonqualification. By the 1980-83 period, however, there was a clear tendency (as in the case of the men) for the non-qualified, and those with CSEs below grade 1, to go on schemes - relative to the qualified, and the non-qualified constituted a larger proportion of female entrants to schemes than in 1975-79. But, as there were far more YOP and other scheme places by this period, every category in the female sample was much more likely to go on a scheme in the 1980-83 group of entrants than in the group of earlier entrants.

## Employment histories of scheme participants
In Chapter 3 various summary measures of labour market histories were described, and these can be used to assess how far the experience of those who had attended government schemes differed from that of the whole sample.

People who had been on schemes were likely to have had a more fragmented experience of the labour market than those who had never attended a scheme. Although this difference of experience was in part real, it could be argued that it was also partly artificial. For example, someone who has been unemployed, then goes on a scheme, and then becomes unemployed again, will have two spells of unemployment counted, even though the total period involved was the same as someone else who was unemployed throughout.

A better comparison can be based on proportion of time spent in employment. But there is the complication that any time spent on a government scheme subtracts from the possible time available for employment. In official statistics, time spent on government schemes is treated as a separate category from economic activity. In earlier chapters we departed from this convention, since it seemed more realistic to regard jobs, schemes and unemployment as the main parallel alternatives for this group of young people. But now that the requirement is to make direct comparisons between those who have been on schemes and those who have not, it seems more appropriate to take the schemes themselves out of the calculation.

**Table 5.2    Proportion of time in employment, and scheme participation**

*Mean per cent of time in employment*

|  | Number of schemes attended | | |
|---|---|---|---|
|  | None | One | Two |
| **Male** | | | |
| 1975-79 entrants to labour market | 50 | 34 | 21 |
| 1980-83 entrants to labour market | 20 | 15 | 11 |
| **Female** | | | |
| 1975-79 entrants to labour market | 57 | 37 | 17 |
| 1980-83 entrants to labour market | 23 | 14 | 13 |

Note:    Each figure is the time spent in employment expressed as a percentage of time spent economically active, for that group.

Table 5.2 shows the results of such an analysis, with separate figures for men and women and for those entering the labour market in 1975-79 and 1980-83. The results show clearly that, even when separate comparisons are made in the way indicated, and even when time spent on schemes is excluded from the calculation, those who went on schemes spent a lower proportion of time in employment. In terms of absolute differences, the gap between the scheme participants and the non-participants was greater in the earlier period, when only a minority was going on schemes. But in proportionate terms, non-participants had as much of an advantage over participants in 1980-83 as they had in 1975-79. In interpreting these findings, of course, one should recall the point made earlier, that YOP participants in the present survey were not representative of all YOP participants. Hence there can be no general inference that YOP caused a deterioration of participants' prospects.

Since the non-qualified were more likely to go on schemes in 1980-83, the effect of qualifications should be controlled. This was done in two separate sets of analyses, one combined with sex of respondent and the other with period of entry to the labour market. As expected, this somewhat reduces the contrasts in labour market fortunes of those going on schemes and those not going. However, the differences in proportions of time spent in work remain clear, within every level of qualification. The results shown in Table 5.3 are by period of entry to the labour market, across both male and female groups. Considering those with some school examination passes, who entered the labour market in 1975-79, we find that those who went on one scheme spent 43 per cent of their available time in work; those who never went on a scheme spent 56 per cent of their time in work. Those participating in more than one scheme fared worst in terms of employment.

Similarly, of those entering the labour market in 1975-79, and having no qualifications at all, those who went on one scheme spent 27 per cent of their time in work; those who never went on a scheme spent 48 per cent of their time in work. Again, those who went on more than one scheme did worst. The group with the smallest differences in employment record was those with vocational qualifications, but even here the differences were in the same direction, resulting in more employment for those who did not go on a scheme.

Similar comparisons can be drawn for those entering the labour market in 1980-83, when jobs were much scarcer and it was becoming more normal for young people to go on a scheme. For example, in this period, of those who passed any school examination and did not go on a scheme, the proportion of time spent in work was 23 per cent - to be compared with 16 per cent for those in this category who did go on one scheme.

**Table 5.3** **Proportion of time in work, and scheme participation, controlling for qualification level**

*mean per cent of time in employment*

| | Entry to labour market | |
| | 1975-79 | 1980-83 |
| --- | --- | --- |
| **Those with school qualification** | | |
| Number of schemes: | | |
| None | 56 | 23 |
| One | 43 | 16 |
| Two+ | 23 | 15 |
| | | |
| **Those with vocational qualification** | | |
| Number of schemes: | | |
| None | 58 | 26 |
| One | 49 | 18 |
| Two+ | 35 | 16 |
| | | |
| **Those with no qualification** | | |
| Number of schemes: | | |
| None | 48 | 18 |
| One | 27 | 13 |
| Two+ | 18 | 8 |

Note:   Male and female are combined. Each figure is the time spent in employment expressed as a percentage of time spent economically active, for that group

The same kind of results appeared in the analysis which controlled for qualification within male and female groups. The results are not shown here, since they merely repeat the picture which has already been established.

**Initial outcomes of schemes**
The preceding analyses have shown that participation on schemes, within our sample, was associated with a relatively low proportion of time spent in employment. This, however, refers to the entire period in the labour market, hence does not distinguish between periods of work or unemployment prior to schemes, and those following entry to schemes. It has been customary, in the various studies carried out to

monitor the effects of YOP or other schemes, to take as a chief measure of outcome the proportion in employment within a certain period of leaving the scheme - for example, the proportion after three months or after six months[3].

Table 5.4 shows the result of such an analysis, based upon the first scheme attended by young people in our sample. We have chosen six months after the completion of the scheme as the point at which to take the 'snapshot', since some of the earlier research has shown that the proportions in work tend to rise over such a period following YOP.

**Table 5.4   Labour market status six months after leaving first schemes**

*column percentages*

|  | Male entry to labour market | | Female | |
|  | 1975-79 | 1980-83 | 1975-79 | 1980-83 |
|---|---|---|---|---|
| Unemployed | 48 | 59 | 41 | 59 |
| Job | 31 | 11 | 40 | 14 |
| Scheme | 11 | 23 | 15 | 22 |
| Sick | 1 | — | 0 | 0 |
| Full-time education | 1 | 3 | 2 | 1 |
| Unregistered, not working | 1 | 1 | 1 | 0 |
| Other | 2 | — | 0 | 2 |
| Not stated | 5 | 3 | 2 | 3 |
| *Total (weighted)* | *1424* | *1686* | *494* | *1001* |

— Less than 0.5 per cent

There was a much better chance of schemes being followed by jobs for 1975-79 entrants than for 1980-83 entrants. This is consistent with what has previously been reported about YOP outcomes, which were affected by the more difficult labour market of 1980 and after.

Although precise comparisons with previous YOP research are not possible, for reasons already noted, it seems sufficiently clear at an impressionistic level that the present sample fared considerably worse than the average for YOP schemes. In the pre-1980 period, job placement rates of 60-70 per cent after YOP have been reported. The 1975-79 entrants in our survey had employment rates, at six months after schemes, of only 31 per cent in the case of men and 37 per cent in the case of women. Even by 1982, post-YOP placements seem to have been around 40 per cent according to some reports, but among the 1980-83 entrants to the labour market in our sample, the rate of placement was no more than one third of this. Indeed, for the 1980-83 entrants to the labour market, almost 60 per cent were unemployed six months after leaving their first scheme, with a further 20 per cent or so back on another scheme.

It seems therefore that the former YOP participants in long-term unemployment were a selected group which had to an exceptional degree failed to make the transition from schemes to employment.

### Selection effects in the operation of schemes

The evidence examined so far shows that those within the sample who went on schemes, notably YOP, fared appreciably worse in the labour market than the average of all 18-24 year olds in long-term unemployment. Nor can this be attributed to particularly disadvantageous social background or personal attainments among the YOP or other scheme participants. What, then, can explain the different outcomes which they experienced?

Commentators have sometimes observed that, in addition to its functions as a form of work experience, the YOP could serve as a form of extended selection process[4]. Employers had the opportunity to observe the work behaviour of young people for several months and form an assessment of their suitability for employment. Those who were favourably evaluated might therefore be likely to get the offer of a job, or perhaps a recommendation might be passed on to another employer.

If the YOP served as an extended selection process, with any reasonable degree of reliability, then certain consequences would follow. Those selected into employment after YOP should have had an above-average chance of finding a good fit between themselves and the employment offered, and this should in turn have led to an above-average degree of stability in the ensuing period. The problem in testing this inference lies in finding an appropriate group with whom to make a comparison. However some support appears to come from findings by Collins and colleagues, reporting on the MSC's 1983 follow-up of YOP participants[5]. This showed that, of those entering a job immediately upon leaving YOP, 88 per cent were still employed six months later. Such a finding appears to contrast with evidence pointing to a high level of instability among young people who go into jobs after a period of unemployment, as shown in the MSC/PSI study of the unemployed flow[6].

But the extended selection process of YOP-type schemes may also have adverse implications for those not successful in gaining access to jobs after their placements. These may be regarded as in some sense having failed a test, or as having been rejected after a lengthy assessment, and this might tell against them subsequently. The failure to move into employment after YOP might also be compounded by a period of ensuing unemployment.

In part, presumably, success or failure in getting employment after a scheme placement would reflect personal attributes as evaluated by employers. However, as various studies of YOP have shown, outcomes could depend not only on individual differences but also on the kinds of scheme entered and the timing of entry[7]. In the present survey, we did not attempt to differentiate between the various categories of YOP scheme (since recall would have been unreliable), and so cannot evaluate that source of influence. However, we can identify two other circumstances: when in an individual's work history he or she entered a scheme, and whether it was the first scheme entered, or a subsequent placement.

In fact, we have already shown in passing that large proportions of the young long-term unemployed had been on more than one scheme. Even among the 1975-79 entrants to the labour market, nearly one third of those who had been on any scheme had been on two or more schemes. With the 1980-83 entrants, who joined a youth labour market in which scheme participation had become the norm, 47 per cent of male scheme participants and 37 per cent of female participants attended two or more schemes. As Tables 5.2 and 5.3 demonstrated, those who went on more than one scheme spent well below average proportions of time in employment. We can again interpret this as partly the result of personal attributes which we are unable to measure in this survey - so that the individuals offering less to employers found themselves forced back on a further scheme placement. But we can also visualize that the very recourse to a second scheme might look problematical in the eyes of (some) employers, and would later compound difficulties in finding work.

Late entry to schemes is another circumstance which has been singled out in the literature on YOP as causing problems. We therefore once more used our 'snapshot' of status six months after leaving the first scheme, but this time cross-tabulated the results by period after entering the labour market when this first scheme was joined by the individual. The findings are shown in Table 5.5.

**Table 5.5   Labour market status after schemes, by timing of entry to scheme**

| | Months after entering labour market when joined scheme* | | |
|---|---|---|---|
| | 0-6 | 7-12 | 13-24 |
| **Male entry in 1975-79** | | | |
| Unemployed | 43 | 41 | 53 |
| Job | 37 | 41 | 34 |
| **Male, entry in 1980-83** | | | |
| Unemployed | 56 | 68 | 73 |
| Job | 13 | 9 | 4 |
| **Female, entry in 1975-79** | | | |
| Unemployed | 36 | 37 | 49 |
| Job | 40 | 46 | 39 |
| **Female, entry in 1980-83** | | | |
| Unemployed | 55 | 67 | 76 |
| Job | 14 | 13 | 8 |

Note:    Only the first scheme attended is included.

For men joining the labour market in 1975-79, the first scheme was followed (at six months' remove) by a job in around 40 per cent of cases, provided that the scheme was entered in the first year in the labour market. This proportion fell to 34 per cent if the scheme was entered in the second year in the labour market. (Schemes entered after two or three years in the labour market have been excluded from the analysis, as many of these would not have been YOP schemes.) For men entering the labour market in 1980-83, provided they entered the schemes within the first year the rate entering jobs thereafter was about 13 per cent. But almost nobody who started a scheme after the first year in the labour market went on to a job.

With women the effect of time and entry to the scheme was less clear cut. Those coming into the labour market in 1975-79 found that the time at which they entered schemes made little difference to employment prospects. But for those entering the labour market in 1980-83, timing was more influential. Entry within the first year was followed by employment in about 15 per cent of cases; this fell to eight per cent for those entering a scheme in their second year in the labour market.

When the results for the men and the women are taken together, there was evidently a disadvantage in coming late to the first scheme. YOP was envisaged primarily as a scheme for young people in their first year after leaving school. Entering the scheme late might have in part had tactical disadvantages connected with it. Since the availability of jobs was contracting in 1980-82, it was generally better to start sooner rather than later. In addition, and perhaps more important, late entry within any year's intake might put individuals at a disadvantage, since earlier starters would have taken up many of the available jobs for people in the 16-17 age group.

In addition, as we have speculated in regard to those not getting jobs after YOP, and in regard to those entering more than one scheme, the latecomers to schemes may have been disadvantaged by the logic of employers' selection processes. In an over-supplied labour market, employers can aim to reduce their risks in recruitment by narrowing the range of applicants they will consider. Those with irregular or 'non-standard' characteristics of their work record may have decreased chances or re-employment under such circumstances. It seems plausible that those who have entered YOP at unusual points may have this additional constraint to contend with. Selection processes tend to be cumulative in their effects.

**CEP and CP scheme participants**

From our examination so far, we have concluded that selection effects help to account for the particularly adverse labour market histories of former scheme participants within the young long-term unemployed. To test this notion further, it is of value to consider a much smaller group - those who participated in the Community Enterprise Programme or its successor, the Community Programme. For convenience' sake, we will refer to this group simply as 'CP participants'.

There were rather few CP participants in the sample. Women in particular included a mere handful who had entered CP schemes, partly no doubt because they are under-represented on CP schemes as a whole (8). This limits the possibilities for detailed analysis, which must be confined to the male section of the sample. But there is one valuable possibility for analysis which does not exist in the case of YOP participants. The CP group could be divided into two parts of roughly similar size, one of which consisted of those who had formerly been on CP and were now back in long-term unemployment, while the other group consisted of those who had been long-term unemployed at the time of sampling, but had subsequently entered a CP scheme. This latter group was enlarged in size by consideration of the follow-up survey which took place in 1985, hence providing a period of 16 months' entry on CP in addition to the four-month period between sampling and interview.

As well as comparing CP participants as a whole with the remainder of the survey sample, we are able to compare former with current entrants to CP. The characteristics of current entrants should say something about selection processes into CP, while the characteristics of former participants should tell us something about 'selection' back into unemployment.

### The sample of male CP participants
As already noted, there were so few female CP participants (24 at the time of the 1984 interview; a further 11 in the follow-up) that it was not feasible to carry out any detailed analysis of them. Of men, however, the survey obtained a total of 184 CP participants. There were 65 who had been on CP schemes before reverting to long-term unemployment, 64 who were actually on CP at the time of the 1984 interview, and a further 55 who were in the follow-up sub-sample and had entered a CP scheme during the 16-month interval before the follow-up.

It should be noted that these figures from the follow-up show the rapid expansion of the CP scheme around the time of this study. The entrants to CP during the 16-month period between interview and follow-up constituted 16 per cent of the male sample (on a weighted basis), or an annual rate of entry of around 12 per cent. This was about in line with the stated plans of the MSC concerning the coverage of the scheme.

In presenting the findings concerning CP participants, we depart from the conventions used in most of this report. As the numbers are small, and since the comparisons run from the interview survey to the follow-up survey, the latter constituting a sub-sample of the former, the most practical form of reporting is in terms of unweighted numbers.

It is also important to keep separate the three groups of CP participants, namely those entering before the sample was drawn, those entering between sampling and the 1984 interview, and those entering after the 1984 interview. It is only the second of these three groups - those entering in the period between sampling and interview - who may approximate to a flow sample from long-term youth unemployment into the Community Programme. The entrants during the follow-up period do not represent such a flow sample, since we no longer include those recently becoming eligible for CP (that is, those recently completing six months in unemployment). The group of earlier participants in CP represent a particular form of selection - not only into the scheme, but also (after it) back into unemployment. As will soon become apparent, these differences in the constitution of the three groups also result in systematic differences in their composition.

## Characteristics of male CP participants

Differences between the three groups of CP entrants immediately become apparent upon examining their school and vocational qualifications. Those who were in CP schemes at the time of the 1984 interview on some criteria were better qualified than the other two groups, and also better qualified than the male sample as a whole. In particular, this group contained 25 per cent with vocational qualifications, by comparison with 14 per cent in the whole male sample (unweighted basis), 13 per cent in the group entering CP after the 1984 interview, and six per cent in the group of earlier CP entrants. Similarly, if O-level and A-level passes are considered, the respective proportions holding either of these were 34 per cent, 30 per cent, 20 per cent, and five per cent.

But a different ordering applied when CSE passes below grade 1 were considered. Here it was the group entering CP schemes after the 1984 interview, and appearing in the follow-up sample, which had much the highest proportion of these lower-level qualifications, at 38 per cent. Those who had entered CP in earlier years included 29 per cent with CSEs, and entrants at the time of the 1984 interviews 19 per cent, which was close to the overall figure for the male sample.

U—J

The impression given by these findings is of different layers of entry to the CP schemes. Those on schemes at the 1984 interview may, we suggest, represent those who were 'at the head of the queue', hence containing disproportionate numbers of those with better levels of qualification from among the young long-term unemployed. Those from the sample entering with more delay represent the next layer of entry, and hence contain many with the lower-level qualifications. Those, finally, who entered CP at an earlier stage represent, as we have already suggested, a quite different kind of filtering process - one which leads them to return to unemployment. This group, despite a substantial proportion with lower qualifications, had so few with the higher qualifications that its overall rate of non-qualification was particularly high - 65 per cent compared with 48 per cent for the male sample as a whole.

Similar differences could also be discerned between the various groups of male CP participants, in the case of a number of indications of social background. Of these the two most significant were:

(i) CP participants in 1984-85 were more likely to come from owner-occupied households than were former participants, and correspondingly less likely to come from local authority rented accommodation. Both those on CP at the 1984 interview, and those on it prior to the follow-up, came in 33 per cent of cases from households with owner occupation, while the proportion among the earlier participants was 19 per cent. The overall proportion for the male sample was intermediate, at 28 per cent.

(ii) CP participants at the time of the 1984 interview on average came from smaller families than did either earlier or later participants. Only 38 per cent of the former had three or more siblings, while this figure was 65 per cent in the case of the subsequent entrants, 66 per cent in the case of the earlier entrants now returned to long-term unemployment, and 56 per cent for the survey as a whole (unweighted basis).

These findings broadly confirm the interpretation that CP participants in the three groups were systematically different. The view that the group in CP schemes at the time of the 1984 interview was in some sense a 'top of the queue' group was also supported by some further evidence, concerning the form and degree of activity in the labour market. On most of the available indices, that group was more competitive in its search for employment than were the later entrants to CP schemes, or the previous participants who had returned to long-term unemployment. If at the 'top of the queue', this did not seem undeserved in terms of the approach to job search which they were displaying.

(i)   They were prepared to travel further to work. Hence 58 per cent of this group stated they would travel 10 miles or more, while in the more recent group of CP entrants the proportion was 37 per cent, and in the group of earlier entrants 47 per cent (48 per cent in the male sample as a whole, on an unweighted basis).

(ii)  They had more frequently visited other areas or considered moving house, and the great majority said they were willing to move if a job was available.

(iii) They had a greater tendency to make use of many sources of information about jobs than the other two groups.

(iv)  More of them had made large numbers of job applications during the previous year: 26 per cent had made more than 20 applications, compared with 14 per cent in the group entering CP during the follow-up period, and 13 per cent among the former CP participants now back in unemployment.

**Table 5.6   Labour market experience of different groups to CP participants**

|  | On CP at 1984 interview | On CP during 1984-85 | On CP before 1984 |
| --- | --- | --- | --- |
| Proportion of time in work (mean % of time) | 24 | 27 | 13 |
| Held at least one previous job (% of sample) | 80 | 73 | 80 |
| Held a job lasting 2+ years (% of sample) | 16 | 20 | 2 |
| Changed labour market status at least 3 times (% of sample) | 38 | 42 | 55 |

Surprisingly, the systematic differences between the three groups of CP participants did not carry over so clearly into their previous experiences in the labour market. Four measures of this previous experience are shown in Table 5.6. It can be seen that, in general, the entrants to CP in 1984 and 1985 had had more settled employment than the earlier entrants to CP. But those on CP at the 1984 interview had not consistently fared better than the later entrants to CP of 1984-85, even though they had better qualifications and few social disadvantages. This lack of previous success, relative to their advantages, did not reflect a poor attitude towards job-seeking, since as we have shown they were particularly vigorous in their efforts to find employment. CP participation might be expected to give them the chance to 'relaunch' their job-seeking efforts from a better position than long-term unemployment.

**Concluding comments**
It seems clear, then, that current entrants to CP schemes differed systematically from former entrants who had returned to long-term unemployment and hence were found in our sample. These differences may be quite plausibly explained in terms of differential selection effects, along the lines of the earlier discussion of all scheme participants in the sample.

Those recently entering CP schemes seem to have been selected for these schemes because they have positive things to offer, such as vocational qualifications, and a vigorous approach to job-seeking.

Published results from an MSC follow-up survey of CP participants showed that about 40 per cent could expect to find employment while they were on CP placements, or immediately after (9). This is an unusually high job placement rate for a long-term unemployed group. Presumably the high placement rate reflects in part the actual qualities of the intake. In addition, CP itself may provide the young people concerned with a position from which they can get a better hearing from employers. As we have already remarked, selection processes tend to be cumulative, so that selection into CP may tend itself to act as a partial recommendation to an employer. To this may be added the possibility of obtaining a recommendation from the CP scheme management.

The group selected into CP schemes after a longer delay can plausibly be regarded as the next group along in the queue. They have relatively few of the 'better' qualifications, such as vocational certificates or O-levels, but more of the lower CSEs. They are not exceptionally active job-seekers, but have a little more experience to offer.

Those entering CP but failing to obtain employment, and hence returning to unemployment, are also likely to be a 'selected' group, in a double sense. The basis of their original selection into CP was probably largely remedial, to judge from their disadvantaged backgrounds, lack of qualifications, and extremely adverse employment record. After CP, they may have failed to gain employment because of low qualifications or lack of personal attributes which employers favour. Hence the CP 'residue' in long-term unemployment has different average characteristics from the CP intake. Moreover, once that an individual has had an opportunity on CP, but failed to convert it into a job, this evidence of rejection may tend to become a subsequent disadvantage in job search, quite apart from any personal characteristics which were involved.

This set of interpretations has been based on small samples, and cannot therefore be regarded as more than tentative on that score. On the other hand, the network of mutually reinforcing evidence which supports the interpretation would be difficult to explain as the operation of chance.

More important than the specific issue of CP schemes, however, is the more general notion of sequential selection processes which this analysis illustrates. The introduction of new schemes, such as YOP or CP, may through these selection processes - both into the schemes, and from the schemes into jobs or unemployment - have considerable repercussions on the workings of the labour market and the separation of the labour force into groups with different career chances. While there has been relatively little research into the selection processes themselves, the contrasting characteristics of those who have, and have not, passed through YOP or CP at various stages and with various results, indicates both the existence of those selection processes and the practical importance of understanding their action. A possible suggestion from the evidence is that the introduction of schemes of the type discussed here provided employers with two distinct kinds of information. Initially, it provided them with information to appraise and select young people for jobs. In addition, however, it provided signals about those young people who were not selected into jobs but returned to unemployment, and these signals may have continued to polarize the labour market prospects of those selected as against those rejected.

This tendency to polarization would be reduced, however, if the human capital acquired through scheme participation was recognized by employers. In that case, former participation in a scheme providing work experience or training would be valued in its own right, irrespective of the immediate outcome of participation in terms of getting, or not getting, a job. In the next chapter, we will examine the influence on job prospects for the young long-term unemployed of various forms of human capital.

# 6　New Jobs

The most important practical question about the young long-term unemployed is whether they are able to find jobs. The rate at which they return to work gives an indication of the difficulty or feasibility of reducing the levels of long-term youth unemployment, and the type of work to which they gain access may show both the best opportunities for their future employment and equally what other types of employment appear foreclosed to them.

The study was designed to provide three types of information about new jobs:

(i)    The period between sampling in February 1984, and interviewing in June of that year, was sufficient to permit an assessment of the rate at which the young long-term unemployed were flowing into employment, based on information which they supplied about new jobs obtained.

(ii)   The follow-up survey in October 1985 (described in more detail in Chapter 1) obtained information from a random sub-sample of the original sample, and provided a view of the prospects for this group of getting new jobs over a longer period of 16 months.

(iii)  In addition to the subsample representing the whole survey, the follow-up included a 'booster' sample of those with new jobs at the time of the 1984 interview. By this means, we were able to examine the stability of those jobs over the 16-month period.

The purpose of this chapter is chiefly descriptive. An account is given of the movement into jobs, and of some of the characteristics of those getting jobs, but discussion of possible explanatory factors, such as wage flexibility or qualifications, is deferred until later chapters when the role of these influences can be treated not only in relation to new jobs but also in relation to other aspects of experience in the labour market.

## The proportions finding work

Of the entire sample, 14 per cent had returned to work within the period of four months at interview in 1984. The results from the initial four months cannot be extrapolated into an annual rate, for two reasons. In the first place, there is the possibility of seasonal variations in the job market. More important, however, is the consideration that young people with the most to offer in terms of experience, qualifications or personal qualities are likely to obtain work soonest, so that the remainder will be on average weaker competitors for jobs, and likely to leave unemployment at a slower rate. Hence over a longer period the outflow from an initial stock of long-term unemployed into jobs is likely to be progressively reduced.

This point was confirmed by the findings from the follow-up questionnaire survey, which took place approximately 16 months after the interview. During this period, 40 per cent of the sample had held a job, which had either terminated or was still continuing at the time of the follow-up. If the rate of movement into work of the initial four-month period had been sustained, about 56 per cent would have had a job.

It should be noted that these two findings represent different measures of the employment prospects of the young long-term unemployed, each equally appropriate if correctly interpreted. The movement into jobs over a short period (an even shorter period than four months would be better) approximates to the flow out of long-term unemployment, for this age group. The movement over a longer period underestimates the overall flow from long-term youth unemployment into jobs because it does not reflect the (on average better) job chances of those newly flowing into long-term unemployment over the period. But it permits a more realistic assessment of the average chances of finding work for young people with the longer periods of unemployment.

## Differences between the main survey groups

The rate of movement into work was next compared between the four main groups which we have found it helpful to distinguish in this survey - by gender, and (within gender) by age/period of entry to the labour market. The details for these four groups are shown in Table 6.1.

**Table 6.1   Initial flow into new jobs, 1984 (4 months)**

*percentages*

| | | |
|---|---|---|
| **Female** | entry in 1975-79 | 12 |
| | entry in 1980-83 | 17 |
| **Male** | entry in 1975-79 | 13 |
| | entry in 1980-83 | 15 |

At this stage the differences between the four groups were fairly small. The younger group of women (entering the labour market in 1980-83) did somewhat better than the others, with almost 17 per cent entering jobs. The young men in the same age group came next, with around 15 per cent. The 1975-79 entrants, somewhat surprisingly, did less well, the men getting new jobs in 13 per cent of cases and the women in 12 per cent. The results for this latter group of women may have been affected by their rising tendency to leave the labour force, although this in itself could have partly been influenced by difficulties in finding employment.

By the time of the follow-up survey in 1985, the differences were much more marked, and perhaps surprising. They can initially be summarized as follows:

**Table 6.2   Proportions moving into work 1984-85 (16 months)**

*percentages*

| | | |
|---|---|---|
| **Female** | entry in 1975-79 | 42 |
| | entry in 1980-83 | 39 |
| **Male** | entry in 1975-79 | 35 |
| | entry in 1980-83 | 49 |

A direct comparison between the male and female groups was by this time difficult to achieve, because of the increasing proportions of young women leaving the labour force (20 per cent of the younger women and 26 per cent of the somewhat older group). In addition, the young men's results were also partly affected by the high proportions going into Community Programme schemes (15 per cent of the younger group and 19 per cent of the older).

These complications do not affect the main feature of the results, which was the unexpectedly large gap in employment prospects in favour of the 18-20 over the 21-25 year old group of men. There were good reasons why the opposite might have been predicted. The over-20s had entered the labour market before 1980, in a more favourable job market, and had far more work experience to offer to prospective employers. In addition, the 18-20 age group might be thought to suffer more in competition with recent school leavers both by reason of wage costs and by virtue of the latter's improved initial training. Yet these results clearly suggest that, once in long-term unemployment, it is the over-20s who constitute the eventual problem group.

An explanation of this difference will only become possible when we have examined the evidence concerning the role of qualifications and training, in the next chapter. For the moment, it is worth bearing in mind that the explanation should also account for the fact that, among the young women, the over-20 group was not at a competitive disadvantage.

A broader view of the labour market position of the young long-term unemployed sample, in the 16 months until the follow-up survey, is available for 85 per cent of the sub-sample. These completed in full a month-by-month record of their employment status over the period, so that we can calculate the average proportions of time spent in each status. This information is condensed into Table 6.3.

**Table 6.3    Time distribution in 1984-85 (follow-up sample)**

|  | Female | | Male | |
|---|---|---|---|---|
|  | older | younger | older | younger |
| **Percentage of time spent in:** | | | | |
| employment | 21 | 29 | 24 | 33 |
| unemployment | 56 | 56 | 68 | 57 |
| schemes/f.t.e. | 2 | 4 | 7 | 10 |
| inactive | 22 | 12 | 1 | 0 |

This analysis reveals rather a larger difference than the previous one in the labour market position of women in the two age groups. It also clarifies the divergent positions of young long-term unemployed men and women, with passage of time. The older group, among whom the longest periods of unemployment are concentrated, exhibit the sharpest gender differences. The over-20 males have the highest likelihood of continuing in unemployment, while the over-20 women tend to move out of the labour force into domestic roles.

## Differences by length of unemployment period

As explained in the Introduction, the survey was based on a 'stock sample' and therefore contained a larger proportion of those with long periods of unemployment than would be obtained by a longitudinal follow-up on the intake into unemployment. The declining chances of return to work as unemployment becomes more prolonged are illustrated in Table 6.4. For both men and women in the sample, the chance of finding a job by the time of the 1984 interview rose to a peak towards the end of their first year of unemployment; around 20 per cent of this group (slightly more for the women) were in work at interview. Those with between one and two years of continuous unemployment at the time of the sampling were considerably less likely to be back in work at interview: 12 per cent in the case of both men and women. For the quite substantial group with two years or more of continuous unemployment at sampling, the chances of being in a job were even lower.

**Table 6.4    Proportions obtaining new jobs in 1984, by period of unemployment**

*percentages in work at interview*

| | Total (weighted) | Period of unemployment at sampling (months) | | | |
|---|---|---|---|---|---|
| | | 6-9 | 10-12 | 13-24 | 25+ |
| Male | 6492 | 20 | 20 | 12 | 9 |
| Female | 3508 | 19 | 22 | 12 | 7 |

The effect of duration of unemployment was further confirmed by the follow-up survey. Over the 16-month period, about one half of those with the shortest durations of unemployment (6-12 months at sampling) had obtained a job, but this proportion fell to 36 per cent among those with between one and two years of unemployment at sampling, and to 15 per cent among those with more than two years of unemployment at sampling.

### Comparison of 1985 with 1981

This analysis by duration also leads to a comparison with the 1980/81 DE/PSI survey of long-term unemployment. The sampling, interview, and follow-up points were similarly timed in that survey and the present one, hence a comparison is particularly straightforward, although the 1980/81 survey included a small number aged 17 years at sampling. The earlier survey however covered only people with one year or more of unemployment at the time of sampling. In fact, after excluding from the present survey the group with 6-12 months of unemployment at sampling, an almost identical rate of movement into work was found in the two surveys, at 29 per cent. Hence it appears that the chances of obtaining a job, for the young long-term unemployed, have remained virtually constant from 1981 to 1985, despite the improvement of business conditions over that period.

### The stability of new jobs

Even if jobs are temporary or for other reasons short-lived, they may be of considerable value and benefit to young people in long-term unemployment. But other things being equal, a stable and lasting job would clearly be of greater value and benefit. Moreover, from the viewpoint of economic efficiency, stable jobs offer greater possibilities of training and development of human capital. Hence it is important to assess not only whether individuals were able to move into new jobs, but also whether they were able to hold them. This constituted one of the main objectives of the follow-up survey.

There were two methods available for assessing this issue, neither of which provides a complete perspective upon it. On one hand, we can consider how many, of all those within the follow-up survey who had been in work, were still actually in work at the point when they replied to the inquiry. The limitation in this case is that the point during the 16-month interval at which individuals entered a job could vary greatly, and in particular some who were in work at the time of the follow-up might have held their jobs for a very short period.

The booster sample, of those with jobs at the 1984 interview, was intended to remedy this, and to provide a more substantial period over which the question of stability might be assessed. In total we had 151 young people in the follow-up (main sample and booster combined) who were in work in June 1984. We can ask what happened to their jobs over the period of 16 months up to the follow-up. The limitation here is that (as we have already suggested) this group is likely to be biased in its composition towards those people with better than average abilities, relative to the sample as a whole. Accordingly, they may also have better than average chances of holding onto jobs once that they have them. In addition, because they do not constitute a random sample on the same basis as the original survey sample, it would be incorrect to treat them statistically in the same way as the main follow-up sample, and in fact we have analysed them only in unweighted form. However, as they constitute such a large fraction of those with jobs at the 1984 interview (about 45 per cent), we can be confident that they provide an excellent picture of that particular group.

Considering first the whole follow-up sample, we find that of those with jobs at any time (40 per cent), about two in three (27 per cent of the sample) were actually in work when they replied to the follow-up. In addition, it was possible to analyse how much of the 16 months had been spent in work, for that 85 per cent who completed the month-by-month labour market record. For those who had held a job, this proved to be a surprisingly high figure - 10.6 months, or about two thirds of the period between interview and follow-up. When it is taken into account that some jobs started late in the period between interview and follow-up, this indicator seems to suggest a substantial degree of stability in the new jobs. A further complication, however, is that some individuals (seven per cent of the follow-up sample, or 17 per cent of those who got jobs) actually had more than one job during the period. They spent a large proportion of their time in employment, but their jobs could not really be called stable.

Turning next to the 'boosted' analysis of those in work at the 1984 interview, we find that a very similar proportion to the main follow-up sample - 63 per cent - were actually in work when replying to the follow-up. This again suggests a fairly substantial degree of stability, but again it is over-estimated because of transitions between jobs. In this group, 16 per cent were in their second job by the time of the follow-up, so that the proportion holding employment continuously over the 16-month period was actually 47 per cent.

It seems, then, that not more than one half of jobs obtained by the young long-term unemployed last as long as 16 months; and if we, perhaps a little optimistically, assume that this applies to the whole sample, then it would seem that about one in five of the young long-term unemployed could hope to leave unemployment for jobs with this kind of stability. In addition, however, there may be a smaller set, around 7-8 per cent of all young long-term unemployed, whose move into employment is initially short-lived but who then succeed in finding a further job.

It is difficult to find any independent yardstick against which to assess whether the observed degree of stability was 'good'. On an impressionistic basis, we are of the opinion that it represents an encouraging development for the young long-term unemployed. In coming to this judgement, we would particularly point to the very low level of stability in new jobs observed in the 1980/81 DE/PSI survey of long-term unjemployment, although that study did not separately consider the issue of stability for the 18-24 age group because of insufficient sample size; and we would also point to the low level of stability, or high level of 'fragmentation', in the work histories of the present sample since 1980.

Here one should particularly note the contrast in the case of the 18-20 year old group (those entering the labour market in 1980-83). In their past histories, jobs lasting as long as one year were few and far between (see Chapter 4). Yet, in the follow-up period, those obtaining jobs within this age group held them on average for 11.2 months. This was a longer average period than in the case of the over-20 age group, and of course the majority (two thirds) of these jobs had not been terminated at the time of follow-up, so that their completed duration could be expected to be considerably longer. If we cannot absolutely demonstrate the matter, we nevertheless feel that these were strong signs of a restabilization of the youth labour market in the aftermath of the recession of the early 1980s.

One of the assumptions which has led us to attach importance to the distinction between stable and unstable jobs is that the former are more likely to involve training and so contribute to the future supply of skills. While the subject of training will be pursued in more detail later, it is worth noting briefly at this point that the assumption was supported by the findings of the follow-up on those with jobs at the 1984 interview. Those continuously in work during 1984-85 had had some form of training in 82 per cent of cases, and in 13 per cent this included off-the-job training. Those who had lost their job and were not working at follow-up had received training in 66 per cent of cases, and in no instance did this include off-the-job training.

## How and where new jobs were found

It is becoming increasingly appreciated that the functioning and structure of labour markets may be shaped by the detailed mechanisms of job search. Two aspects likely to be of particular significance are the channels through which jobs are sought and found; and the spatial extent of job search and of new jobs.

The young long-term unemployed, as a whole, made use of a wide range of channels of information in seeking jobs, with each individual on average referring to four such channels of information being used in parallel. This is in accordance with other evidence, which always indicates that the unemployed are not dependent on any one source of job information. The most commonly used channels, among the present group, were Jobcentres, contacts with family, friends and acquaintances, and press advertisements. Direct approaches to employers were also used by more than one half, and around one third consulted their Careers Office.

The source through which new jobs were actually found were also broadly in line with the findings of previous studies. As is already well known, the effectiveness of the various channels in leading to jobs is by no means proportional to the frequency wich which they are used. By far the most prominent source of information leading to new jobs was personal contacts - family, friends and acquaintances - which led to nearly half the jobs for young men and to nearly 40 per cent of the jobs for young women, at the time of the 1984 inter view. These sources also grew more important with the passage of time. New jobs in the period of 16 months up to the follow-up survey came from personal networks for 52 per cent of young men and for 62 per cent of young women. Moreover, in both 1984 and 1985 it was those with longer periods of unem ployment who particularly benefited from these personal networks. Lack of such a network would, therefore, be an extremely serious disadvantage for a young person in long-term unemployment.

The other two methods most frequently used - the Jobcentre and the press - produced new jobs each, in proportions which varied by gender and by stage of unemployment, within the range of 12 to 22 per cent. Direct approaches to employers, although used by smaller proportions, led to around the same proportion of jobs overall, and were particularly productive at the later stage, recorded in the follow-up survey. Over that period they produced 19 per cent of all new jobs, and 23 per cent of new jobs for young men. The full details are shown in Table 6.5.

**Table 6.5    Channels through which new jobs were found**

*column percentages*

| | Year | Male | Female | Months of unemployment | | |
| | | | | 6-12 | 13-24 | 25+ |
|---|---|---|---|---|---|---|
| Family/friends | 1984 | 48 | 38 | 37 | 48 | 60 |
| | 1985 | 52 | 60 | 47 | 50 | 59 |
| Jobcentre | 1984 | 22 | 17 | 22 | 18 | 16 |
| | 1985 | 13 | 18 | 17 | 12 | 1 |
| Careers office | 1984 | 1 | — | 1 | 1 | 2 |
| | 1985 | 1 | 0 | 3 | 0 | 0 |
| Private agency | 1984 | — | 4 | 2 | 0 | 2 |
| | 1985 | 1 | 0 | 1 | 0 | 0 |
| Direct approach to employer | 1984 | 12 | 15 | 13 | 13 | 13 |
| | 1985 | 23 | 14 | 21 | 22 | 15 |
| Press advertisement | 1984 | 10 | 14 | 14 | 12 | 1 |
| | 1985 | 10 | 18 | 12 | 12 | 14 |
| Advertisement in shops/on notice boards | 1984 | 0 | 7 | 4 | 2 | 0 |
| | 1985 | 3 | 5 | 0 | 8 | 0 |
| Other | 1984 | 6 | 4 | 5 | 5 | 3 |
| | 1985 | 2 | 3 | 4 | 2 | 0 |

\*         At time of sampling
—         Less than 0.5 per cent
Note:    Those entering self-employment were not asked this question

At the 1984 interview, those in new jobs were not asked the distance of those jobs from their homes. In view of significant findings concerning the extent of job search (to be discussed in detail in Chapter 8), it appeared that this was an unfortunate omission, and the gap in the information was partly filled by a question in the follow-up survey. This did indeed yield striking information.

Of the jobs obtained in the 16-month period up to the follow-up survey, 35 per cent of men's, but 71 per cent of wopmen's, were within a three-mile radius of their homes. Women in particular, therefore, but also a considerable section of young men, appeared to be operating in highly localised labour markets. So far as the men were concerned, however, there was also a degree of polarization, with 29 per cent working more than five miles away from home, and a further 16 per cent - many of whom had become self-employed - working at a variety of places.

As the evidence to be discussed in Chapter 8 will show in more detail, these young people were for the most part prepared to travel much longer distances to work than the location of new jobs would suggest, and many of them had searched for jobs completely outside their immmediate locality. And it does not seem entirely fanciful to suggest a parallel here with the wide range of job-seeking channels used, but eventual dependence on local and informal information networks. Many of the young long-term unemployed, one might say, want to operate in the wider and more formalised labour market, but their best chances remain in a local and informal labour market.

## Industries and occupations of new jobs

In Chapter 4 it was shown that the industries and occupations in which the young long-term unemployed had spent their 'main' or most recent jobs were very different in composition from those of a national cross-section of 18-24 year olds. In examining the new jobs obtained by members of the sample, it is naturally of interest to compare them with previous jobs. If the new jobs have a very similar composition in terms of industry and occupation to the former jobs, then the new jobs can be regarded as a continuation of the patterns already described in the preceding chapter. If however there are substantial differences in composition between the new jobs and the former jobs, then this may signal some fresh departure or emerging trend. Such differences however could arise in two distinct ways. They could arise because the types of jobs on offer were changing in composition and the young unemployed were adapting to different opportunities. Or they could arise because the young people best able to find work are already concentrated in the industries or occupations offering the most opportunities. While it is not possible to decide between these two possibilities in a rigorous way, sensible inferences can sometimes be made.

For the purpose of this rather detailed type of analysis, we have judged it preferable to concentrate on the evidence provided by the new jobs in being at the time of the 1984 interviews, rather than considering also the new jobs obtained up to the time of the follow-up survey in 1985. The reasons for this decision are practical ones. Although a far larger proportion obtained jobs by the time of the follow-up, this procedure only covered about 20 per cent of the original sample, so that in terms of actual numbers of jobs, the material from the 1984 interviews is more extensive. It is also of superior quality, since the descriptions of their jobs and employers provided in the self-completion questionnaires of the follow-up were often rather sketchy. On balance, then, the complications introduced by considering the two groups of information in parallel would not be justified by the gains.

Because of its detailed nature we do not show a complete table comparing the occupations of new jobs in 1984 with the 'main' or most recent jobs prior to unemployment. However several points of interest can be abstracted from the analysis, and they seem to indicate the effects both of job market opportunities and of individual differences.

*For the young men:*
(i)     there was an increase in the proportion of new jobs located in non-manual occupations - from 15 per cent in the 'main' or most recent prior jobs to a new figure of 19 per cent. Jobs in selling rose from five per cent to seven per cent, and in technical jobs from one per cent to three per cent. It seems likely that this increase reflects the advantages of those of the young unemployed who have experience or abilities fitting them for the non-manual segment of the labour market;
(ii)    whereas nine per cent of the male sample had previous jobs in catering, cleaning and personal services, nearly 13 per cent of the new jobs were in this group of occupations. These are generally jobs with low skill levels and the increasing movement into them is likely to reflect job market opportunity rather than personal advantages;

(iii) fewer of the new jobs for young men than of former jobs were located in the manual occupations of the manufacturing and construction sector. The largest decline was in the processing, making and repair occupations of the metal and electrical industries - that is, of the engineering, electronics and associated industries. Here the new jobs accounted for just 12 per cent of the total, compared with 18 per cent of the former jobs. As pointed out in Chapter 4, these engineering jobs were already markedly under-represented among the young unemployed men. The new jobs, then, probably reflect a lack of opportunities in these occupations for young men without recognized skills.

### For the young women:

(i) there had been some increase in the proportions of new jobs in the non-manual categories - notably a rise in professional occupations from four (in the former jobs) to six per cent, and an increase in clerical occupations from 22 to 25 per cent;

(ii) but this was offset by a large decline in the proportion of jobs in selling, which for the femal group means primarily shop assistants. Here the proportion in the former jobs had been 17 per cent but was only 11 per cent in the new jobs;

(iii) as in the case of the young men, there was a substantial movement into jobs in catering, cleaning and personal services: the 'former' proportion was 22 per cent, the 'new' proportion 37 per cent - more than one third of all new jobs;

(iv) again as with the young men, there appeared to be a decline in the jobs in manufacturing for this group. In the non-engineering processing, making and repair occupations, the fall was from 15 per cent in the former jobs to six per cent in the new jobs. The corresponding figures for the painting, packing, assembling and inspecting occupations were from 13 per cent down to five percent. These are generally unskilled or semi-skilled occupations so it seems likely that it is lack of demand rather than lack of qualifications or experience which was limiting the numbers of such jobs;

(v) there were several very marked differences in the composition of new jobs by occupation between the younger and older group of women - those entering the labour market in 1980-83 and those entering in 1975-79. In particular:

- whereas 12 per cent of new jobs in the 1975-79 entrants' group were clerical, the proportion in the younger group was 34 per cent;
- whereas five per cent of new jobs in the 1975-79 group were in selling (shop assistants), 15 per cent of new jobs for the younger women were in this category;
- the 1975-79 group of entrants had no less than 59 per cent of all their new jobs in catering, cleaning and personal service occupations, whereas these accounted for only 21 per cent of the new jobs in the 1980-83 group. These occupations provide many part-time jobs which may be for that reason attractive to women in the older age-groups caring for a family.

The corresponding analysis for industries of new jobs is shown in full at Table 6.6. In Chapter 4, attention was drawn to three industries which dominated the 'main' or most recent jobs prior to unemployment: 'other manufacture', distribution and hotels and catering, and (in the case of men only) construction. It is notable that these industries had not increased their representation in the new jobs. Among the men with new jobs, they were about as important as in the former jobs, but among the women both 'other manufacture' and distribution hotels and catering provided a lower proportion of the new jobs than hitherto.

More generally, the new jobs for men had a broadly similar industrial composition to former jobs, while for women there were greater differences. There was a greater proportion of jobs in transport and communications for both men and women, but particulary for women, and for women jobs in banking and finance also rose from the previous figure of four per cent to eight per cent of the new jobs. The most conspicuous feature of Table 6.6, however, applies to both men and women. Seventeen per cent of men's new jobs were in the 'other services' group of industries, by comparison with 13 per cent of former jobs. For women, the proportion of new jobs in this industry group was 31 per cent, compared with 21 per cent of former jobs.

All of these comparisons are cross-sectional - they set all new jobs on one side and all the 'main' or most recent jobs on the other. They therefore reflect changes in the spectrum of jobs, but not necessarily changes which individuals had experienced in their personal movements from job to job. The latter will be taken up in Chapter 9 under the heading of 'industrial and occupational flexibility'. It may however help to give a perspective on the new jobs to note, anticipating Chapter 9, that there had in fact been a great deal of individual change on the part of those who took the new jobs.

**Table 6.6    Industrial divisions of new jobs (1984)**

*column percentages*

|  | Male | | Female | |
| --- | --- | --- | --- | --- |
|  | | entry to labour market | | |
|  | 1975-79 | 1980-83 | 1975-79 | 1980-83 |
| Agriculture etc | 1 | 2 | 0 | 1 |
| Energy and water etc | 1 | 1 | 2 | 0 |
| Metals and chemicals | 2 | 1 | 1 | 0 |
| Engineering | 9 | 13 | 6 | 11 |
| Other manufacture | 12 | 12 | 16 | 8 |
| Construction | 21 | 18 | 0 | 2 |
| Distribution, hotels, catering etc | 20 | 29 | 34 | 34 |
| Transport and communications | 9 | 3 | 5 | 6 |
| Banking, finance and business services | 2 | 5 | 9 | 6 |
| Other services | 23 | 16 | 27 | 32 |
| Other/not stated | 0 | 0 | 0 | 0 |
| *Total in new jobs (weighted)* | *497* | *391* | *210* | *298* |

## Characteristics of new jobs

It was shown in Chapter 4 that in their former 'main' jobs the young long-term unemployed were over-represented in the small-firm sector and under-represented in the public sector. A similar analysis for the new jobs held at the time of the 1984 interviews showed marked differences in the types of employments obtained by young men and young women, and also some puzzling differences between the groups entering the labour market in 1975-79 and 1980-83.

Among the men, there was a marked shift (by comparison with the 'main' jobs) away from large-firm employment and into new jobs with small firms or into self-employment. Nearly half the new jobs for men were in small firms or self-employment, which is possibly about twice the proportion in the whole economy.[1]

Among women, the shift was if anything towards employment in the public sector: 15 per cent of 'main' jobs had been there, but now there were 18 per cent of new jobs in the public sector. But the older group of women (1975-79 entrants to the labour market) were much more likely to go into small firms or self-employment, and much less likely to get new jobs in the public sector, while the reverse applied to the younger women (1980-83 entrants to the labour market).

To pursue these possibly significant pointers, Table 6.7 breaks down the types of employers in new jobs in detail. For men, this reveals in particular the importance of self-employment in the new jobs: 19 per cent of the older group of men had become self-employed, 12 per cent of the younger group, and 16 per cent overall (one in six of all new jobs for men). Whereas the older men more frequently went into self-employment, the more recent entrants to the labour market more frequently took jobs in small firms.

**Table 6.7   Types of employer in new jobs (1984)**

*column percentages*

| | Male | | Female | |
| --- | --- | --- | --- | --- |
| | entry to labour market | | | |
| | 1975-79 | 1980-83 | 1975-79 | 1980-83 |
| Self employment | 19 | 11 | 5 | 2 |
| Small local firm | 22 | 31 | 27 | 11 |
| Large or medium-sized firm or chain | 39 | 42 | 45 | 52 |
| Nationalized industry | 4 | 3 | 5 | 8 |
| Civil service | 1 | 0 | 0 | 3 |
| Local authority | 11 | 6 | 5 | 8 |
| Health or education authority | 1 | 1 | 0 | 7 |
| Other | 3 | 5 | 13 | 9 |
| *Total (weighted)* | *497* | *391* | *210* | *298* |

Since self-employment has emerged as one of the main sources of growth in employment for the whole economy in the mid-1980s, it is of special interest to look at the young men in our sample entering self-employment. As the sample size in this respect was small, we can only look at them in broad terms, but two points are worth making. First, nearly all the self-employment is in construction or services. Second, nearly all the young men entering self-employment were wholly without educational or vocational qualifications.

Among women, the consistently greater success of the younger group in getting all categories of public sector jobs is clearly visible. The table also reveals that a not insignificant number of jobs were categorised as 'other'. On the basis of experience with the question in the 1980-81 DE/PSI survey of long-term unemployment, it was decided to reclassify these 'other' jobs to the small-firm category (for example, they would include such cases as domestic service or jobs in private schools).

By the time of the follow-up 16 months later, the contours of these findings had generally been somewhat softened, although there were no radical changes of direction. There was a slight slackening of the movement into self-employment among the men (13 per cent in the later period against 16 per cent at the time of the 1984 interview), but more conspicuous was a reduction in the proportion of jobs in the small-firm sector, which in the later period provided 22 per cent of the jobs for men and 28 per cent for women - only a little above national proportions. More generally, the differences between the new jobs of the young men and of the young women, in terms of size and the public-private split, were much smaller than in 1984, except for the relative absence of young women from self-employment. It is difficult to know whether these over-time differences were related to stages of unemployment or to changes in the labour market. In either sense, it seems that as time went on the new jobs tended to revert more towards a 'customary' distribution.

## Pay in new jobs

From the viewpoint of economic theory, the quality of jobs may be gauged by the pay received in them. The analysis of pay data does provide at least a first assessment of the quality of the new jobs, and a means of comparing them with the jobs most representative of the young long-term unemployed as a whole - the 'main' or most recent jobs before unemployment.

The average pay levels in the new jobs are summarized in Table 6.8, with the usual divisions into male and female, and 1975-79 and

1980-83 intakes to the labour market. The comparative figures for all 'main' or most recent jobs before long-term unemployment are shown below. The main points which emerge are:

(i) the average pay for all men in the new jobs was the same as for all men's main or most recent jobs before unemployment, and this (insofar as pay is a valid indicator of job quality) indicates that the new jobs on average were at the same level as those previously held by all long-term unemployed men;

(ii) the new jobs of women, in contrast to those of men, were on average considerably lower-paid than all women's main or most recent jobs before unemployment. This suggests (according to the economic criterion of job quality) that on average the new jobs were of lower level than former jobs;

(iii) however, the fall in average pay was attributable only to the older women who had entered the labour market in 1975-79; their average weekly earnings were about 42 while those of all women of this group in their 'main' jobs had been about 58. The younger women who entered the labour market in 1980-83 had higher average pay than in the former jobs for their group.

**Table 6.8  Pay in new jobs (1984), with comparisons to 'main' or most recent prior jobs**

|  | Male | | Female | |
| --- | --- | --- | --- | --- |
|  | entry to labour market | | | |
|  | 1975-79 | 1980-83 | 1975-79 | 1980-83 |
| **New jobs:** | | | | |
| mean £/week | 77.7 | 61.2 | 42.4 | 48.3 |
| standard error | 3.54 | 3.05 | 3.48 | 2.00 |
| **Main or most recent prior jobs:** | | | | |
| mean £/week | 76.5 | 54.2 | 58.3 | 43.5 |
| standard error | 1.33 | 1.57 | 1.13 | 1.46 |

Note: Pay in prior jobs adjusted to May 1984 values by means of RPI deflator

The improvement in pay for the younger women (the only group to have clearly achieved such an advance) is consistent with the occupational analysis presented earlier in this chapter. There it was shown that the women entering the labour market in 1980-83 were much more likely to have obtained non-manual jobs, especially clerical jobs. The older group of women as we have shown were highly concentrated in catering, cleaning and personal services and in small-firm employment.

These occupational contrasts are also likely to be linked to contrasts between full-time and part-time employment, and there had in fact been a considerable increase in the propensity to part-time working in the new jobs, by comparison with former jobs. We analysed hours of work into 'full-time' (30 or more hours per week) and 'part-time' (less than 30 hours). There was some problem with missing information, since many respondents were unable to quote a typical working week, possibly because they had spent too short a time in the job or because they were self-employed or in casual jobs. The salient finding, as one would expect, was the large number of women who had entered the labour market in 1975-79 now going into part-time work. Whereas in the 'main' jobs for all women in this group only six per cent had been part-time, no less than 42 per cent of the new jobs were part-time, a figure which is close to the proportion for women in employment in all age-groups. To some extent this shift might be explained as a normal process whereby women become more interested in part-time work as they marry and have children, and whereby equally employers open jobs with part-time hours to women as they leave the juvenile category.

In Table 6.9 the relationship between marital status and part-time work is illustrated - a relationship which contrasts for men and women in this age-group. Among the latter part-time work constituted the majority of jobs for married women. But of course single women outnumbered married women by a considerable factor, and many of the part-time jobs went to these single women. Of those men who got part-time work, virtually all were single; married men with young families (as most of these were) do not seek part-time jobs. Marital status accounts for a large number of the new part-time jobs, but the position is not as simple as it might seem to be.

In any case, an increase in part-time work is apparent among all age-groups and among men as well as women. For women entering the labour market in 1980-83, 15 per cent of the 'main' jobs had been part-time, but 19 per cent of new jobs had part-time hours. For men entering the labour market in 1980-83, the corresponding comparison is of five per cent against 17 per cent; and for the older men, entering in 1975-79, three per cent against 11 per cent.

Table 6.9    Full-time and part-time hours in new jobs, by marital
            status

*column percentages*

| | Male | | Female | |
| --- | --- | --- | --- | --- |
| | Married | Single | Married | SIngle |
| Full-time | 81 | 72 | 26 | 67 |
| Part-time | 1 | 17 | 50 | 21 |
| Not stated | 18 | 11 | 24 | 12 |
| *Total in new jobs* *(weighted)* | *189* | *687* | *130* | *372* |

Note:    Respondents were asked to state the typical hours per week. Part-time was
        classified as less than 30 hours. The high proportion not stating typical hours
        may be partly a consequence of self-employment or of casual work.

The tendency for quite substantial minorities of single young men to move into part-time jobs appears to be one of those signs of increasing flexibility in the operation of labour markets which many commentators have in recent years been seeking. But by the time of the follow-up survey in 1985, this sign (if such it was) had faded. Of the new jobs obtained by young men in our follow-up sample over this longer period, only six per cent had part-time hours.

This is the second point at which was have noted a reversion from an unusual to a customary pattern between 1984 and 1985. It is worth asking also whether the pay provided by new jobs underwent any turn of direction over this period. In fact, however, it did not. The average pay for the new jobs in the follow-up period, in 1985 money, was about £80 for the young men and £48 for the young women (36 per cent of the latter were part-timers). Allowing for inflation of around five per cent, this is very close to the level of the new jobs in 1984, and (in real terms) to the 'main' jobs held previously. The new jobs continue along the pay plateau which already seems to have been entered by these young people in the early 1980s (see Chapter 4).

### Training in new jobs
In Chapter 4 it was noted that only a small proportion of the young long-term unemployed had participated in a formal traineeship or

apprenticeship, but that in their 'main' or most recent jobs before unemployment the majority had received some type of instruction or training. In most cases this was on-the-job training by a supervisor or trainer, but in the case of 17 per cent of young men and 13 per cent of young women there had been some element of formal classroom instruction. The indications from the study of young people in the labour market by Ashton and Maguire[2] are that formal training tends to take place early in the young person's career and becomes less available with successive jobs. Our expectation, therefore, was to find relatively low levels of training in the new jobs.

The findings were that the majority of young people getting new jobs by the time of the 1984 interview received some on-the-job instruction, but that other forms of training were relatively infrequent especially among the 21-24 year old group. Overall only seven per cent of young men and nine per cent of young women had received any form of training other than on-the-job instruction. Nearly all of these were in the younger age-group of each sex, and relatively large proportions of the older group - 43 per cent in the case of young men and 48 per cent in the case of young women - had had no training at all. The reduced availability of training was also apparent in the jobs obtained over the longer period up to the 1985 follow-up, but at this stage the female group got far less training than the male. (No training in these new jobs was provided for 33 per cent of women, compared with 24 per cent of men; and only two per cent of women, compared with 11 per cent of men, got anything more elaborate than on-the-job training.) These observations are consistent with those of Ashton and Maguire in suggesting a 'tapering off' of training as young people (at least those within the lower part of the labour market) get further from their point of entry.

## Concluding comments

The purpose of this chapter has been primarily descriptive and comparative. The rate of movement into new jobs, and their distribution within the major groupings of the sample, have been documented. The characteristics of the new jobs have been outlined and compared with the former jobs considered to be most representative of the employment history of the young long-term unemployed. Attempts to explain the individual attributes or circumstances which make it more or less likely that a new job will be obtained, are left until subsequent chapters.

One finding of possible practical importance was that much the slowest rate of moving into jobs was among young men over 20. The disadvantages of the 18-20 year old group in unemployment may seem more obvious because of wage and training differentials with younger people. On our evidence, it seems rather the young men in long-term unemployment who have reached 21 who are in the weakest competitive position.

Another finding of interest was that the chances of getting a job, for a young person with one year or more of unemployment, had barely changed between 1981 and 1985. The prospects of finding a job within a period of one year and four months remained at around 30 per cent. But there were much better chances for those with six to 12 months of unemployment, so that the overall rate (for all durations of unemployment) was 40 per cent over the period.

In addition to examining the rate of moving into jobs, we also devoted much effort, through the follow-up survey, to assessing the stability of those jobs which were obtained. It is difficult to establish an objective yardstick for this assessment. However, in the context of the other information gathered both by this survey and by previous surveys of the unemployed, our judgement is that the degree of stability in the new jobs was surprisingly high. We suggest that the period 1984-85 may have witnessed a reversion towards more stable patterns of employment in the youth labour market.

This conclusion is doubly surprising, because much of the evidence of the chapter can be interpreted as indicative of movement on the part of the long-term unemployed in this age group into what is often termed the 'secondary' labour market, where unstable jobs are supposed to be prevalent. The evidence on this score included the large proportion of new jobs in catering, cleaning and personal service occupations; the further reduction in jobs in the engineering and associated industries which provide one of the main paths to skilled manual worker status; the large numbers of jobs in small firms and, for men, in self-employment; the increase in part-time jobs as a proportion of the total; and the low level of training provided in the new jobs.

Against this, it seems that in some respects the new jobs obtained at a later stage during 1984-85, and reflected in the follow-up survey, conformed to a more 'normal' pattern. In particular, there were fewer jobs in small firms and fewer young men taking part-time jobs.

This reversion to a more customary mix of small- and large-firm, and private and public sector, employment, would appear consistent with the notion of a 'restabilizing' tendency in the youth labour market at around this time. But our data are not extensive enough to make such an interpretation secure. A full understanding of what was taking place requires more knowledge of changes in employers' policies around the mid-1980s, and this will have to await the results of other research studies.

# 7   The Value of Qualifications, Training and Experience

In the preceding chapters we have analysed the labour market experience of the young unemployed.  In this and the next two the intention is to examine a number of influences which could help to explain variations in that labour market experience.  Why, for example, have some of the young people been able to spend a large part of their time in employment while others have spent very little or none?  Why have some succeeded in getting new jobs while others remain unemployed?

Throughout these chapters we are of course only concerned with variations within the group covered in our survey, and not variations across the whole labour market.  As was made clear in earlier chapters, the young long-term unemployed are located to a very large degree within the lower part of the labour market of 18-24 year olds.  But this does not mean that we can never say anything about the operation of the labour market as a whole.  In Chapters 3 and 4 we took pains to show how the young long-term unemployed compared with broader groups of their age, and where we are equipped with information about the overall distribution of some characteristics, it may be possible to widen our interpretation accordingly.

The possible influences of qualifications and training are brought together in this chapter because they appear to relate to a group of ideas which are among the most important advanced by labour market economists in recent years to explain variations in individual job successes.  On the one hand, investment in job-relevant knowledge through education, training and on-the-job experience is expected to enhance the value of the individual to the employer. Although this reasoning has usually been applied as a means of predicting wages, it appears relevant to an explanation of relative chances of employment or of time spent in unemployment. A further development of human capital concepts, in what has come to be known as 'signalling theory', stresses the value of qualifications or other accredited characteristics as a means of lowering employers' information costs in recruitment[1]. However we will not dwell on the theoretical aspects. From a common-sense viewpoint, it seems likely that anything which contributes to making a young person better qualified (in the widest sense) is likely to raise his or her chances of employment, and indeed of an improved quality of job. The proviso is, of course, that employers must recognize the qualification as being of worth to them.

## Educational and vocational qualifications

*Influence on time in work 1975-84* The time spent by the individual in employment (including self-employment), as a proportion of the total period spent in the labour market, has been established in previous chapters as a measure of the conditions in the labour market over a medium-term time span. In addition, however, it is likely to differ between individuals faced with similar labour market conditions. We begin, therefore, by assessing whether this measure differs according to levels of qualification. The analysis is repeated for each of the four main groupings of the sample - by male and female and by period of entry to the labour market (1975-79 and 1980-83). These divisions can also be thought of simply as 'age within sex', since period of entry to the labour market corresponds fairly well with age in this sample, few of whom have gone on to further education.

As Table 7.1 makes clear, qualifications made a considerable difference to the cumulative labour market experience of all four groups. To have no qualification pushed down the time spent in work as a proportion of the total.

In addition a number of more detailed findings emerge from this set of analyses, some of which are not entirely expected.

(i)   There was a marked difference in the relative value of school examination passes and vocational qualifications between young men and young women. For young men, it was important to have vocational qualifications (which in this group means apprenticeships, City & Guilds, and so on - see Chapter 3 for

**Table 7.1    Qualifications and time spent in employment, 1975-84**

*percentages (weighted)*

| | Male | | Female | |
|---|---|---|---|---|
| | Time in employment | | | |
| | entered labour market in | | | |
| | 1975-79 | 1980-83 | 1975-79 | 1980-83 |
| No qualifications | 38 | 12 | 42 | 10 |
| School examination only | 40 | 14 | 54 | 19 |
| - of which, CSE below grade 1 | 44 | 12 | 56 | 16 |
| School and vocational qualification | 54 | 19 | 52 | 24 |
| Vocational qualification only | 62 | — | — | — |

—    Mean not shown as cell total was too small

details); school examination passes conferred only a marginal advantage on their own. For the young women, on the other hand, school examination results were the important influence for 1975-79 entrants, while vocational qualifications on top of school qualifications began to pay dividends only in 1980-83. For the young women, it should be recalled (see Chapter 3), vocational qualifications mostly consisted of clerical, secretarial or commercial subjects.

(ii)   Although the differences of time spent in work appear smaller in the 1980-83 than in the 1975-79 period, it should be borne in mind that the availability of jobs was less in the later period, so that proportionally the advantage of having some form of qualifications persists.

(iii)  It is sometimes asserted that the lower grades of CSE passes (below grade 1) confer little advantage on school leavers. However in Table 7.1 we have included a separate analysis of those with CSE passes below grade 1, which suggests that for this group of young people lower CSEs were worth having. For those entering the labour market in the 1975-79 period, particularly, those with lower CSEs fared as well or better than the average of all in the groups with school examination passes; this was true of both men and women. It was only in 1980-83 that this advantage began to diminish. Even so women in this age group (18-20) who had lower CSEs spent 16 per cent of time in jobs, compared to 10 per cent in the case of the totally unqualified. Among the younger group of men, however, there was no difference on this measure between the lower CSEs and the unqualified. It seems, then, that lower CSEs may have declined in value to some extent, perhaps through being crowded out as the availability of people with higher grades and qualifications has increased. Alternatively, one could argue that in the 1975-79 period employers were insensitive to differences in examination grades when recruiting (since those with lower grades did as well or better than those with higher grades). In that case the poorer level of job market success of those with lower CSEs in 1980-83 would reflect a growing awareness or sensitivity on the part of employers to differences of grade in qualifications.

(iv) Although the analysis confirms the influence on job market success of qualifications, the size of the differences because of qualifications was much smaller than the differences in success between the 1975-79 and the 1980-83 entrants to the labour market. For example, men with vocational qualifications who entered the labour market during 1980-83 only achieved 19 per cent of time in work, while those men entering the labour market in 1975-79 without any qualifications spent 28 per cent of their time in work. Actually this understates the contrast, because (as was demonstrated in Chapter 4) the 1975-79 entrants spent higher proportions of their time in work up the 1980, after which they too were affected by the adverse labour market conditions.

The evidence summarized above constitutes a confirmation of the importance of qualifications even within the lower part of the labour market and over a medium-term time span. A wider review of the labour market would presumably produce even stronger results, since common observation as well as a variety of research studies show that entry to higher occupations depends to a great extent on qualifications, and in this higher stratum the proportion of time spent out of work is much lower. The survey also has produced potentially important new insight into the way that different types and levels of qualifications have different market values for men and for women and can also change in value over a short period of time.

*Influence on uncompleted periods of unemployment* The length of time spent in unemployment in the current uncompleted spell may also be affected by qualifications. At the time of drawing the sample the date when each individual's benefit claim had commenced was obtained from the NUBS computer, so that we had as accurate a measure of the period of unemployment as might be found. At an earlier point (Chapter 3, Table 3.2) we have already shown that there was a relationship between qualification and period of unemployment. We do not show a further table here, but there are some more detailed points worth noting.

Among the men, those with vocational qualifications were least likely to have prolonged spells of current unemployment. Conversely, those with no qualifications at all formed a progressively larger proportion of those with increasingly long spells of unemployment. Those with school examination passes, but no vocational qualifications were intermediate. The same patters held for women and were if anything more marked than in the case of men. Also, the influence of qualifications or lack of qualifications on time in unemployment was at least as marked for the 1980-83 entrants to the labour market as for the 1975-79 entrants, even though the former group (because of their shorter time in the labour market) had on average shorter spells of unemployment.

*Qualifications and new jobs* One might expect that the new jobs obtained by the young long-term unemployed would continue to show the influences present in the work histories as a whole, unless something was changing in the labour market. The test of the influence of qualifications, which is of the greatest current concern, lies in examining differences between the group in work and the group still out of work. The comparison is presented in Table 7.2. In interpreting this analysis, it must be remembered that the actual numbers concerned are quite small: 209 men and 123 women from the sample were in work at the time of the 1984 interview.

The overall conclusions to be drawn from Table 7.2 are similar to those put forward for our first analysis in this chapter, relating to time in work throughout the labour market history. Qualifications certainly continued to influence the chances of getting a job in the first part of 1984, but there also continued to be differences between types of qualification and between the four sub-groups of the analysis.

**Table 7.2   Qualifications and entry to new job at 1984 interview**

*percentages (weighted)*

| | In new job | | | |
| | Male | | Female | |
| | entered labour market in | | | |
| | 1975-79 | 1980-83 | 1975-79 | 1980-83 |
|---|---|---|---|---|
| No qualification | 11 | 13 | 10 | 6 |
| School examination only | 9 | 14 | 14 | 22 |
| - of which, CSE below grade 1 | 10 | 15 | 21 | 20 |
| School and vocational | 24 | 24 | 13 | 28 |
| Vocational only | 39 | — | — | — |

—    Percentage not shown as cell total was too small

For young men who entered the labour market in 1975-79 (in 1984 aged about 21-24) vocational qualifications, with or without school examination passes to back them up, were very important influences on job-getting. School examination passes on their own conferred no advantage; they had conferred little advantage in the previous work history (see Table 7.1). But it must be remembered that very few in this group had the kind of educational qualifications which would get them into higher-level careers.

If the results are taken across the two age-groups, to give a kind of overall snapshot of the current state of the labour market for these young men, then the striking point is the importance of vocational qualifications. Those with such qualifications were twice as likely to be in a new job as those without, or as those with only school qualifications.

Among the young women, on the other hand, any qualification appeared to be of advantage, even for the older group (aged about 21-24), and there was not much difference in the job-getting chances of those with school examination passes only and those with some vocational qualification as well. In fact, it is also notable that among the women (though not among the men) to have a lower CSE pass (that is, lower than CSE grade 1) was useful.

In short, when reviewing the time in work throughout the job history, there were differences in the influence of qualifications depending both on sex and on age or period of entry to the labour market.

*Progressive impact of qualifications* It might be supposed that qualifications are mainly of importance for entry to occupations, and thereafter decline in influence. In a long time perspective, this is indeed well documented[2]. But in the present study, perhaps the clearest evidence concerning the influence of qualifications came from the follow-up survey conducted in Autumn 1985, when the sub-sample contacted had acquired another 16 months' experience of the job market. Not only did presence and absence of qualifications distinguish between those who did and those who did not get new jobs in this period, but graduations of qualification were clearly reflected in chances of getting work.

Taking all groups together (as sample size was relatively small), we found that the rates of movement into new jobs ran as shown in Table 7.3.

**Table 7.3    Proportions having a new job in 1984-85, by qualification**

*percentages*

| | |
|---|---|
| No qualifications | 26 |
| CSEs below grade 1 | 42 |
| O-level or equivalent | 58 |
| A-level or equivalent | 65 |
| Any vocational (with or without any of the above) | 60 |

Note:    O-levels, A-levels and vocational qualifications are non-exclusive categories

The impression given is that as young people fall deeper into long-term unemployment, the possession of some educational or vocational qualification becomes still more important in order to gain acceptance by employers. This could happen, for instance, because job experience is progressively receding into the past and being given less weight by employers, whereas formal qualifications retain their worth, at least for people in this age band.

It is also noteworthy that whereas in 1984 educational qualifications were on their own of little advantage to the young men, during the extended period of 1984-85 all kinds of certificated qualifications became important.

## Qualifications and the 'quality' of main jobs

If qualifications give young people a competitive advantage within their own section of the labour market, then it should be possible for them to exercise more choice over the kind of jobs they take. It has sometimes been assumed that qualified people will naturally tend to go into the large-enterprise, high-paying sector, but this seems far from self-evident. We examined what type of employers people had in their main job (or latest job, if none stood out as the main one) and how this related to qualifications. We also examined the influence, if any, of qualifications on pay, further training at work, and whether full-time or part-time hours were worked. The full results from these analyses are not tabulated here, but the main findings are stated.

(i) *Type of employer.* There was in fact little relationship between qualifications of the young long-term unemployed and the type of employer in their 'main' or most recent jobs. Type of employer was divided into small firms or self-employment, large private firms, and public sector. The only consistent influence was that those with a combination of school examination passes and vocational qualifications were about twice as likely as other groups to get into public sector jobs. However the relatively small proportion of public sector jobs in the young unemployed's background (see Chapter 4) means that this tendency had little impact on the overall pattern. Large firms in fact took slightly fewer with school plus vocational qualifications than would be expected, but small firms about the expected number, if the calculation is based on the assumption that young people are equally likely to go to the different kinds of employer whatever their qualifications. These results are important in showing that, although the young unemployed came disproportionately from a small-firm background, it is far from true that the small firms were recruiting only the least qualified end of the spectrum.

(ii) *Pay* Qualifications did affect the average pay level in the 'main' or more recent job, but there were quite large variations in the influence depending on sex and age-group. The combination of school and vocational qualifications came consistently top of the pay league, and this was the clearest finding.

(iii) *Training* The influence of qualification on training depended on sex. Among the men, those with vocational qualifications had the most training (as would be expected), but those with school qualifications only, also got much more formal training than those without qualifications. Among women, however, it was only those with vocational qualifications who had had more training.

(iv) Although it is sometimes supposed - for example within the literature of 'secondary' labour markets - that part-time work is mainly taken by less qualified people, there was no indication of that within the present sample. Among both men and women, those considering that their 'main' job was part-time, or whose most recent job was part-time, were as likely to have some school or vocational qualifications as to be unqualified.

## Where qualifications do not count: ethnic minorities

Because the influence of qualifications on the labour market position of the young long-term unemployed is so marked, it is of interest also to consider any groups where it does not have the expected impact. Such a group was constituted by the members of Asian and Afro-Caribbean minorities within the sample. (For the latter, we will use the more customary if less accurate term 'West Indian minority'.)

Although they formed only a small proportion of the whole sample (see Chapter 3 for details), the members of ethnic minority groups were highly concentrated in a few major centres. To get a comparison with the white majority in the sample which took account of location, we decided to confine attention to those areas of high ethnic minority concentrations: Greater London, Greater Manchester, West Yorkshire, the West Midlands, Nottingham, and Southampton. This reduced the sample size for the ethnic minorities from 178 to 145 (81 per cent of the total), while reducing that for the white majority from 2294 to 756 (33 per cent of the total). Since this departure from our normal base in this report affects population weighting to an unknown degree, we present the analyses in this section in unweighted form.

Detailed analysis of patterns of qualification showed that it was necessary to distinguish Asian from West Indian, and male from female within these, in order to make valid comparisons with the white sample. Broadly speaking, we found that young Asian women and young West Indian men were similar in their qualifications to their white counterparts, but that young Asian men and (especially) young West Indian women in the sample were clearly better qualified than both their corresponding white groups and their gender-opposites in their own ethnic groups. This appears clearly in the following summary of the proportions having no qualifications whatever:

**Table 7.4   Proportions without qualification, by ethnic group and sex**

*percentages*

|             | Male | Female |
|-------------|------|--------|
| Asian       | 32   | 40     |
| West Indian | 54   | 15     |
| White       | 51   | 41     |

Note:     See text for definition of sub-sample used

The superior qualifications of the young Asian men and the young West Indian women were confirmed by the details concerning O-levels and A-levels also. The Asian males had 30 per cent O-levels and 11 per cent with A-levels; the West Indian females had 35 per cent with O-levels and 19 per cent with A-levels. White males got O-levels in 20 per cent of cases, and white females in 27 per cent of cases; both had seven per cent with A-levels. As before, the Asian women and West Indian men had similar levels of attainment, on these measures, to their white counterparts.

In view of what this chapter has shown about the influence of qualifications on labour market outcomes, and in view also of the fact that we are comparing ethnic and white groups only within common labour markets, it would be predicted that the ethnic minority groups would have either been on a par in terms of employment with the corresponding white groups, or in the case of Asian males and West Indian females, appreciably ahead of them. But five different measures of labour market experience all showed that the ethnic minority groups had been faring considerably worse in the labour market than their white comparators. They were, thus, failing to receive the returns to qualifications which appeared to apply in the sample as a whole.

The full results of this analysis have been documented in a separate paper[3], which also shows that the differences in returns to qualifications between white and non-white groups cannot plausibly be attributed to intervening influences such as disadvantages of social background or current labour market activity. Here one measure of labour market experience will suffice to illustrate the nature of differences and their lack of correspondence with qualification levels. The measure chosen is proportion who have never had a job, since entering the labour market.

**Table 7.5    Proportions without any employment, by ethnic group and sex**

*percentages*

|             | Male | Female |
|-------------|------|--------|
| Asian       | 36   | 48     |
| West Indian | 32   | 54     |
| White       | 20   | 24     |

Note:    See text for definition of sub-sample used

One of the features of these results, and of the other labour market measures examined, is that female members of the ethnic minority groups have experienced particularly severe problems. The young West Indian women - the best qualified sub-group in the sample - also had the most extreme employment problems.

**Driving licence as a form of qualification**
In Chapter 3 we suggested that possession of a driving licence would, up to a point, be regarded as a kind of personal attainment, and should confer similar advantages to educational or vocational qualifications. It is in this light that we now examine its influence on success in the labour market. Of course, it must also be recalled that possession of a driving licence, it coupled with access to a vehicle, may provide the competitive advantage of being able to look for jobs more rapidly, further afield, and away from public transport routes. Hence there is an aspect of mobility as well as of qualification about having a driving licence; and these are aspects which the present survey cannot separate, although we return to the question of mobility in the next chapter.

Among men, 36 per cent overall held a driving licence: 38 per cent in the older group (who joined the labour market in 1975-79) and 34 per cent in the younger group. Among women, the overall proportion was 23 per cent with 20 per cent in the younger group and 25 per cent in the older. Being able to drive, among this group of young people, was therefore less common than having some type of school examination qualification, but more common than having some type of vocational qualification.

We begin by looking at the relationship of having a driving licence with proportion of time spent in work. This is done in Table 7.6. The total effect of having a driving licence was in fact, rather greater for the men who entered the labour market in 1975-79, and for the women who entered the labour market in 1980-83. In the former group, males with driving licences spent 49 per cent of their time in work, while those without driving licences spent only 36 per cent of their time in work. Even sharper was the difference in the case of the younger group of women: drivers, 26 per cent of their time spent in work, non-drivers, 14 per cent. The young men entering the labour market in 1980-83 were also affected by whether or not they could drive, although not quite so much as in the case of the young women.

**Table 7.6   Possession of a driving licence, and time spent in employment 1975-84**

*mean percentages (weighted)*

|  | Time in employment | | | |
|  | Male | | Female | |
|  | entered labour market in | | | |
|  | 1975-79 | 1980-83 | 1975-79 | 1980-83 |
| --- | --- | --- | --- | --- |
| With driving licence | 49 | 18 | 60 | 26 |
| No driving licence | 36 | 12 | 44 | 14 |

The notion of driving as a competitive advantage is also supported when we look at new jobs which the young people had entered between the time of sampling and the time of the survey interview - a more up-to-date picture of success in the labour market. Here the possession of a driving licence had its most conspicuous impact, and one which was clearly greater than that of qualifications.

In fact, as Table 7.7 shows, having a driving licence about doubled the chances of having a new job, at the time of the interview in 1984, for the young men, and more than doubled it for young women. Those men without a driving licence had a new job in 10 per cent of cases, but those with a driving licence in 20 per cent. Young women without a driving licence got new jobs in 11 per cent of cases (similar to the corresponding group of men), but those with a driving licence got a new job in 25 per cent of cases.

**Table 7.7    Possession of a driving licence, and entry to a new job in 1984**

*percentages (weighted)*

|  | In new job at 1984 interview | | | |
|  | Male | | Female | |
|  | entered labour market in | | | |
|  | 1975-79 | 1980-83 | 1975-79 | 1980-83 |
|---|---|---|---|---|
| With driving licence | 20 | 21 | 20 | 32 |
| No driving licence | 9 | 11 | 10 | 13 |

There was an even stronger effect for the young women who entered the labour market in 1980-83 (the younger age group). Non-drivers in this group got new jobs in 13 per cent of cases, drivers in 32 per cent. As the actual numbers involved were small, too much stress should not be put on this result; but it could be that, exactly because a smaller proportion of this group had a driving licence, the competitive advantage within the group was correspondingly greater. For men in the two age-groups, between which there was little difference in the proportions able to drive, the influence of having a driving licence on getting a new job was the same.

**Progressive impact of driving licence**
If these results appear strong, they are exceeded by the findings from the follow-up survey held 16 months after the 1984 interview. Among the sub-sample covered by this follow-up, the contrast in fortunes between drivers and non-drivers can only be described as remarkable, as simply stated in the following rates of movement into new jobs during the 16-month period:

     drivers        68 per cent
     non-drivers   20 per cent

To put this in perspective, drivers did better in getting into work than did young people with A-levels (65 per cent in new jobs). But that is not all. Drivers got their jobs sooner, and/or were less likely to lose them subsequently, so that they had appreciably longer average periods in employment (drivers in jobs: 11.5 months; non-drivers in jobs: 9.8 months). This difference was not discernible between qualified and non-qualified in new jobs.

In the previous chapter, it was noted that the influence of qualifications seemed to become stronger as unemployment continued. An interpretation advanced for that was that as the previous period of employment recedes into the past, the experience formerly gained loses its pull with prospective employers, but that qualifications continue to be regarded as relevant. The same argument could apply to possession of a driving licence.

## Driving as a competitive advantage for young women

Some of the results which have been described seem to suggest that to have a driving licence is even more of an advantage for the young women than for the young men, and particularly so for the younger group of women who entered the labour market in 1980-83. As the possession of a driving licence is less common for the women than for the men, and least common for the younger group of women, our interpretation of the findings is that they are consistent with relative competitive advantage. The differences in advantage would not appear if all the men and all the women were in totally open competition with all others, but we know that this is not so: the youth labour market is partially segmented by age and sex. For example, the young women drivers who entered the labour market in 1980-83 are likely to be competing particularly against the others in that specific group. Although of course these younger women drivers are far outnumbered by young male drivers, they are likely to be relatively little in direct job competition with these and their advantage remains in relation to young women in their own age group.

## Training in the main or most recent job

The process of human capital formation does not end with educational or vocational qualifications. Training within employment, because it is so directly relevant to work, should have a value to the individual when competing for jobs. This however depends upon the new employers' ability to recognize and utilize the training which the individual has formerly received.

We obtained information about the type of training received in the 'main' job before unemployment, or if the respondent could not say which was the main job, the most recent one. Details are presented in Chapter 4. The main distinctions which we use here are between those who received two or more types of training - which usually implies a combination of on-the-job instruction with some classroom instruction; those who received one type of training only, which usually means on-the-job instruction by a trainer or supervisor; and those who received no training whatever.

Of course, training which took place in a job (especially in a recent job) cannot be regarded as an influence on the overall level of success in the labour market since much of that labour market experience may have taken place before the training was obtained. It could however influence events towards the end of the labour market history - notably the length of time in the current unemployment, the chances of getting a new job, and the type of job obtained.

*Training as an influence on duration of current unemployment*
Earlier in the chapter if was shown that those without qualifications tended to accumulate at the 'tail' of long-term unemployment - at durations of more than two years of continuous unemployment. Conversely relatively few with qualifications were found at the longest durations. One might expect a parallel finding with training, and this is considered in Table 7.8. Because the older group (those entering the labour market in 1975-79) had longer spells of unemployment on average, we have looked at the proportion with more than two years in their current spell for this group, but at the proportion with more than one year for the younger group with shorter average spells.

As can be seen, the results were not consistent across the groups and do not lend much support to the view that training within the job was influencing the duration of unemployment. The clearest support for this supposition was among the older group of women, where those with no training were most likely to have long unemployment, those with one form of training (that is, on-the-job instruction) were somewhat less likely, and those with two or more forms of training least likely by a considerable margin. Among the younger women, however, those with no training were no more likely to have long unemployment spells than those with on-the-job instruction; and there were too few in the group with the more formal types of training for a comparison of these to be possible. Among the older group of men, those with no training at all were only slightly more likely to appear at the longest durations of unemployment than were those with two or more types of training, while the highest probability of protracted unemployment fell to those with just on-the-job training. Finally, in the case of the younger group of men (1980-83 entrants to the labour market) there was simply no consistent difference in length of unemployment between those with different amounts of training.

**Table 7.8  Training in main (or most recent) job, and prolonged unemployment**

*percentages*

| | With 'prolonged' unemployment | | | |
| | Male | | Female | |
| | entered labour market in | | | |
| | 1975-79 | 1980-83 | 1975-79 | 1980-83 |
| --- | --- | --- | --- | --- |
| No training | 33 | 55 | 29 | 46 |
| One type of training (usually 'on-the-job') | 38 | 54 | 20 | 47 |
| Two or more types of training (includes 'off-the-job') | 28 | 58 | 8 | 29* |

\*      Unreliable; cell total too small
Note:   For those entering the labour market in 1975-79, prolonged unemployment is defined as more than 24 months in the spell at date of sampling. For those entering the labour market in 1980-83, it is defined as more than 12 months.

*Training and new jobs*

As well as considering whether training has influenced the persistence of long-term unemployment, we wish to assess whether training affects chances of getting new jobs after that period of unemployment. It has already been shown that qualifications had a progressive influence on labour market chances, as far as this group was concerned. It could be that the value of training would, similarly, emerge once that the current situation was examined.

To examine this possibility, we considered those new jobs obtained between the time of drawing the sample and the survey interview in 1984. It is possible to consider not only whether previous training in work influenced the chances of getting a new job in this period, but also whether training was connected with getting different types of jobs - especially better-paid jobs. The analysis of whether a new job was obtained or not is shown in Table 7.9.

**Table 7.9    Training in main (or most recent) job, and new job in 1984**

*percentages (weighted)*

| | With new job at 1984 interview | | | |
| | Male | | Female | |
| | entered labour market in | | | |
| | 1975-79 | 1980-83 | 1975-79 | 1980-83 |
|---|---|---|---|---|
| No training | 15 | 23 | 26 | 27 |
| One type of training (usually 'on-the-job') | 12 | 15 | 11 | 24 |
| Two or more types of training (includes 'off-the-job') | 14 | 11 | 8 | 17* |

\*      Unreliable; based on small number

It can readily be seen that training in the main or most recent job did not influence success in getting a new job. In fact, the best chances of getting a new job seemed to be enjoyed by those who had received no training in their main or most recent job. This was particularly the case for women in the 21-24 age group. Among younger women, however, those with on-the-job training in their main job had possibly a slightly better chance of a new job than those with no previous training. Among the men, those without training did best in getting work, and there were negligible differences between those with just on-the-job training and those with two or more types of training. One should not stress too heavily the paradoxical negative relationship between past training and chances of a new job at this stage, because, first, the differences involved were small, and second, they had disappeared in the results of the follow-up survey. These latter (not tabulated here) show simply a lack of any systematic difference between those with various levels of training when it came to getting a new job during 1984-85 as a whole.

The impression given by this evidence - and by the previous findings concerning the duration of the current spell of unemployment - is that training in previous jobs carries little weight in getting new jobs. One must of course bear in mind that this applies only to the occupational strata of the labour market in which the young long-term unemployed are seeking work.

It is however still possible that training in previous jobs could influence the quality of any new jobs obtained. For example, training could raise an individual's expectations or sense of personal value, and lead him or her to be more selective about taking a new job thereafter. This could lengthen the time in unemployment but should have some returns, for example through higher subsequent pay levels.

Our analysis which examined this question, however (not tabulated here), once more suggested a negative conclusion. For the men who entered the labour market in 1975-79, in particular, higher levels of training in their former jobs were associated with lower pay in their new jobs, although the differences were statistically non-significant because of small sample size. Among the remaining groups, the only indication of higher pay for more training was among the women aged 21-24, where those with on-the-job instruction got higher pay than those with no training at all. Taken overall, however, the results were best interpreted as showing no relationship between previous training and pay in the new job.

In short, then, the various analyses concerning training in the main job prior to unemployment have failed to reveal any effect on subsequent outcomes in the labour market.

## Work experience and subsequent success

Qualifications, training, and work experience have all been regarded as forms of human capital. A substantial body of research by human capital economists has shown that work experience, as reflected in the number of years in an occupation or within a particular employment, positively influences earnings[4]. Indeed, in the mid-1960s Blau and Duncan[5] had already demonstrated that, as work experience grew longer, the preceding job became the strongest predictor of the current job, while the influence of initial educational attainments progressively waned.

However, with our survey group, young and with disrupted labour market experience, we have now seen that while certificated attainments influenced success in finding new jobs, previous job training did not. It would be consistent with this contrast to find, also, that prior work experience had little value in reestablishing these young people in jobs.

To show that this was so, we do not need to introduce any new evidence, but only to recall one of the important findings from Chapter 6 and reinterpret it. There was some suggestion that in 1984, those who had entered the labour market during 1975-79 were falling behind the younger people, who entered in 1980-83, in their chances of getting new jobs. Moreover, by the time of the follow-up survey in late 1985, the younger group of men had forged well ahead of the older group, while in the case of women there was no difference by age. The groups which had entered the labour market earlier, it should be remembered, had enjoyed much more stable employment conditions up to 1980 and therefore had far more work experience, on average, than the younger group.

This finding can be interpreted simply in the light of the present chapter's findings. After a prolonged spell of unemployment, young people's work experience ceases to have any influence upon their ability to find new work (much the same as with training in previous jobs). Since, however, certificated qualifications continue to be influential, or even grow progressively important, the younger male group, with a higher level of qualification, progressively pulls ahead of the older, more experienced male group. In the case of women, there was no difference in qualification levels between earlier and later entrants to the labour market, so they remain equal in their chances of finding new work.

**Qualifications in their social background**
The evidence of the two preceding sections suggests that non-certificated training and work experience can be ruled out as significant influences upon the young unemployed's chances of getting new jobs. Having simplified matters in this way, we can therefore turn our attention back, once again, to certificated qualifications, including possession of a driving licence. What further needs to be done to strengthen our understanding of this apparently important influence?

The most obvious limit of the findings earlier in this chapter is that they are based on separate analyses which do not take account of possible overlap between the two kinds of attainment considered. It seems quite likely that educational and vocational qualifications will, in fact, overlap considerably with possession of a driving licence. The very fact that we have considered both to be forms of qualification suggests that personal attributes may be common to both. In the extreme case, it is conceivable that a driving licence is an entirely spurious influence on success in the labour market, because of its association with qualifications tapping more basic abilities.

Moreover, we have already pointed out that qualifications are in their turn influenced by a number of social background variables (see Chapter 3). Social background could provide another common influence upon the various forms of attainment. How can we be sure that, when we portray influences of qualifications or of the driving licence upon labour market success, we are not presenting the shadow rather than the substance? Could it not be, in particular, that both educational attainment and possession of a driving licence reflect a relatively affluent family background, which would continue to provide other advantages for young people seeking jobs?

A further complication concerns the implications of differences between the young men and young women in our sample: differences in attainments, in marital and household circumstances, and in labour market behaviour, as well as in job-seeking success rates.

To assess all these possible complications, we developed a more unified statistical analysis, making use of the method of log-linear modelling. The full details are presented in Appendix 3 (see table M1). Here we merely summarize what was included in the analysis and the main conclusions reached.

The data consisted of a five-way cross-tabulation of the whole survey, with these dimensions:

(i)   gender;

(ii)  housing tenure: owner occupied or other. This we considered to be the best general indicator of social background or social class which we had available (for further discussion of this measure in relation to social class, see Pahl)[6];

(iii) educational and vocational qualifications: coded into five categories, vocational qualifications being assumed to add to educational (for further details, see Appendix 3);

(iv)  driving licence: possessed, or not possessed;

(v)   whether in a new job at the 1984 interview (yes or no).

We sought to account for or explain the complete five-way table in terms of all the pairs of associations between the variables. (With five variables, there are 10 such pairs.) The statistical method used permits one to assess whether this does yield a satisfactory view of the data, and in addition permits the contribution or importance of each pairwise association to be measured. Here, of course, we are particularly interested in whether the associations between educational qualification and getting a new job, and between having a driving licence and getting a new job, continue to hold their own when jostling with other variables.

This analysis resulted in a well-fitting model: that is, all the interrelationships between the five variables could reasonably be reduced to the pairs of associations. Moreover, eight of the 10 pairs contributed strongly to the overall model, while two were somewhat weak. The former, strong relationships included those between educational qualifications and getting a new job, and between having a driving licence and getting a new job. The weak relationships were those between gender and getting a new job, and between housing tenure (our social class proxy) and getting a new job.

The composite analysis, therefore, much strengthens our explanation of job-getting in long-term youth unemployment. In brief, we have found that:

- educational qualifications and driving licence have distinct influences on job-getting: the one cannot substitute for the other;
- gender and housing tenure, our two social background variables, are both related to the two attainments variables, and to each other; but only weakly to job-getting.

It follows that one cannot interpret either educational qualifications or possession of a driving licence merely as an indicator of social advantage.

The findings are summed up in diagrammatic form in Figure 7.1, overleaf.

## Qualifications and unemployment duration

There is one further practical question to be considered. In Chapter 6 it was shown that the chances of getting a new job declined as the period of unemployment grew longer. And the non-qualified are particularly concentrated at the longest periods of unemployment. Are there two separate influences here - an effect of duration, as well as an effect of qualification - or is the effect of duration merely the cumulative expression of the qualification effect?

**Figure 7.1  Influences on getting jobs**

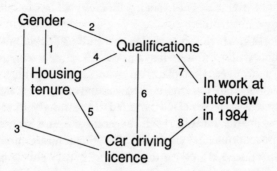

The interpretation of the diagram is as follows:

1,2,3:    Women in the samples were more likely to have qualifications and to be in owner occupied housing, but less likely to have a driving licence;

4,5:    Those in owner occupied housing were more likely to have qualifications or a driving licence;

6,7,8:    Those with qualifications were more likely to have a driving liicence, and someone with either was more likely to get a job.

An analysis similar to that described in the previous section of the chapter was performed to assess this question. However, the social background variables (gender and housing tenure) were removed from the analysis and replaced with two variables reflecting the potential influence of time. The first, unemployment period, was divided into three categories (6-12 months, 13-24 months, and more than 24 months). The second expressed the distinction, used throughout this report, between those entering the labour market in 1975-79 and those entering in 1980-83. It is essential to include this second variable, for recent entrants to the labour market had a lower probability of having, as yet, a long period of unemployment.

The other three variables in the analysis were as before (educational and vocational qualifications, driving licence, and whether in employment at the 1984 interview). But educational and vocational qualifications were now reduced to a three-category, instead of a five-category, scale, in order to make the analysis technically manageable.

The result, which is reported in Appendix 3 (Table M.2), showed that unemployment duration had a powerful influence on the chances of getting a job, even when placed in an analysis alongside educational and vocational qualifications, and possession of a driving licence. The two attainment variables also continued to be strongly associated with job-getting in this analysis. But, by comparison with the previous analysis, educational and vocational qualifications appeared to have a somewhat reduced effect, resulting from the very strong association with unemployment duration.

While the analysis further confirms the robustness of the explanation based on qualification or attainments, it also poses more sharply the problem of interpreting the part played by unemployment duration. If unemployment duration does not merely 'carry forward' or accumulate the previous influences of qualifications on job-getting, what else does it do? There seem to be two main possibilities.

(i)   Just as unemployment duration transmits or expresses the (previous) influence of educational and vocational qualifications, so it may also transmit the influences of other personal attainments or personal attributes not measured by the survey. Anything which affects the chances of getting a job both at earlier and at later times in unemployment will be reflected, to some extent, in unemployment duration. There are many attributes which the survey does not assess (for example, appearance, speech, handwriting), and the apparent influence of unemployment duration will, to an unknown degree, be increased by the hidden influence of these.

(ii)  Unemployment duration may, in its own right, act as a signal which affects the behaviour of both young people seeking jobs and employers selecting among applicants. The longer the time during which employment has been unsuccessfully sought, the more discouraged the individual may become. Employers may also use information about periods in unemployment as a method of screening applicants, in the belief that long periods of unemployment reflect undesirable personal attributes or lead to a loss of work motivation[7].

The next chapter concerns job search, and in it we take further the notion of unemployment duration as a labour market signal. The more immediate need is to consider the implications for an assessment of the role of qualifications and attainments in helping young people to leave long-term unemployment.

The first, and most important, conclusion is that the importance of certificated qualifications, including possession of a driving licence, is further confirmed by the analysis. The second, and more cautionary, point is that while certificated qualifications are easily identified, other personal attributes may be missing, and these also could be important. The strong link between unemployment duration and success in getting a new job reminds one of these missing aspects.

## Qualifications and local labour market structure

We have now placed the influence of qualifications alongside both social background variables and the effect of period of unemployment. There is one further link to be examined. In Chapter 2 we showed that the aggregate changes of employment during 1971-81 in 20 travel-to-work areas, from which much of the present sample came, could to a substantial degree be accounted for by the local industry structure together with national trends in labour market demand by industry. It is possible (if not plausible) that the influence of qualifications on our young sample was no more than a reflection of local structural conditions. For example, an industrial structure heavily biassed towards manufacturing could at one and the same time lead to low educational attainments among young people and adverse employment prospects for them. We need to test, by joint analysis with a measure reflecting local structural conditions, whether qualifications have an independent influence on young people's employment chances. It is equally of interest to examine whether the general structural background 'shows through' in the labour market experience of the young unemployed once that differences in individual attainments have been controlled. We used two different analysis methods to approach these issues.

(i)   We used the 11-fold area-type stratification of the sample (described in Chapter 1 and Appendix 1) as a variable, within a four-way analysis with qualifications, possession of a driving licence, and whether or not in a job at the 1984 interview. The area-type variable is, of course, a relatively crude way to represent spatial differences in labour market structures, but it was designed to reflect points emphasized as important by economic geographers: for instance, the different employment chances of the metropolitan regions (except London) at one extreme and the rural high-growth and suburban localities at the other. And, in fact, there were large differences apparent between these area-types when it came to young people in our sample getting new jobs. From the suburban and high growth areas, 22 per cent had got jobs by the time of the 1984 interview, while for some metropolitan regions the figure was only 10 per cent.

However, the mutlivariate analysis (see Appendix 3, Table M3) showed that the relationship between area-types and getting new jobs become non-significant when qualifications and possession of a driving licence were alongside. This suggests that the differences between area-types were entirely reducible to differences in personal attainments; or that the area-type differences were fully expressed in these terms.

(ii)  The second analysis improved the spatial dimension by making use of the 20 travel to work areas (defined in Chapter 2 and Appendix 2) in which two-thirds of the sample were located. It also introduced a direct measure of industrial structure, namely, manufacturing employment in 1981 as a percentage of total employment in the travel to work area. This measure of local industrial structure was attached to each individual. A multiple regression analysis was then performed of individual proportion of time in work on qualifications, driving licence and the local structural measure. (Certain other complications of the analysis are described in Appendix 3, Table M4). The analysis accounted for 29 per cent of the individual variation in time spent in employment. Qualifications, driving licence and prevalence of manufacturing employment in 1981 had substantial and highly significant influences on time spent in employment during 1975-84. Those in areas of high manufacturing concentration, if entering the labour market during 1975-79, spent more time in employment; but if entering the labour market in 1980-83, spent less time in employment.

So far as structural influences are concerned, the two analyses appear to yield different conclusions. But there are two good reasons for that. The first is purely technical: it is reasonable that the structural influences should show through only when they are more specifically defined and measured, as in analysis (ii). The second reason is more substantial. Analysis (i) considers a very particular kind of transition, from long-term unemployment into employment, and it could well be that structural influences are not directly involved at that particular level of individual competition. Analysis (ii), on the other hand, reflects the overall impact in the medium-term of a range of labour-market influences - not only individual competition in getting jobs, but also the loss of jobs, which could involve closures, redundancies and other circumstances in which structural changes would be directly involved. We should stress that the linking of structural variables with individual survey data is a relatively recent development, so that interpretation should at this stage be cautious. It is nevertheless a striking evidence of the significance of structural change that the influence of manufacturing employment concentration should change its direction so precisely in step with the labour market experiences of this group of young people.

So far as qualifications are concerned, the conclusions from these two further analyses are straight forward. Whatever kinds of variables we introduce alongside qualifications, the latter continued to have an important bearing on both the past labour market experiences and the current job prospects of these young people in long-term unemployment. The same applies to the possession of a driving licence.

**Concluding comments**
This chapter has reviewed the influences of qualifications training and experience on labour market outcomes of various kinds. The result has been to demonstrate a sharp difference between the influence of qualifications and that of training or experience; and, within qualifications, to point to differences in the value of school and vocational certificates.

181

Within this group of young people, qualifications brought obvious benefits in terms of getting and holding jobs. This is an important and by no means self-evident conclusion, in view of the fact that most of the survey group were confined to manual and lower nonmanual jobs, where qualifications are often supposed to matter least. So far as young men were concerned, however, it was vocational qualifications rather than school examination passes which mattered. This was much less the case with the young women, for whom any kind of qualification appreciably improved prospects in the job market. The strong parallel influence on job prospects of possession of a driving licence was, as we interpreted it, a further indication of the value of certificated personal attainments.

Against this positive set of findings concerning qualifications, the negative findings concerning the relationship of training at work and of work experience to subsequent prospects in the labour market create a strong contrast. Training received in former jobs (other than training which forms part of certificated vocational qualifications) appears to be completely disregarded by employers when considering the applications of young people in the present group. The underlying reasons for this lack of positive influence from training may lie in the field of information. However worthwhile the training has been in reality, it cannot serve to improve job prospects unless it can be communicated to employers. Lack of standards and certification in training supplied in-the-job, coupled with the high rate of inter-industry and inter-occupational mobility of this group, may be sufficient to explain the findings.

# 8   Job Search

Up to this point, we have been looking at long-term unemployment among 18-24 year olds in what might be called a 'structural' way. We have been trying to account for their experience in the labour market, and their current prospects of obtaining jobs, in terms of a structure of opportunity shaped by educational and vocational attainment, occupational segregation, and economic change. Now, in turning to the topic of job search, we are faced with an apparently different kind of task, that of accounting for the behaviour of the young people. This does, in fact, require some new lines of reasoning and analysis. But we will also seek to show that the influences already identified as important in the labour market experience of the young long-term unemployed carry over into their current labour market behaviour.

It is generally considered to be desirable, in a market or mixed market economic system, that unemployed people should maintain a reasonable level of activity in seeking work. Without job seeking by individuals, the labour market cannot function competitively and work cannot be allocated either efficiently or justly. If those who are long-term unemployed drop out of competition from jobs, then downward pressure on wages is reduced and a wage-led restoration of employment becomes less likely. So, if large proportions of the long-term unemployed have low levels of job search activity, or altogether cease to look for work, this affects not only their own future but the total level of unemployment as well. The popular argument, that it is pointless to encourage unemployed people to look for jobs when there are not enough jobs to go around, is fallacious because it ignores the longer-term effects of job competition on the labour market.

An important purpose of analysing job search among the young long-term unemployed, therefore, is to identify those factors which help to maintain activity, and also to assess the prevalence, and reasons for occurrence, of declines in activity.

It would be mistaken, however, to focus too narrowly on the quantity of job search while ignoring qualitative aspects. There has been growing recognition of the role of spatial mobility, whether in the local labour market or through movement into new labour markets, in helping the economy to respond to imbalances in employment. Spatially extensive job search may be the necessary precursor of actual mobility in the labour market. These are additional aspects which we examine in this chapter, although the relevant information collected by the survey was rather limited.

Finally, there are those aspects of job search which are referred to collectively as 'flexibility'. These include willingness to work at lower wages, in response to an altered labour market, or to move from customary types of job to the kinds of job currently available. These matters are discussed in the next chapter: the argument of the present chapter is not affected by this subsequent discussion.

## Two contrasting viewpoints

The main viewpoint from which we approach the analysis of job search is one of expecting broadly rational behaviour on the part of the young long-term unemployed. We imagine that the activity of job seeking is largely controlled by the expected returns to be obtained from it. The attractiveness of any course of action depends not only on the gain to be made from it, if it succeeds, but also on how good are the chances that it will succeed. In addition, the known or expected costs of the action in question will be taken into the reckoning. Costs and gains are not necessarily confined to financial terms: whatever the individual likes or dislikes can weigh in the balance.

The present survey did not obtain information about individuals' expectations of the costs and gains from job seeking. However, assuming the view which we have put forward leads to predictions about which groups of young unemployed people are likely to be persistent job-seekers. The analysis can test these predictions and hence, indirectly, the underlying viewpoint.

If young people seek jobs in proportion to the returns which they can objectively expect from them, then those who are most likely to obtain jobs will also, other things being equal, make the most job applications, since there will be more jobs available with which they have an appreciable chance of success. Similarly, those with low chances of getting a job will tend to make relatively few job applications. This difference might not appear if the costs of seeking jobs were negligible, for then even the slightest chance of gaining a job would be preferable to doing nothing and being without. But common sense tells that job seeking does have both financial and psychological costs, especially the pain of disappointment.

In the preceding chapter, we have shown that success in competing for new jobs once among the young long-term unemployed depends partly on certificated attainments (educational and vocational qualifications, and possession of a driving licence) and partly on the time already spent in unemployment. The number of job applications should be based on just these same circumstances, if young unemployed people's job search is rational.

## Complications for assessing rationality

So far we have tacitly assumed that the choice facing young people in long-term unemployment is simply between seeking a job and doing nothing, and between having a job and having nothing. But matters are not as simple as that. There may be alternative roles, outside the labour market, providing both activities and rewards, and if these alternative roles offer the expectation of better net returns than job seeking, then they will be preferred. Our analysis should in some way take account of this possibility.

The popular media have frequently suggested, in recent years, that youth unemployment may breed a 'drop-out culture' or 'street corner society' in which employment is no longer a cornerstone and leisure values predominate. Social scientists have generally regarded such notions as fanciful, and studies conducted in parallel with the present research have shown traditional, job-centred values still to be firmly in place among young unemployed people[1]. We do not devote much further attention to this line of thought.

A much more substantial possibility, however, is that of withdrawing from the labour market, wholly or in part, in favour of a household role. Young women losing jobs or facing difficulties in entering employment may fall back upon their customary roles in the home, and especially upon their role in child bearing and motherhood.

Or a period of unemployment may form part of a more or less planned or voluntary transition out of the labour market and into a household or maternal role. There could also be some move, among young men, towards an acceptance of household roles as a substitute for the role of jobholder and breadwinner; although available evidence suggests that such a move would apply, at most, to a small proportion.

The other complication to be considered is financial choice. Here the financial returns to be expected from employment have to be compared with the financial returns from remaining in unemployment. The notion that the existence of unemployment benefits establishes a wage threshold below which people are unwilling to be employed, was once controversial but is now an accepted part of orthodox economic thought. If, as we propose, people are assumed to act in accordance with rational expectation of returns, then it is clearly necessary to take account of benefit payments in an analysis of job search. However, it is also necessary to appreciate the complexity of the matter. It would be somewhat simplistic, for example, to assume that job search will always be at a lower level where benefit entitlements are relatively high. If the individual has some reasonable hope of employment which will yield a significantly higher return than benefits in unemployment, then job search should continue; and this should hold, however high the level of benefits. It is only where the type of employment which the individual could reasonably hope to gain offers a wage below or in the vicinity of benefit levels, that job search would be reduced through the 'masking out' of such employment from the field of interest.

Moreover, it should not be assumed that the individual assesses the returns from employment purely in terms of the initial wage on offer. Even leaving to one side the non-financial advantages of employment (for example, social status, self-esteem), there remains the important matter of employment as the entry to a career, offering the possibility of continued financial returns and increasing security.

It seems plausible, on this interpretation, that the disincentive effects on job search of benefits would be greater among groups in lower-paid jobs and with the lowest long-term career expectations. Such a group would be those lacking educational and vocational qualifications.

We can now briefly state the items which need to be brought together in the analysis, in order to take account of the various aspects of job search which we have discussed.

(i) First, of course, we need a measure of job search: we have several, but initially we can focus upon the number of job applications made.

(ii) Next, the circumstances with most influence on actual success in obtaining jobs must be included. These consist of educational and vocational qualifications; possession of a driving licence; and the period spent in unemployment.

(iii) Third, we must make provisions in the analysis for choice of a non-employment role. As the most obvious example of this is provided by women as housewives and mothers, we should include gender, and whether with or without children.

(iv) Fourth, the influence of variable levels of state benefits should be accommodated. But, again, it is children who have much the greatest impact on benefits: we refine the analysis a little by incorporating the number of dependent children.

(v) Finally, benefits have to be viewed relative to the expected returns to employment. But we have argued that such expected returns are related to educational and vocational qualifications, already included in the specification for the analysis.

Further details of the variables used in the analysis, and of the considerations in their formulation, are given in Appendix 3 (section M5).

## Actual influences on job search

Figure 8.1 summarizes the results of the analysis which brought together all the items described in the preceding section. (For full statistical details, see Appendix 3, M5). The complete set of relationships between the six variables was satisfactorily accounted for by:

(i) the three-way interactions involving gender, children, and each of the other four variables;

(ii) the set of six pairwise associations between the four variables other than gender and children.

**Figure 8.1 Rational choice and job search**

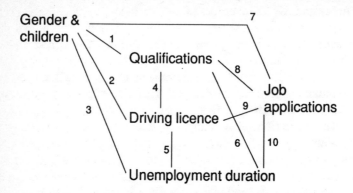

The interpretation of the chart is as follows:

1,2,3,7:   Women with children differed from both women without children and from men in the sample, in having higher qualifications, lower unemployment duration, and lower levels of job search.

4,5,6:   Those with qualifications were more likely to have a driving licence, and those with either tended to have shorter unemployment durations.

8,9,10:   Qualifications or a driving licence were linked to more job search while lengthy unemployment was linked to less.

*The maternal role.* The interactions between gender, children, and the other variables play a crucial part in explaining job search, and we will begin with them. What these results say, in essence, is that among the young long-term unemployed, women with children are quite unlike men with children, both in their background and their labour market behaviour. Young unemployed men with children, for example, have lower qualifications, on average, than young unemployed men without children. Conversely, young unemployed women with children have higher qualifications, on average, than young unemployed women without children. The contrast between men and women in the survey in terms of marital status and period of unemployment, was already emphasised in Chapter 3. Consistent with that, young mothers in the survey were likely to have relatively short periods of unemployment while young fathers in the survey were likely to have relatively long periods of unemployment.

But these relative advantages were not enough to maintain the level of job-seeking among young mothers, against the calls of their household and maternal roles. Whereas the level of job-seeking among young women without children remained at the same level as for young men, having one or more children led to a great reduction in job applications and a great increase in withdrawal from the job market. These findings are summarised in Table 8.1.

The table, as well as showing clearly the expected impact of motherhood on young women's job market activity, suggests that household roles other than motherhood were having no influence on job search. The young women without children were just as active in the job market as were the young men.

**Table 8.1    Gender, children and job search**

*row percentages*

| | Total (unweighted) | Not seeking work | Seeking work number of job applications | | |
| | | | none | 1-10 | 11+ |
|---|---|---|---|---|---|
| **Male** | | | | | |
| - no child | 1312 | 8 | 12 | 43 | 38 |
| - child | 308 | 9 | 13 | 43 | 35 |
| **Female** | | | | | |
| - no child | 683 | 6 | 13 | 45 | 35 |
| - child | 169 | 42 | 12 | 37 | 9 |

*Benefits* Young men's job search, on the other hand, was unaffected by whether or not they had dependant children. This finding has a double significance. In the first place, it tends to confirm that household and paternal roles do not, as yet, offer a real alternative to an economically active role, when young men experience prolonged unemployment. In the second place, since the presence of children to a large extent determines the level of state benefits, the finding indicates that those receiving higher levels of benefits do not for that reason reduce their job search activity. (This was further confirmed by the more comprehensive multivariate analysis (see Appendix 3, M6) in which the *number* of children was also taken into account.)

Indeed, young men with children might have been expected to have somewhat lower levels of job search activity than found, because of their lower levels of qualification and longer periods in unemployment.

As was pointed out in Chapter 3, the great majority of women with children had working husbands, hence were not entitled to supplementary benefits linked to number of children. The lower level of job search among mothers cannot be attributed to a disincentive effect of state benefits, as ordinarily understood, for this would entail that their much reduced levels of job search were associated with high benefit levels. It is possible none the less that the existence of insurance based unemployment benefits influences unemployed young women who already have children to drop out of the labour market; or, if they do not have children, to begin a family. But the ways in which experience of employment and unemployment interacts with benefit entitlements to influence such decisions seems likely to constitute a fairly complex field, requiring special inquiry. Much research on unemployment has been male-centered, and our own survey, with its focus on the labour market, lacks the information which would be necessary to disentangle the complex issues involved on the side of family income and family formation.

*Rational search*  The remaining aspects of the results of the analysis were straightforward and in line with our expectations. The level of job search was associated with all three of the influences which were shown, in Chapter 6, to be most important in relation to finding a new job: educational and vocational qualifications, possession of a driving licence, and the period spent in current unemployment. Those with educational or vocational qualifications of any kind, or with a driving licence, or with a relatively shorter period of unemployment behind them, were much more likely than the remainder to be making frequent job applications. Those without some or all of these advantages were, conversely, more likely to be making no job applications, or few. All three advantages were strong influences, the possession of a driving licence somewhat less so than the other two, but still of considerable importance.

Hence the composite analysis was consistent with the view which we outlined, in that the job seeking activity of young long-term unemployed people was proportional to the real advantages or disadvantages which they possessed in the job market. There was no indication that the influence of real advantages declined with longer periods of unemployment, although, of course, those with longer unemployment tended less often to have such advantages. Young people in long-term unemployment, in short, had solid reasons for being either less active or more active in the job market.

The analysis has also simplified the potential complications for a 'rational expectations' view of job search. Young mothers in long-term unemployment are clearly a special case; but to explain the job search both of young women without children, and of all young men in the sample, we have to take account neither of alternative roles outside the labour market, nor of the disincentive effects of benefits.

One of the points to be drawn from this analysis, and applied in other ways, is that the efficacy of one or another kind of job seeking can only be assessed after taking account of young people's advantages, especially their qualifications. For example, there are data from the survey which suggest, if taken at face value, that there is a considerable advantage in young unemployed people seeking jobs through the less frequently used routes of private employment agencies or direct 'on spec.' applications to employers. Of those who made no job applications, only 24 per cent contacted an employer direct to find out about possible jobs; this proportion climbed to 78 per cent among those who made more than 20 job applications. However, whereas direct contact with employers was attempted by 53 per cent of those without educational and vocational qualifications, the proportion was 62 per cent among those with 0-levels or equivalent, and 71 per cent among those with A-levels. Hence qualifications might be said to facilitate direct search more generally. It is where there is little or no association between an aid to job seeking and the qualifications of those using it, that an additional influence on job applications might be expected. We will shortly look at two such aspects.

## Complete withdrawal from the labour market

But first there is one possibly questionable aspect of the preceding analysis, which we must consider. In defining job search, we included in the same category those who directly stated that they had not been looking for a job during the past year, and those who, though still seeing themselves as job-seekers, had not actually made any applications. (The two groups are, however, separately identified in

Table 8.1.) It might be that the former were a distinctive group, because they had made a clear decision to move out of competition for jobs, and should therefore be the subject of a separate analysis.

It should first be noted that the group was not a large one, as a proportion of the young unemployed. On a weighted basis, they constituted eight per cent of the male sample and 14 per cent of the female. Nearly one half of the women gave pregnancy or child-rearing as their reason for ceasing to look for work, a point which tallies with our preceding analysis, and fully accounts for the differences in proportions between men and women. Although not a large group, however, those withdrawing from job search had increased by comparison with the 1980 DE/PSI survey.

**Table 8.2    Increase in withdrawals from job search**

*per cent of total*

|  | Male | Female |
| --- | --- | --- |
| 1984  (1 year or more unemployed) | 9 | 13 |
| 1980  (1 year or more unemployed) | 5 | 8 |

This increase in 'opting out' of the job market, although gradual, might give some cause for concern in the long run, and so adds to the case for a separate analysis.

The composite analysis described in the preceding section was repeated, with 'opting out' replacing 'job applications' in the specification. The details are, once again, presented in Appendix 3, M7.

Complete withdrawal from the job market was even more strongly a reflection of young women's maternal roles than in the case of our preceding analysis. Indeed, young women with children were almost five times as likely to withdraw from the job market as young women without children, or young men. The relationships between withdrawal from the job market on the one hand, and educational and vocational qualifications, possession of a driving licence, and period of unemployment, were all reduced by comparison with the earlier analysis. In the case of the driving licence, the estimated relationship was no longer statistically significant, but the other two estimated relationships remained at a substantial level. Those with more than two years' unemployment were, similarly, estimated to have a 57 per cent higher chance of withdrawing than those with 6-12 months', and the corresponding figure was 50 per cent for those with between one and two years' unemployment.

In short, the analysis of complete withdrawal or 'opting out' from the job market was still broadly consistent with the view that young people's labour market behaviour in long-term unemployment reflects a reasonable assessment of their real situation. However, the maternal role was a larger consideration and qualifications and (especially) possession of a driving licence, somewhat smaller.

## Supporting job search

If young unemployed people's job search activity is attuned to the real chances of success, that might seem to leave less scope for those who wish to guide and support them through their difficulties. If, for example, young people scan jobs on offer and decide that they will not apply because their qualifications or employment record is not up to the competition, would there be any point in giving them contrary advice?

Correct interpretation of the findings which have been presented depends on the level at which it is being directed. At the aggregate level, these findings certainly give no reason to suppose that there is much scope for improving the operation of the labour market by stimulating competitive behaviour in itself. Those who are not competing, or competing only weakly, would be helped to compete chiefly by getting qualifications or other real advantages. If everyone started to apply for additional jobs where the chances of selection were negligible, this would raise the costs of operation of the job market without contributing to its efficacy.

But support from others may still be important in forming young people's appreciation of the job market and so in providing the very basis for their rational behaviour. Their ability to judge chances of success depends on getting information, and others play a part in this process. Moreover, but for external support and encouragement, even those with some advantage such as qualifications might become despondent as a result of prolonged unemployment, and their job seeking activity decline. There is no necessary inconsistency, then, between considering that young unemployed people tend to act realistically in the labour market, and examining how their activity may be influenced by outside support.

Two contrasting kinds of support seem of particular interest: the relatively 'formal' support provided through Jobcentres (the part of the employment services most relevant to 18-24 year olds), and the relatively 'informal' support supplied by parents, relatives and friends. We carried out two separate analyses to examine how the presence or absence of each kind of support was linked to job search. The analyses were similar to those presented earlier, but to keep them within technically manageable proportions, the item about possession of a driving licence was omitted. (The earlier analyses showed this to have a smaller influence on job search than did qualifications.) Those who had completely ceased to seek work were necessarily excluded from these analyses, as the questions about forms of support and forms of information about jobs were not asked of them.

*Support from Jobcentres* The first of the two analyses introduced, as its new item, whether the Jobcentre had given any information concerning possible jobs, either by telephone or by post. The period considered was the preceding year. The results of the anlaysis are summarised in Figure 8.2; the details are provided, as usual with this type of analysis, in Appendix 3, M8.

The results again displayed the relationships, already established in our other analyses, between the level of job search and educational and vocational qualifications, and between the level of job search and period of unemployment. There were also, as before, strong interactions between the maternal role and other aspects of the data. The basic interpretation of job seeking is not, therefore, affected by introducing Jobcentre support into consideration.

The main interest of the analysis, however, lies in the relationships of Jobcentre support to the other aspects, and here the findings were striking.

(i)   First, this support was clearly and strongly related to the level of job search. Indeed, the underlying relationship between job search and Jobcentre support was estimated to be somewhat larger than that between qualifications and job search or that between duration of unemployment and job search.

(ii)  Jobcentre support was estimated to be significantly related to educational and vocational qualifications: the qualified were more likely to get support. However, this relationship was not a large one. Moreover, there was no significant relationship between Jobcentre support and period of unemployment, sex, or parental status. It is particularly interesting that Jobcentre support was as likely to be given to those with long periods of unemployment, as to others, a marked change since the 1980-81 DE/PSI survey. Taking the findings as a whole, Jobcentre support appeared to be available on a highly even-handed basis.

**Figure 8.2  Job centre support and job search**

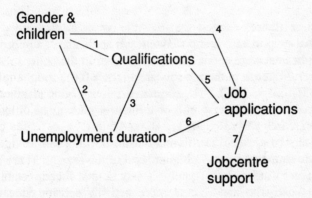

The interpretation of the diagram is as follows:

1-6:      Similar relationships to those described in Figure 8.1.

7:      Jobcentre support was linked to more job search.

These two aspects of the findings about Jobcentre support are, in fact, intimately connected. Since young unemployed people tend to select a level of job search in accordance with their qualifications, period of unemployment, and parental status, the support provided by the Jobcentres to a degree appears to counteract or balance this tendency. The multivariate statistical analysis takes account of this, and states that the underlying relationship between Jobcentre support and job search is considerably stronger than appears from a simpler analysis. The simple relation is shown in Table 8.3:

**Table 8.3    Job search and Jobcentre support**

*percentages*

|  | Whether contacted by Jobcentre about a job | |
|---|---|---|
|  | Yes | No |
| No job applications | 11 | 18 |
| 1-10 applications | 46 | 49 |
| 11 or more applications | 43 | 34 |
| *Base (unweighted)* | *568* | *1652* |

These figures suggest that the relative odds of those getting Jobcentre support also being frequent job applicants, as opposed to non-applicants, were about 2 to 1. (The odds in the bottom row are 43/34 = 1.26, those in the top row are 11/18 = 0.61, and the relative odds 1.26/0.61 = 2.07). The estimated relative odds after making allowance for the contrary pull of influences such as qualifications upon job search was calculated as about 3.5 to 1.

It must be stressed that this relationship does not demonstrate that Jobcentre support 'causes' a higher level of job search. There could be such an influence but, equally, it may be that Jobcentres tend to choose those who are already more actively seeking jobs when distributing job information. It is also quite plausible that influences work in both directions: Jobcentre support boosts job search, while young people increase their chances of support by showing a high level of activity.

*Family and friends* In Chapter 6 we saw that new jobs most frequently came from information supplied by parents, relatives and friends. It is of particular interest, therefore, to ask whether the availability of this kind of information is also connected with high levels of activity in the job market.

The findings from this analysis were highly similar to those concerning Jobcentre support, but if anything even more striking (Appendix 3,M9). Approaching family or friends for job information was highly related to the level of job applications, according to the estimates from the multivariate model. At the same time, this support from family and friends was not significantly related to other aspects of the analysis, except (to a marginal degree) to gender (young women being slightly less likely to seek job information from family or friends). Because 'informal' support was independent of young people's qualifications, time in unemployment, and parental status, like Jobcentre support it was pulling - or being pushed - against the tendencies underlying activity levels in job search. A simple analysis would suggest that the relative odds of high job search with informal support, compared with low job search, were less than 2 to 1. But the multivariate anlaysis, after allowing for the contrary influences of qualifications and other aspects, estimated the effect as close to 6 to 1.

The interpretation is as in the case of 'formal' Jobcentre support. Young unemployed people may have their job search stimulated by seeking information from family and friends; or such a flow of information is most likely to be forthcoming where young people are already active seekers of jobs; or a combination of both.

In any case, it seems that the support which young unemployed people get, whether formal or informal, is available largely irrespective of their qualifications, period of unemployment, gender and parental status. So this kind of external support works in a way which is complementary to the main influences already identified on job search and on success in getting jobs. External support may either stimulate job search, or may be a means of backing up those who are already active job seekers. In either case, it seems likely to be an equalizing influence in the job market.

## Job search and success in finding jobs

So far in this chapter we have considered the circumstances which influence, facilitate or support job search among the young long-term unemployed, but not the consequences of job search. We now turn to the question of whether, or how far, job search improves the chances of getting a new job.

This is, at one level, an extremely easy question to answer, but at another level perhaps the most difficult, both conceptually and technically, of the issues addressed in this study. The easy answer to give is that it clearly makes an enormous difference to continue to seek work and to apply for some jobs rather than none, because those who do not seek work or make no job applications are almost certain to remain out of work, while even the most disadvantaged of job seekers has some small chance of getting a job. This is by no means an academic point, since as Table 8.1 showed, even excluding young mothers around 20 per cent of the young unemployed had either 'opted out' of the job market or had made no job application in the preceding year.

As we go beyond this simple and basic point, and consider methods of assessing the possible gains from various levels of job seeking activity, complications arise. In the first place, as we have already shown that factors such as qualifications influence both job search and chances of getting new jobs, any serious attempt to show how job search and success in getting jobs are related must include and take account of these background influences.

More fundamentally, there are judgements to be made about whom to include in the scope of the analysis. If we include those who have ceased to look for work we will obtain an artificially inflated estimate of the influence of job search. This is because those not seeking work include many young mothers, and some with other household ties or with serious illnesses, who have effectively moved out of the labour market. Indeed, even when young mothers remain in the job market, their job search continues to be sharply different from that of the remainder. We conclude, therefore, that it is preferable to exclude from the analysis both those who describe themselves as not seeking work (for whatever reason), and young mothers if not already included in this group. Of course, we have to be aware of these groups when considering a final interpretation.

But this still leaves many individuals who made no job applications, even though apparently seeking work. Should these be regarded as a distinct group, and so be kept separate in the analysis, or should they be regarded as akin to those who reported making just one or two job applications? For technical reasons, we adopted the latter view, and formed those with no job application and those with just one job application into a group. The other groups were those with between two and 10 applications, and those with more than 10 applications. Even with this simplification, it also proved necessary to collapse our five-point scale of educational and vocational qualifications into a two-point contrast (no qualifications against any) in order to keep the overall analysis to manageable proportions. As mothers were excluded from the analysis, it was not necessary to include gender and dependent children.

In the light of these considerations, two parallel analyses were designed. Both considered the relationships between qualifications, possession of a driving licence, period of unemployment, job search, and whether or not getting a new job. The difference between them consisted in the sixth variable treated. This was Jobcentre support in the first analysis, and support from family and friends in the second.

The statistical details of the analyses are to be found in Appendix 3, M10. Before turning to the conclusions of the analyses, however, we must note that the first analysis (involving Jobcentre support) resulted in a less good fit than the other composite analyses reported in this chapter. More generally, the analyses are of a complexity which fully stretches what is possible with the present sample size. The compromises made in order to conduct the analyses may reduce their efficacy somewhat. For these reasons, caution is necessary and inferences at a fine level of detail must be avoided.

Setting aside differences of degree, we found that all the relationships identified in the analyses previously described reappeared here. So, for example, qualifications, possession of a driving licence, and period of unemployment were related both to job search (in its redefined form) and to getting a new job. Similarly, in their separate analyses, the relationships of Jobcentre support and of support from family and friends with job search were further confirmed.

The analyses also show the expected relationship between job search (number of job applications) and getting a new job. The relationship was, indeed, a highly significant one in both analyses. This shows that the amount of job search influences chances of getting a job, even when other influences on both, such as qualifications, have been taken into account. The initial indications are, therefore, that whatever the position of a young unemployed person, additional job search will tend to pay off. There was, however, an additional feature of the results which made a slightly different interpretation at least equally plausible.

The disconcerting feature of the results lies in the lack of any appreciable advantage for those making more than 10 job applications, by comparison with those making between two and 10. For each of these groups the analyses computed the relative odds of getting a new job compared with those making none or only one job application, and these estimates are picked out and summarised in Table 8.4.

**Table 8.4    Relative odds of getting a job, estimated in two
six-variable models**

|  | Model 1 | Model 2 |
|---|---|---|
| Those with 2-10 job applications compared to those with 0-1 | 2.39 | 2.56 |
| Those with 11+ job applications compared to those with 0-1 | 2.54 | 2.80 |

The differences within each model were statistically not significant, although in the expected direction.  Hence the major difference appears to be between making no job applications or just the odd one, and making a few job applications at least.  The important thing is not to drop out, or virtually drop out, from trying one's hand with employers.  There seems to be an essential minimum level of activity, but above that, sheer activity does not seem to bring reward in itself.  This, however, must be seen in the context of the whole analysis. People with qualifications or other advantages tend to make more job applications anyway.  Young unemployed people tend to choose a level of job search which reflects their realistic chances, but the danger to guard against, in their own interests, is that of ceasing to compete.

The final question to be considered by the analyses was whether the two kinds of support for job search, 'formal' and 'informal', were related to chances of getting a job.  The answer was positive.  Even after allowing for the other influences represented in the composite analyses, both Jobcentre support and support from family and friends emerged as having significant, moderate-sized, relationships with getting a new job.

It is here more plausible to interpret the result as showing that Jobcentre support improves chances of getting new jobs, over and above the other aspects considered in this analysis, including the link between such support and job search.  Similarly, support in the form of information about jobs from family and friends makes an appreciable difference to the chances of getting a new job, as well as or on top of being associated with higher levels of job search activity.

The set of analyses as a whole suggests three simple precepts for helping young people in long-term unemployment:

(i)    do everything to prevent such young people from sticking on the sidelines of the job market;

(ii)   that achieved, have confidence in their ability to judge what jobs they should try to get;

(iii)  offer direct support in the form of information about job openings; and encourage others to provide job information.

In addition, of course, young unemployed people's medium-term or longer-term prospects are likely to be served by chances to acquire qualifications or other attainments, a point to be further discussed in the concluding chapter.

## Mobility in job search

We pointed out, in the introduction to this chapter, that as well as viewing job search in terms of levels of activity, it would be useful to consider it in terms of mobility. A high overall level of mobility should help labour markets to adjust and adapt. And individuals who are more mobile (in the sense of looking further afield, or in a greater variety of places) should have a competitive advantage over those who are less mobile. The information gathered in the survey permits us to provide some simple indications both of the degree of job mobility in the sample as a whole, and of the advantage which young people were getting from efforts to be mobile.

*Driving licence as mobility*  Mobility already, in a way, forms part of the analyses presented in this chapter. For, as we have stated on several occasions, the possession of a driving licence can partly be considered as a form of qualification or personal attainment, but also partly as an advantage in travelling in search of work, and in travelling to work, without the constraints of public transport. It has been shown that possession of a driving licence was linked, among our sample of young unemployed people, with more frequent job applications. This is consistent with the driving licence being a kind of qualification, which opens up more jobs to application, but it is also consistent with the driving licence being an aid to mobility. The survey cannot separate the two aspects or put weights on their relative importance. The survey did, however, ask young people more directly about the distances they were prepared to travel to work when taking a new job, and this can be related to possession of a driving licence.

*Acceptable distance to work* In answering the question about acceptable distance to travel to work, the young unemployed people were asked to think in terms of certain standard intervals: 'less than one mile', 'one mile but less than three miles', ranging up to '10 miles or more'. It was found, as expected, that the acceptable travel-to-work distance was linked to possession of a driving licence, and to availability of a car or van. Having a driving licence, with or without access to a car or van, made the respondent more likely to think of a long journey to work as acceptable. The results are shown in Table 8.5. These findings tend to confirm the interpretation of the driving licence as, in part, an aid to mobility within the local labour market.

**Table 8.5 Personal transport, driving licences, and acceptability of lengthy journey to work**

*percentages*

| | Willing to travel | |
| --- | --- | --- |
| | Male<br>10 miles<br>or more | Female<br>5 miles<br>or more |
| Those with driving licence | 58 | 62 |
| Those owning or regularly using a car or van | 65 | 62 |
| No personal transport | 42 | 49 |

It is also worth noting that quite large proportions of the young long term unemployed said that they were willing to travel long journeys to work, including many who were without a driving licence or a means of personal transport. Those not actively seeking work were not asked the question and so have been omitted from Table 8.5, so that those in the table are all active job-seekers. Of these, one half of the men stated their willingness to travel 10 miles or more to work, while almost the same proportion of women said that they would travel five miles or more. As already noted in Chapter 6, acceptable distances were far greater than the actual spatial spread of the new jobs being obtained.

*Acceptable distance, and chances of new jobs* Willingness to travel further should be, like personal transport, a competitive advantage. In Table 8.6 the effect of the acceptance of long journeys is assessed upon chances of getting a new job. The results do suggest an influence, but not at all as clearly as in the case of possessing a driving licence. There is a bimodal distribution, which is more apparent in the case of men: the highest chance of being in a new job was (as predicted) with those prepared to travel 10 miles or more, but those prepared to travel one to three miles also had better chances than the remaining groups. Here there seems to be a hint of differences between extremely localized job markets and others which are more open; we will shortly also show a link with part-time jobs. As was shown in Chapter 6, a large proportion of new jobs (up to the time of the follow-up survey in 1985) were within three miles of respondents' homes. Young people's willingness to travel substantial distances may be partly nullified if in reality their chances depend largely on informal contacts operating within the immediate locality.

**Table 8.6   Willingness to travel, and proportions in new job in 1984**
*percentages (weighted)*

| Longest acceptable travel distance to work | In job at 1984 interview | |
| --- | --- | --- |
| | Male | Female |
| Less than 1 mile | 0* | 13* |
| 1-3 miles | 15 | 15 |
| 3-5 miles | 9 | 11 |
| 5-10 miles | 9 | 15 |
| 10 miles or more | 19 | 26 |
| Other/don't know | 19 | 15 |

\*   Unreliable; small numbers in cells

Just as we saw that the young women with driving licences tended to have the keenest advantage, so those young women prepared to travel the longest distances also had much the highest chances of getting a new job. Of men willing to travel 10 miles or more, 19 per cent were in new jobs, but among women prepared to travel this distance the proportion was 26 per cent. Quite possibly if we had extended the question to distinguish those who would travel (say) 15 miles or more, we would have identified a smaller group of men with a corresponding advantage in the job market.

Whereas possession of a driving licence did not lead to significantly higher pay in new jobs, willingness to travel long distances was associated with higher pay. Those prepared to travel 10 miles or more in 1984 averaged £75 in the case of men - a differential of £11 over the remainder; and £54 in the case of women - a differential of £13 over the remainder. It is notable that there were no clear differences in average pay among the groups prepared to travel various distances between one and 10 miles, so there appears to be a definite threshold where acceptance of longer journeys begins to pay dividends.

**Table 8.7    Willingness to travel, and proportions in part-time jobs (those in new jobs at 1984 interview only)**

*percentages (weighted)*

| Longest acceptable travel distance to work | Working part-time | |
|---|---|---|
| | Male | Female |
| Less than 5 miles | 21 | 42 |
| 5-10 miles | 15 | 32 |
| 10 miles or more | 10 | 13 |

A definite influence here was the tendency for those who took part-time jobs only to be willing to travel moderate distances; and equally, for those willing to travel further to be set on full-time jobs. The lower acceptable travel distances thereby become linked to the lower earnings of part-time jobs.   Table 8.7 summarizes the information on this association. As one might expect, the relationship was much clearer in the case of women, with their much greater propensity to part-time work. The 'threshold' of a 10-mile journey to work, above which most work full-time, is again apparent in this table.

*Acceptable distance to work, and frequency of job applications*
The same argument which suggested that drivers would tend to make more frequent job applications than non-drivers can be applied plausibly to those willing to make long journeys to work by contrast with those limiting their journey distance. In turn, if it can be shown that those accepting long journeys make more job applications, this will tend to confirm the nature of their competitive advantage.

**Table 8.8    Willingness to travel, and job search in past year**

*row percentages*

| Longest acceptable travel distance | Number of job applications | | | | | | | |
| | Male | | | | Female | | | |
| | Total* | 0-5 | 6-10 | 11+ | Total | 0-5 | 6-10 | 11+ |
| --- | --- | --- | --- | --- | --- | --- | --- | --- |
| Less than 3 miles | *388* | 62 | 10 | 25 | *621* | 69 | 11 | 16 |
| 3-5 miles | *773* | 54 | 18 | 26 | *690* | 57 | 14 | 28 |
| 5-10 miles | *1561* | 46 | 16 | 37 | *789* | 42 | 20 | 33 |
| 10 miles or more | *2832* | 35 | 18 | 44 | *763* | 33 | 17 | 48 |

Note:    Rows add to less than 100 per cent because those not stating number of job applications have been omitted.

Table 8.8 shows the details of such an analysis, and clearly demonstrates the expected connection. The association is, indeed, rather stronger than it was in the similar analysis concerning drivers and non-drivers. Among men, 62 per cent of those wanting to travel less than three miles had made less than six job applications in the previous year; this fell to 46 per cent among those willing to travel between five and 10 miles, and to 35 per cent among those accepting a journey of 10 miles or more. Conversely, those willing to make the longest journeys had made more than 10 job applications in 45 per cent of cases, but this fell to 37 per cent in the group willing to travel between five and 10 miles, and to 25 per cent among those putting a limit of three miles on their journey. The contrasts were still more marked in the case of the young women; while those women willing to travel 10 miles or more had made about as many job applications as the men in that category, the women wishing for shorter travel distances had generally made fewer job applications than the corresponding male groups. This might again be connected with the topic of part-time work, since women seeking jobs which are not only local but part-time will often be particularly limited on what is available.

**Wider geographical mobility**
So far in this chapter we have considered aspects of travel-to-work mobility - the propensity of individuals to have wider or narrower access to a labour market around their home. A more radical type of mobility concerns willingness to move home in order to have better

access to job opportunities. Ideally one would like longitudinal data on individuals who have relocated themselves, to assess the impact on their job chances, but a cross-sectional survey is unable to provide this.

Our information is limited to three questions which were asked of everyone except those no longer actively seeking work. The first, and perhaps most objective of the three, asked whether the individual had visited, in order to look for jobs, a completely different area from the area normally considered. Some 30 per cent of the men, and 19 per cent of the women, said that they had done so. The second question was whether the individual had ever considered moving house in order to help with getting a job. Rather higher proportions said that they had, than had actually visited a different area; this makes one suspect that some of the consideration given to moving had been of a fairly vague kind. Finally, and least satisfactorily, we asked a hypothetical question: 'would you move if you had a job lined up?' Here nearly two thirds of the young men, and more than 40 per cent of the young women, said that they would. This should not be regarded as a forecast, but only as an expression of attitude.

**Table 8.9    Main reasons given for not wanting to move in search of job**

*percentages*

|  | Male | Female |
|---|---|---|
| Family/friends live here | 44 | 34 |
| Like this area | 28 | 22 |
| House/home is here | 10 | 13 |
| Spouse's/boyfriend's/<br>  girlfriend's job is here | 2 | 21 |
| Don't want to live on own | 9 | 9 |
| *Total unwilling to*<br>  *move (weighted)* | *1196* | *1307* |

Note:    The categories are derived from an open-response question, asked only of those stating that they were unwilling to move. More than one reason could be given.

Before considering the influence of geographical mobility, or attitudes thereto, it is of interest to look at the reasons given by those who were not willing to move, even if a job was lined up. The reasons are summarized in Table 8.9 which consists of a classification from open-ended comments. There is not much in these reasons which common sense would fail to predict. The ties of family, friends, homes and familiar localities predominate.

To assess whether geographical mobility, even in the very limited way in which we can approach it, has an influence on what takes place in the job market, we see whether new jobs have come more frequently to those giving positive answers to our three questions. The results are shown in Table 8.10. It is immediately apparent that the men's new jobs have not been influenced by these aspects of mobility, but that there was some small but consistent influence in the case of the women. For example, those young women who had visited an unaccustomed area to look for work were actually in new jobs in 21 per cent of cases, while those who had not looked further afield had new jobs in 16 per cent of cases. The differences were of a similar order in the case of the other two questions. Moreover, inspection of the separate results for the two age groups (not shown here) revealed that while there was no real difference for the women who had entered the labour market in 1975-79, the younger group had more substantial differences which accounted for the overall result for women.

**Table 8.10  Considering other areas, and new jobs in 1984**

*percentages (weighted)*

|  | In work at 1984 interview | |
|---|---|---|
|  | Male | Female |
| **Whether visited a different area to look for a job:** | | |
| Yes | 18 | 21 |
| No | 14 | 16 |
| **Whether considered moving to a different area:** | | |
| Yes | 15 | 20 |
| No | 15 | 16 |
| **Would move to a different area if a job was lined up:** | | |
| Yes | 14 | 20 |
| No | 14 | 15 |

Similarly, when the pay levels in the new jobs were examined, it was found that there were no consistent differences for men between those with a positive approach to geographical mobility and the remainder. In the case of women, once more, there was a substantial and consistent difference in these pay levels. For example, of women in new jobs at the time of interview, those who had visited an unaccustomed area had average pay of £54, while those who had never done so had average pay of £43. Similar differentials existed between women who had considered moving and those who had not, and between those who said they would have moved if a job was lined up for them and those who said they would not.

These results seem to continue a part of the findings in the earlier sections of this chapter, where it has been noted that mobility - in various aspects - seems to confer more advantage on young women than on young men. A link has also been pointed out earlier on between limitation on mobility, part-time working, and hence of course differences in pay levels. The connection with part-time working is therefore pursued with the analysis presented in Table 8.11.

**Table 8.11  Considering other areas, and part-time jobs in 1984**

*percentages (weighted)*

|  | In work at 1984 interview | |
|  | Male | Female |
| --- | --- | --- |
| **Whether visited a different area to look for a job:** | | |
| Yes | 19 | 9 |
| No | 10 | 35 |
| **Whether considered moving to a different area:** | | |
| Yes | 15 | 29 |
| No | 12 | 29 |
| **Would move to a different area if a job was lined up:** | | |
| Yes | 15 | 22 |
| No | 12 | 39 |

Here the surprise is that among men, a positive approach towards geographical mobility seems, to some small extent, linked with part-time working in new jobs. The opposite might have been expected - as is clearly the case with the young women in new jobs. In fact the men who entered the labour market in 1975-79 have conformed to the expected pattern, with part-time jobs taken more often by those not interested in geographical movement. But the younger group of men, who were twice as likely to have taken part-time jobs, were also much more likely to have taken a part-time job if they had shown an interest in moving away. Perhaps with this group we are beginning to see a more extensive kind of job search - in which willingness to take part-time work and willingness to think of moving away go together. But (as explained in Chapter 6) this innovation seemed to be losing momentum during 1984-85, since the proportion of men's new jobs which were part-time fell considerably during this period, by comparison with the initial set of new jobs visible at the 1984 interview.

**Concluding comments**
The majority of the 18-24 year olds in long-term unemployment did not find a new job in the year or more for which we followed their progress. The capacity to sustain job search over long periods, therefore, was important both to preserve individuals' chances of eventual employment, and for the effective working of the labour market.

The survey found that the great majority did continue to seek jobs. But the minority who either completely withdrew from the labour market, or whose rate of job applications fell to near zero, was of a size which could not be ignored. And there was some evidence that this minority had been slowly growing over the period 1980-84.

In attempting to explain the influences upon job-seeking and upon dropping out from the job market, we were able to apply and build upon the findings of Chapter 7. The new consideration which had to be added was that young mothers in unemployment tended to leave the labour market for a household role. Apart from that, the same aspects which raised the likelihood of finding a new job also raised the rate at which new jobs were applied for. Conversely, those aspects which depressed chances of finding a new job also suppressed job search. Specifically, those without educational or vocational qualifications, without a driving licence, with prolonged unemployment, were more likely to cease looking or to apply for jobs only rarely. Search was broadly in agreement with reasonable expectations of success.

This did not mean, however, that job-seeking could not be influenced from outside. The common-sense view that external support will encourage job search was well borne out by our findings. This applied both to support from Jobcentres, and support from family and friends. A particularly important feature of both these kinds of support was that they were as much available to those with obvious disadvantages in the job market, such as prolonged unemployment or lack of qualifications, as to others. Hence support of these kinds was playing an equalizing rather than a polarizing part in the workings of the market. It must be appreciated, however, that young people are more likely to get help where they themselves 'show willing', so that one is talking about a mutual process rather than a directive one.

We also examined, in the manner of an initial exploration, the spatial spread of job search among our samples of young people. To put the findings here into perspective, one must think back to Chapter 6. New jobs, that chapter showed, included a large proportion within highly localised job markets, requiring only short journeys to work by those getting them. By contrast, the majority of the young people seeking jobs claimed that they were prepared to travel long distances to work. Again, although the conventional ties of family, friends and neighbourhoods made many feel that they could not consider moving out of their home areas, there was a substantial proportion who had either looked further afield, on occasion, or would be willing to move if a job was in prospect. Of course, these can only be taken as expressions of attitudes, as the survey had no means of testing willingness to move in practice.

Mobility in job search was closely connected to numbers of job applications made, and to the type of job obtained and the wages and hours of work involved. Our analysis does enough to indicate how important these aspects may be for further study. The most significant point, however, remains the contrast between young unemployed people's attitudes to mobility and the relatively constrained or narrow job markets which appear to confront them. To explain this tension between supply and demand, we would need more information about employers' recruitment policies, and about the spatial structure of local labour markets. In the next chapter, we will find further questions arising about the role of demand.

# 9 Two Kinds of Flexibility

The present chapter pursues the theme of job search and competitive advantage by considering two kinds of flexibility in the pursuit of employment. One concerns the willingness to make changes of industry or occupation if the opportunities are available. The other concerns the willingness to take jobs at a lower real rate of pay than in the past, or at a lower rate of pay than one's current expectations or target. It is appropriate to consider both types of flexibility together, since there is an obvious connection between them. If a person leaves his or her customary line of work and moves into another industry and occupation, then it may often be the case that a lower wage will have to be accepted.

The two types of flexibility have, like job search and spatial mobility, long been given a place by economists in relation to unemployment. They were extensively discussed in the writings of the pre-Keynesian economists, who argued that attachment to declining industries, and wage rigidities brought about through collective bargaining, prevented the labour market from adjusting to new conditions, and hence generated unemployment. Economists working within the neoclassical tradition continue to advance these interpretations. However, it should also be noted that, from the viewpoint of some more recent theoretical developments, flexibility of the kinds described may involve economic risks. In particular, flexibility may lead to occupational downgrading, the loss of returns from investment in human capital, and the trapping of workers in the lowest segment of the labour market which is economically most vulnerable.

An important consideration with flexibility, therefore, is whether jobs obtained in different occupations and at lower rates of pay prove to be stable or provide a fresh starting point for long-term employment.

In this chapter, we assess how much flexibility has actually been displayed by the young people in long-term unemployment, and we examine what part flexibility has played in the new jobs obtained. We also evaluate the extent to which flexibility has been associated with occupational downgrading.

### Development of pay flexibility

In Chapter 4 it was shown that the average pay levels of jobs which the young long-term unemployed regarded as their 'main' or most important employment to date had fallen sub stantially, in real terms, between the late 1970s and the early 1980s. This downward trend (or possibly a step-change) cannot be attributed to a lower quality of worker, since as was also shown in Chapter 3, the qualification levels of the young people in the survey were on average higher in the group entering the labour market in the later period. It might however be in part accounted for by the decreasing duration of jobs after 1980, since the pay figure considered was that which applied at the end of the job, and pay was higher in longer lasting jobs. Nevertheless, the likelihood is that, in a period of rising unemployment, the members of a group particularly affected by unemployment would accept lower paid jobs, whether through downward mobility or through pay cuts for similar work.

The survey interview included questions to assess the pay expectations of the young unemployed. If still not in work at the time of the interview, they were asked what take-home pay they were looking to get. They were also asked whether they would be prepared to accept less money if the job was suitable in other respects; and then, if they said yes, they were asked what was the minimum they would accept. Those who were in new jobs by the time of the interview were asked what pay they had been looking for when searching for a job. They were not however asked about minimum acceptable pay since it was considered that this would have been unrealistic after a job had been obtained.

The desired or expected pay does not in itself tell us anything about pay flexibility; for that we must introduce a comparison, and the most appropriate comparison here is with the 'main' or most recent job before unemployment, for which we have the reported take-home pay. Since this job can be regarded as the most representative of each individual's attainment to date (except for those who have never had a job, of course), the pay from that job can also be regarded as reasonably representative. In addition, comparing each person's pay expectations against former pay controls for individual differences in age and qualifications, in as much as these have been reflected in previous earnings.

The main limitation of the analysis is in the proportion of the sample covered. As well as those who had never previously worked, for whom a pay comparison was evidently not possible, we excluded those who had ceased to seek work for the whole of the preceding year, since their testimony could clearly not be put on the same level as active job-seekers. This left 64 per cent of the total (weighted) survey sample - 68 per cent in the case of the men and 56 per cent in the case of the women. In addition, 13 per cent of these (both men and women) either could not state what their current pay expectations were, or did not give a figure for their previous pay. Thus the effective comparisons are based upon 59 per cent of the male sample and on 49 per cent of the female sample.

The comparison with previous pay (which has been adjusted to May 1984 values by means of the RPI) yields the following summary of relative pay expectations:

**Table 9.1   Comparison of pay expectations with previous pay**

*column percentages*

|  | Male | Female |
| --- | --- | --- |
| Expected £5 or more less than former pay | 26 | 25 |
| Expected the same as former pay, within £5 + or - | 12 | 18 |
| Expected £5 -10 more than former pay | 7 | 10 |
| Expected £10 or above more than former pay | 42 | 34 |
| (Not available) | 13 | 13 |
| *Total (weighted)* | *4409* | *1945* |

Note:    See text for details of base for percentages

The analysis reveals a marked polarization of relative expectations, with the largest group expecting £10 or more higher than their previous pay, but one-quarter prepared for a reduction of £5 or more. To put these figures into perspective, it must be borne in mind that the 18-24 age group is one in which large differentials by age exist. For example, the New Earnings Survey shows that for young men aged 21-24, average earnings are about 30 per cent higher than for those aged 18-20. On average the sample had been out of work for more than nine months, and in many cases the 'main' job had ended several years before that. Those accepting the need for a relative pay cut, or expecting their wages to remain more or less static, can against this background of age-related pay be regarded as showing considerable flexibility in their pay expectations. On the other hand, those expecting to achieve substantial increases - even if these may only be in accordance with the norms for age-related pay - might be thinking unrealistically when they have been unemployed for a considerable time and jobs are scarce.

To assess this further, however, account must be taken of the fixity or flexibility of the expectations themselves. This is where our question about the minimum pay which would be taken 'if the job was all right in other respects' comes into play. The coverage of the question is somewhat different than in the preceding analysis, since it was not asked of those in new jobs. The analysis once again reveals a striking polarization of positions:

**Table 9.2    Comparison of minimum acceptable wage with expected wage**

*column percentages*

|  | Male | Female |
|---|---|---|
| Minimum £10 or more less than expected pay | 58 | 60 |
| Minimum between £5 to £10 less than expected pay | 5 | 12 |
| Minimum up to £5 less | 0.3 | 0.4 |
| Not prepared to take less | 16 | 12 |
| Unable to answer | 20 | 17 |

Although the summary above applies only to those with previous jobs - and hence is as comparable as possible with the figures shown in the previous table - a similar analysis for those who had not previously worked (not shown here) produced almost the same results, except that those without previous jobs were less likely to say they would not take less than their expected pay figure, and were more likely to feel that they couldn't answer the question.

About two-thirds were willing to envisage pay levels below what they were looking for, and the minimum was nearly always set substantially below the expected level. On the other hand, a minority was not prepared to move from its target wage, while another group amounting to about one in five of respondents either had not considered the possibility or could not answer the question in the somewhat general terms in which it was posed.

If therefore the results concerning minimum acceptable pay levels are taken into account, the impression becomes one of a much higher degree of flexibility than the answers concerning pay expectations would suggest on their own.

## The influence of former pay on flexibility of expectations

The degree of flexibility indicated by the stated pay expectations of the young people seems broadly consistent with the actual decline in pay levels for this group in the early 1980s, to which we have referred earlier. But there must always be some doubt about the reliability of statements about pay when they are divorced from job decisions. It may increase confidence in the statements of the respondents about expected and minimum pay if these can be shown to be systematically related to their position in the labour market.

One possibility is that the type of employer in the 'main' job would influence pay expectations. There are two contrary ways in which this might take place. First, it has to be assumed that in general large firms and the public sector tend to provide higher wages than the small-firm sector, for comparable work. Then, to the extent that young people from the large firms and the public sector are relatively inflexible, they will expect to continue to get their pay advantage in future employment. Alternatively, to the extent that they are flexible, they will appreciate that employment chances in the large-firm and public sectors are lower, and will be prepared to accept the lower wages of the small-firm sector.

Table 9.3 suggests that there has been a tendency for those in the public sector and large firms to shift their expectations downwards more often than those in the small-firm sector. If we jointly consider those who would accept a cut of £5 or more and those who merely want their pay to remain static (plus or minus £5), then for men from former public sector jobs 50 per cent fell into this category, for those from large firms the proportion was 43 per cent, while for those from small firms or self-employment it was only 29 per cent. The corresponding proportions for the women were: public sector, 45 per cent, large firms, 51 per cent, and small firms, 33 per cent. There is some indication that young people coming from the perhaps more advantaged part of the labour market had a tendency to adjust their expectations realistically. Conversely, however, those coming from past employment in the small-firm section of the labour market were more likely to see possibilities of increasing their earnings in the future.

**Table 9.3   Pay expectations, relative to past pay, and previous type of employer**

*column percentages*

| | Type of employer in main job | | |
| | small firm or self-employed | medium or large firm | public sector |
| --- | --- | --- | --- |
| **Male** | | | |
| Expected £5 or more less than former pay | 20 | 28 | 39 |
| Expected the same, within £5 | 9 | 15 | 11 |
| Expected £5-10 more | 8 | 7 | 4 |
| Expected £10 or above more | 49 | 40 | 34 |
| (Not available) | 15 | 10 | 12 |
| *Total (weighted)* | *1628* | *2196* | *552* |
| **Female** | | | |
| Expected £5 or more less than former pay | 18 | 28 | 35 |
| Expected the same, within £5 | 15 | 23 | 10 |
| Expected £5-10 more | 12 | 9 | 9 |
| Expected £10 or above more | 40 | 30 | 34 |
| (Not available) | 16 | 10 | 13 |
| *Total (weighted)* | *707* | *989* | *234* |

More generally, there is an important question as to whether it is the relatively high paid, or the relatively low paid, who are most flexible in their expectations. Table 9.4 demonstrates beyond doubt that for this group, pay expectations were inversely related to former levels of pay: the higher paid were willing to take cuts, while the lowest paid hoped for better. The most striking contrasts are between average former pay levels of those willing to take substantial cuts and the remainder. In the case of men, those willing to take a substantial (£5+) cut had average pay of £105; the overall average for men was £71; and the group seeking to increase pay by £10 or more had average former pay of £51. For women, those willing to take a cut of £5 had former pay of £70 on average; the overall average for women was £52; and the group seeking an increase of £10 or more formerly earned an average of £38.

**Table 9.4    Pay expectations, relative to past pay, and mean pay levels**

*£/week in main job*

|  | Mean pay | |
|---|---|---|
|  | Male | Female |
| Expected £5 or more less than former pay | 105.2 | 69.5 |
| Expected the same, within £5 | 74.7 | 53.4 |
| Expected £5-10 more | 59.7 | 46.4 |
| Expected £10 or above more | 50.9 | 38.2 |
| (Not available) | 65.2 | 55.7 |

The same kind of analysis has also been applied to produce the average former pay levels of those giving various replies to the question about minimum acceptable pay. The results (not tabulated here) showed that former pay levels influenced the replies here too, but in a much less clear-cut way. Those men with a minimum of £10 or more below their expected pay level had formerly earned about £8 per week more than those with a smaller gap between minimum and expected; in the case of women, the former pay of these two groups differed on average by roughly £4. But, in the case of both men and women, those who refused to contemplate a figure below their pay target, or who could not give an answer, did not have particularly low former pay; they did not fit into the pattern. Thus the answers relating to minimum pay were less firmly anchored in the former pay levels of the respondents, and should perhaps for that reason be given somewhat less weight.

In general, however, we can clearly assert that flexibility of pay expectations in this group arises through the better-paid being willing to 'trade down'. But since, on the other hand, those with lower previous pay are still seeking some improve ment despite their period in unemployment, the pay expecta tions as a whole point to a convergence or levelling out of pay in future jobs.

## Pay flexibility and labour market outcomes

If these young people put their pay expectations into effect in job-seeking, then how matters turn out will depend also on the way in which employers respond. Will employers, for example, actually seek recruits at lower rates of pay than have been normal in their enterprises, because young people are offering their labour at these lower rates? And will they prefer relatively experienced young workers, who are offering to take a cut, to less experienced workers who are seeking the same rate of pay? There is no theoretical basis for predicting the answer to these questions, nor much of relevance in previous research. Our survey of course does not cover the employers' side, so we are not in a position to give direct answers. We can however examine how the young people have fared in the labour market, and test whether 'success' has been related to pay flexibility. If it has, then the implication is that the labour market is responsive to flexibility, but if it has not, then the implication is that there are obstacles to that response.

One test is to examine the relationship between pay flexibility and the durations of uncompleted spells of unemployment at the time of sampling for the survey. It might be thought that those showing the least flexibility in pay would tend to have difficulty in getting work and hence would accumulate at the longer durations of unemployment. However, Table 9.5 fails to support this line of reasoning. There is no consistent pattern in this set of results and it appears that those with a high degree of flexibility are as likely to remain long in unemployment as those seeking increased pay.

A clearer test should be to examine the relationship between pay flexibility and the likelihood of being in a new job at the time of interview. If the labour market is responsive to pay flexibility, then those with a flexible approach - in effect, offering their services at less than their former market value - should be at an advantage in getting new jobs.

**Table 9.5    Pay expectations, relative to past pay, and prolonged unemployment**

*percentages*

| | With unemployment of 25+ months | |
| --- | --- | --- |
| | Male | Female |
| Compared to former pay: | | |
| Expected £5 or more less than former pay | 30 | 12 |
| Expected the same, within £5 | 26 | 14 |
| Expected £5-10 more | 19 | 16 |
| Expected £10 or above more | 26 | 15 |
| (Not available) | 30 | 32 |

The evidence in this respect is set out in Table 9.6, and gives no more than marginal support to the notion that pay flexibility has led to jobs. The results are easier to interpret if the pay expectations are reduced to two categories: those accepting a pay cut or static pay ('relatively flexible'), and those expecting an increase ('relatively inflexible'). Among the men, there was no significant advantage for the 'relatively flexible'. But there was a small (non-significant) difference in the case of women. Among them, the 'relatively flexible' in regard to pay were in new jobs in 22 per cent of cases, while the 'relatively inflexible' had new jobs in 18 per cent of cases.

**Table 9.6    Pay expectations, relative to past pay, and new jobs in 1984**

*percentages*

| | With new jobs at 1984 interview | |
| --- | --- | --- |
| | Male | Female |
| 'Relatively flexible'* | 14 | 22 |
| 'Relatively inflexible'* | 14 | 18 |

*        See text for definitions.

Even with these young women, however, it might be misleading to interpret this result simply in terms of pay flexibility, since part-time working also comes into the picture. Many women especially in the 21-24 age group were preparing to move into part-time work. Their greater success in finding new jobs, therefore, and the association of this with lower pay expectations, could both spring from their greater willingness to seek, and higher chance of getting, part-time work.

These results must be regarded as discouraging to any attempt to attribute a strong role to pay expectations in the workings of the lower half of the youth labour market. Part of the reason for this may be - as our earlier analysis of 'minimum acceptable' pay suggested - that pay expectations are hedged by the willingness to take much lower pay under some circumstances. On the whole, employers make pay offers rather than seeking out applicants' pay expectations; expectations may be adapted in the face of these offers from the 'demand side'.

**Table 9.7  Pay flexibility, and pay in new job relative to expected pay (those in new jobs at 1984 interview)**

*row percentages*

|  | Total (weighted) | New pay compared to expected pay | | | |
|---|---|---|---|---|---|
|  |  | New higher | New lower | Equal | (Missing info.) |
| **Male** |  |  |  |  |  |
| 'Relatively flexible'* | *246* | 39 | 32 | 18 | 11 |
| 'Relarively inflexible'* | *297* | 25 | 61 | 5 | 9 |
| **Female** |  |  |  |  |  |
| 'Relatively flexible'* | *187* | 29 | 48 | 11 | 13 |
| 'Relatively inflexible'* | *149* | 17 | 64 | 8 | 11 |

Table 9.7 illustrates this reasoning by considering whether individuals who got new jobs received more or less than they originally desired or expected; and whether this was systematically related to whether their former expectations had been 'relatively flexible' or 'relatively inflexible'. The results have to be treated with some caution, because of gaps in information about the pay in the new jobs, but are nevertheless quite revealing. Of those for whom we have complete pay information, 53 per cent of men and 61 per cent of

women ended up with new pay which was lower than their expectations. Moreover, those who had the highest pay expectations were most likely to finish with less than they expected, while those with the lowest pay expectations - or the greatest degree of 'relative flexibility' - tended to do better than they had expected. There appear, then, to have been two tendencies in play: a tendency for people to be more flexible in practice than their stated expectations would suggest, and a tendency for the outcomes to even out differences in expectations.

This evening out of pay, relative to expectations, is also illustrated in Table 9.8, which can be compared with Table 9.4. The earlier table, which plotted average pay in the 'main' job against degrees of pay flexibility, showed a steep slope, with the formerly highest paid willing to take cuts and the lowest paid seeking increases. The present table shows that in the new jobs, a process of convergence of pay levels has been realized. Those who were willing to take cuts or remain static have come, in terms of their average new pay levels, closer to the young people who wanted increases. Nevertheless, the 'relatively flexible' were still getting more in their new jobs than the 'relatively inflexible'.

**Table 9.8    Pay flexibility, and pay in new jobs in 1984 (those in work at 1984 interview)**

*£/week in new job (weighted)*

|  | Mean net pay | |
|---|---|---|
|  | Male | Female |
| 'Relatively flexible'* | 79.7 | 47.3 |
| 'Relatively inflexible'* | 68.2 | 43.1 |

\* see text for definitions

This process of convergence is further demonstrated in Table 9.9, which shows the average pay levels in the former 'main' jobs for groups who have displayed varying degrees of flexibility in real life - that is, who have taken pay cuts or got pay increases in their new jobs. The numbers in some of the cells are small but the pattern is nevertheless sufficiently evident. Those who took the largest cuts in their new jobs, relative to their main jobs, tended to have relatively high average pay in their old jobs. Those who got increases in their new jobs, relative to their main jobs, tended to have relatively low pay in those previous jobs.

**Table 9.9    Pay in main job, and difference between that and new job's pay (those in work at 1984 interview)**

| | Difference: new job - main job (£/week) | | |
| --- | --- | --- | --- |
| | Less by at least £5 | Within £5+ or- | Greater by at least £5 |
| | Mean net pay (£/week) in main job | | |
| Male | 95.6 | 65.2 | 60.0 |
| Female | 61.7 | 46.0 | 39.5 |

The policies of employers in taking on these young people with a background of recent unemployment seems, one might speculate, to be relatively independent of their pay expectations. It seems as if there is a relatively narrow band of jobs - narrow, that is, as defined by the pay on offer - which the young people can enter; and they can do so either by reducing their expectations from previous higher pay levels or by raising them if their previous earnings (because of their youthful age, perhaps) were low.

**Table 9.10   Pay in former jobs, by success in fixing new jobs**

*£/week in main job (weighted)*

| | Mean net pay | | | |
| --- | --- | --- | --- | --- |
| | Male | | Female | |
| | entry to labour market in | | | |
| | 1975-79 | 1980-83 | 1975-79 | 1980-83 |
| In work at 1984 interview | 82.6 | 60.8 | 53.9 | 48.8 |
| Not in work at 1984 interview | 75.6 | 53.0 | 59.0 | 42.1 |

If this is the case, then one would expect the formerly higher-paid to have on balance some advantage, provided that their former wages indicated their worth. This is confirmed by Table 9.10, which compares the former wages in 'main' jobs of those who obtained new jobs by the time of interview, and those who did not. There is a higher average wage level (in past jobs) for three out of four 'age within sex' groups who have new jobs, compared with those who are still out of work. For example, men in the 21-24 age group in jobs at the interview had average pay in their former 'main' jobs of £83, while men in this group still out of work averaged £76 in their main jobs. The group to which this pay difference did not apply was that of women aged 21-24; here the confounding factor may be, once more, the movement into part-time working which particularly affected this group.

Finally, we can assess the average change in average pay resulting from movements into new jobs, for those who had also held a previous job:

| 'Main' or most recent job: | Male £ | Female £ |
| --- | --- | --- |
| 1975-79 entrants | 82.6 | 53.9 |
| 1980-83 entrants | 60.8 | 48.8 |
| All | 75.5 | 51.5 |
| New job | 74.1 | 45.0 |

The new jobs, therefore, represented an average decrease in weekly pay of 1.9 per cent for the young men, and of 12.6 per cent for the young women; the latter figure, of course, once more reflects the movement into part-time work.

It seems clear, therefore, that despite the low position in the distribution of earnings from which the young long-term unemployed set out, they had been prepared on average to accept reduced wages in order to get new jobs. Although in absolute terms the reductions were not great, they have to be seen against the norms of a 7-8 per cent per annum increase as young people progress into adult wage rates. It seems, therefore, that wages have been flexible in practice despite the very weak relationship of pay expectations to labour market outcomes.

Does this tendency, however, merely reflect the more competitive behaviour of those who have got into jobs? Although some of the earlier analyses in the chapter have already addressed this (with an answer in the negative), it remains of interest to consider the issue anew in the light of the follow-up postal survey of Autumn 1985. With this information it is possible to consider both how pay worked out for those getting jobs in 1984-85, and what were the pay expectations of those who continued in prolonged unemployment.

As we have already reported in Chapter 6, pay in the new jobs at the follow-up was in line with the pay of the new jobs recorded at the time of the 1984 interview. The additional point of interest, however, is how this pay related to the desired or target wage of those who got the new jobs. In the case of the young men who got new jobs, average desired pay, at £82.3, was a little higher than the actual pay, at £80.1. It was the young women who accepted really large gaps between target and actual wages: £58.4 on average for the former, £48.2 on average for the latter. Hence, not only were the young people not achieving the progress in wages which is common within this age range (if in continuous employment), but in addition they were clearly - and especially in the case of women - prepared to go below their wage targets.

Those not successful in moving into work, however, had considerably higher target wages: £89.8 on average among the young men, and £78.6 on average among the young women. This might be taken as some evidence of unrealistic wage expectations tending to keep this group out of work. However, as before we also asked them to state the lowest wage which they would be prepared to consider. From this question it emerged that the gap between target wage and reservation wage was widening with time. Where both answers were given, the average difference was £16.7 for the men, and no less than £29.1 for the women. These reservation wage levels therefore came within the range of wages actually being paid to those moving into work. The longer that people are out of work, the more difficult it may become for them to assess realistically at what pay level they can hope to get a job, and this may result in greater fluctuations in their replies.

## Industrial and occupational flexibility

In Chapter 4 it has already been shown that changes of industry and occupation were notable features of the working lives of the young long-term unemployed before unemployment. There are two further questions to be considered. One is whether industrial and occupational flexibility continues to show itself in the new jobs which have been found - do these tend to be the same as in the main or most recent jobs before unemployment, or do they represent still further changes? The second question is how the changes of industry and occupation which have occurred connect with variations in pay.

The amount of industrial and occupational change involved in the new jobs continued to be considerable. In Chapter 4 it was noted that the amount of change between the first job after leaving school, and the most recent job before unemployment, was great. To recapitulate those findings briefly, the young men had changed industry in 69 per cent of cases and had changed occupation in 82 per cent of cases. The young women's corresponding proportions of changes were 61 per cent and 74 per cent. Turning to the new jobs, obtained by the time of the 1984 interview, we find that (where the individuals concerned had had a previous job) the proportion of change between the main or the latest job before unemployment on the one hand, and the new jobs on the other, was not much less than the figures quoted above. For men, the industry had changed in 65 per cent of cases and the occupation in 75 per cent of cases. For women, the respective proportions were 61 per cent and 62 per cent. In other words, only one third had been able to stay within the industry or occupation of the job which was most representative of their career to date. This general lack of attachment to a particular industry or occupation is one of the most striking descriptive findings of the survey.

**Table 9.11  Industrial flexibility, and pay in new jobs in 1984 (those in work at 1984 interview)**

*£/week in new jobs (weighted)*

|  | Mean pay | |
|---|---|---|
|  | Male | Female |
| **Between main or previous job and new job:** | | |
| Moved industry | 71.0 | 45.4 |
| Stayed in same industry | 81.6 | 44.3 |

Note: The difference in mean pay is significant for males at the 95% confidence level, but not for females.

In Table 9.11 the average pay in new jobs is compared for those who had moved industry (relative to their main or most recent prior job) and for those who had remained in the same industry. By industry, we mean as always the broad grouping into ten categories provided by the Office of Population Censuses and Surveys. The results show an apparent difference between the young men and the young women in the influence of industrial flexibility on pay. For the women, there was no difference in pay between the two groups. For the young men, those remaining in the same industry received on average £82 weekly in their new jobs, while those changing industry received £71. Thus the latter group was receiving 13 per cent lower wages than those remaining in the same industry as before.

The influence of changes in occupation can be analysed in the same way as that of changes in industry. The analysis is based once more on the broad grouping of the OPCS classification, which yields 16 categories. Table 9.12 shows the average pay in new jobs (at the time of the 1984 interview) for those who changed occupation and for those who remained in the same occupation.

**Table 9.12  Occupational flexibility, and pay in new jobs in 1984 (those in new jobs at 1984 interview)**

*£/week in new jobs (weighted)*

|  | Mean pay | |
| --- | --- | --- |
|  | Male | Female |
| **Between main or previous job and new job:** | | |
| Changed occupation | 72.8 | 43.8 |
| Stayed in same occupation | 77.6 | 47.3 |

Note:    The apparent differences are non-significant at the 95% confidence level

In this case the influence of change on the average pay of new jobs was moderate in the case of both men and women: an average difference of £5 for men, and of £3 for women; small sample size means that neither of these is statistically significant. Moreover, a separate analysis (not tabulated) showed that the differences in pay for individuals, between their main or most recent job and their new job, followed no clear pattern in relation to occupational flexibility. Men who had changed occupation had taken a reduction in real pay of £5 or more in 35 per cent of cases, but had achieved an increase of similar size in 38 per cent of cases. Men staying in the same occupations had experienced pay reductions in 37 per cent of cases and increases in only 23 per cent of cases - the opposite of what might have been expected. For the women the pattern was similarly best regarded as inconclusive.

In all, then, the evidence that industrial or occupational flexibility adversely affected these young people's labour market positions receives relatively weak support. At this point the findings of Chapter 4 should also be recalled. There it was noted that, if the labour market histories of the young long-term unemployed were taken as a whole, no clear indication could be found that changes of industry or occupation were related to the various measures of labour market 'success' - such as proportion of time spent in jobs, or the duration of the longest job held. The present evidence, while showing that changes of industry and occupation continued apace among this group, does not call for any substantial modification of the earlier conclusions.

## Occupational downgrading, industrial flexibility, and wages

Industries and occupations are conventionally regarded as providing separate views of employment, and we have so far followed convention. In reality however industries and occupations are interwoven in employment structures. And one of the ways in which this can be shown is by consideration of occupational downgrading.

People who have been displaced from an occupation, and lack transferable credentials for skills in demand, may be obliged to move to less skilled work, or more generally work of lower value, in order to resume employment. We have already pointed out that, when this happens, the flexibility displayed in willingness to move occupations may involve a trade-off or cost, both for the individual and for the economy, in the form of the loss of previously accumulated skills and lowered productivity. It is important to establish how much of the flexibility displayed by the young long-term unemployed involved occupational downgrading.

To do this with a fine degree of discrimination, requires a method of evaluating the relative worth of occupations. In a previous study, this problem was solved by use of the Hope-Goldthorpe scale of occupational desirability[1], but because of the new occupational coding scheme introduced for the 1981 Census, this method was not available to us at the time when our analysis was being performed. We therefore decided to use the average pay levels per occupation, published in the New Earnings Survey 1984, as a means of ranking occupations.

Limitations of the information published in the NES concerning women's earnings, however, forced us to confine this assessment to the occupations of men in the 1984 survey[2].

Using this method, we found that substantial proportions of the young men had moved from higher-paid to lower-paid occupations, and that the proportions were similar whichever of the main comparisons we made. The findings can be summarized as follows:

**Table 9.13  Various measures of downgrading (male sample only)**

*percentages (weighted)*

|  | Experiencing 'downgrading' |
| --- | --- |
| Between first job, and latest job prior to unemployment | 38 |
| Before 'main' job and latest job prior to unemployment | 38 |
| Between 'main' job and new job held at time of 1984 interview | 38 |

In short, in all the job transitions being made among this group of young men, about four in 10 involved movement into a job which appeared to be inferior in terms of the expected pay levels associated with it.

The association between downgrading and inter-industry moves was a clear one, as shown by the following findings:

**Table 9.14  Downgrading by industrial flexibility (male sample only)**

*percentages (weighted)*

|  | Experiencing 'downgrading' | |
| --- | --- | --- |
|  | Moving industry | In same industry |
| Between 'main' and 'latest' job | 44 | 30 |
| Between 'main' and 'new' job | 43 | 30 |

In reading these figures, it must be remembered that there were about twice as many who moved industry as stayed in the same industry, so that in total about three quarters of all occupational downgrading involved a move of industry.

228

It would be expected that downgrading leads to real reductions in pay, and since there was such a high proportion of young men experiencing downgrading, this could be a substantial contributor to the pay flexibility which has been documented. In fact, however, attempts to demonstrate the expected relationship with pay met with little success. For example, downwardly mobile individuals accounted for about the same proportion of those getting increased pay or maintaining their pay, as they did of those taking cuts in pay. As with some of our previous findings, it seems that there are so many sources of variation in the way that pay is determined, that expected relationships between pay and other circumstances fail to show through in a simple manner.

The findings regarding downgrading, therefore, do not directly disturb our conclusions concerning pay. They may, however, cast a somewhat different light on the conclusions regarding flexibility as a whole, since they tend to confirm that there is a risk in industrial mobility of sacrificing skills and productivity.

## Concluding comments on 'flexibility'

The greater part of this chapter has been devoted to analysing the part played by pay flexibility, a topic which has an important place in economic theories of employment and unemployment. We were unable to find any clear evidence that relative pay expectations - relative, that is, to previous levels of pay - influenced labour market out comes. However, from the analyses a picture progressively emerged of how decisions concerning pay were being made - not of course a complete or detailed picture, but at least an outline sketch.

Interpreting freely, we would suggest that these young people perceive a relatively narrow band of pay within which they have the chance of a job. For those who have already in past jobs progressed beyond this band, the decision is commonly made to accept reductions of pay in order to return to work. Among those whose former jobs have been at the lowest levels of pay - and this is most often perhaps a matter of juvenile wages - the hope remains of increasing the pay level when finding a new job. There is thus a convergence between the formerly higher-paid and the formerly lower-paid in competing for jobs.

On the face of it this seems an unequal contest in which the formerly higher-paid must take the majority of jobs. To some extent this is so, as can be seen from the former pay of those in new jobs. But there is by no means a complete crowding out of those who seek more pay than formerly by those who offer their services at reduced wages. Their apparent competitive advantage, as well as the whole relationship between pay expectations and job outcomes, become blurred in actual practice, for a number of reasons. On the side of the job-seekers, minimum acceptable pay tends to be well below the pay expectation or target, and on the whole there was a tendency to accept less money than had been hoped for. But on the side of the employers, there also appears to have been little correspondence between wage offers and pay expectations, presumably in part because of lack of information about the latter. Thus those who were prepared to take reductions in pay often finished in new jobs with more pay than they had expected.

The net result of this process was, in the time-period of February to June 1984, an average reduction of wages when moving into new jobs - despite the fact that only a minority were expecting such a reduction. The relatively low level of pay was also maintained in the 16-month period to the follow-up survey; and once again, those in new jobs had on average accepted pay levels which were lower than their expectations or targets.

The other aspect of flexibility covered in this chapter has been movement between industries and occupations. For the young men, there seemed to be some pay advantage if they could stay within the same industry when getting a new job, but otherwise we were unable to find any relationship between industrial and occupational flexibility and other labour market outcomes.

The remarkable finding, however, is how pervasive industrial and occupational changes are within the labour market experience of this group. There is a similarity between this aspect and the tendency to a highly fragmented pattern of experience, on which attention has been focused in earlier chapters. Both point to an underlying failure to find any firm foothold in the labour market, and at a conceptual level this seems closely akin to their problems of unemployment. The lack of any statistical relationship in our survey between industrial and occupational changes on one hand, and severity of labour market problems on the other, could arise simply because almost all these young people have been affected by a lack of stability. A full evaluation of the effects of industrial and occupational movement would require comparisons between those affected, and those not affected, by long-term unemployment.

# 10 Conclusions and Implications

In this final chapter we attempt to bring together and interpret the findings of the study in two ways. First, we construct as comprehensive an explanation of long-term unemployment among 18-24 year olds as we are able. Second, we identify the main implications or issues for policy which appear to follow from our explanation. Each of these aims requires a brief further discussion, to make clearer both the scope and the limits of what we are seeking to achieve.

Our explanation of long-term youth unemployment is cast in the form of a narrative description of the processes involved, both those processes leading to the aggregate levels of youth unemployment experienced in the 1980s, and the processes of 'selection' into unemployment, and of competition in acquiring new jobs, which affect young people. We have tried to fashion a coherent, we hope persuasive, but not unduly lengthy or detailed account. This has meant that many of the complications, both of data and of interpretation, which were discussed in the earlier chapters, are not referred to in this chapter. Our intention is not to minimize the complications, nor to brush them aside. But, at the end of all the detailed analysis and discussion, we consider that it is possible to make abstractions and judgements which simplify and clarify the lines of an overall explanation. And if it is possible, then it is desirable, especially at a time when social research is receiving much criticism because of the inaccessibility of its results. Making our results accessible has been one of our main motives in preparing this chapter.

At the same time, we have to emphasize that the summary account given here must be seen in the context of the detailed arguments and discussions developed in the earlier chapters. It has only as much assurance or reliability as those chapters give it. Furthermore, our account here does not incorporate all the findings of the study, but only selects those which appear most important. The Summary provided at the beginning of the report lists the findings more completely.

With the second section of the chapter, our procedure has been to pick out those aspects of our explanation which most strongly relate to current concerns or themes of public policy. We do not, however, discuss current government policies or schemes. Nor do we speculate on future policies, nor 'invent' policies to give expression to our own predilections. Rather, we consider policy at a more thematic level, and hope that as a result our discussion becomes less dependent on the particular time at which it is written. For example, we discuss 'qualification policy' rather than the provisions of, say, the Youth Training Scheme or the Job Training Scheme. Each such scheme or development will, in any case, be subject to periodic modification, in the normal course of events. To pay too much attention to current details would be to ensure that our discussion would soon be outdated. We hope, of course, that this study may be of some value to those concerned with short- to medium-term developments of schemes and programmes for the youth labour market. But we also consider that general issues of policy, of continuing long-term importance, are involved in the study in which we have engaged. The chief application of the present research lies in helping to clarify these longer-term issues.

## Explaining long-term unemployment among 18-24 year olds

Youth unemployment can be seen in three perspectives: long, medium, and short. The long perspective permits one to see structural changes, which are imperceptible in a shorter time-frame. The medium-term brings into focus the impact of macroeconomic changes and their impact on the labour market. The short-term perspective provides a close-up of competition for jobs. Each perspective therefore reveals different processes, the signs of which we can read in the histories of young people found in long-term unemployment. Since the shorter-term processes take place in an environment already shaped by the longer-term processes, and cannot be understood except in that context, it is sensible to begin our account with the longest view.

The post-war period has witnessed large changes in the structure of employment, not only in Britain but in all industrialized economies where study of such matters has been made. The change of longest, and most steady, continuance has been a reduction in the relative size of the manual occupations and an increase in the relative size of the higher occupations. Occupations intermediate between these two groups have maintained a fairly stable size relative to total employment. The occupations which we call 'higher' consist of professional, managerial, administrative and technological types of jobs. The additional numbers of such posts which have become available have been filled partly by an expansion of education leading to higher qualification, and partly by high rates of upward mobility from among less qualified people within employment.

This shift in the occupational structure has been one of the mainsprings of opportunity and affluence for the working population throughout the post-war period. The relative contraction of manual occupations at first led to no problems of employment. At least until the early 1960s, economic historians generally agree, output was limited by supply rather than demand; employers could not get enough labour, and young people offering themselves for manual work had no great difficulty in finding it. Then, either through apprenticeships or though accumulated experience, young people could get into skilled employment.

By the early 1970s, however, additional structural changes were becoming visible, and these grew progressively throughout the decade. Manufacturing employment was already becoming a smaller part of total employment, as much of the new employment was created by public and private services. Now, as world trade in manufactured goods stagnated following the 1973 oil shock, employment in manufacturing rapidly contracted, and total employment was sustained only by the continuing growth of services.

But this relative shift between the sectors ensured that the trends in occupations continued despite slower economic growth. The traditional manufacturing industries, obviously contracting by the mid-70s, employed high proportions of manual workers, while the expanding service industries were hungry for white-collar and higher-qualified workers. The decade of the oil shocks was not, therefore, one of declining opportunity, but rather of increasing polarization of opportunity. The growth of the upper occupations if anything accelerated, while the decline of the lower (manual) occupations not only continued but was finally converted into open unemployment.

For young people in their first few years of work, structural changes of the kinds described had particularly large consequences. To be more precise, it was the young people who entered work at age 16 or 17, without the advantage of further or higher education, who were likely to face employment problems. In the first place, such young people particularly depended upon manual and lower service jobs for their start in working life, or upon apprenticeships. But the lower-level occupations were contracting; and manufacturing industry, traditional provider of manual work and of apprenticeships, was also contracting. Moreover, whenever contraction takes place, young workers are among the most vulnerable. They may lack the skills and experience to compete for jobs against workers in their prime years, and may be particularly affected when employers stop recruiting to adjust the workforce numbers. And prime age workers, with financial resources as well as skills, may be better able to move away from areas of declining opportunity than young workers, who are likely to remain dependent upon their families of origin until they get themselves established in work.

In short, our picture of the long-term changes involved in youth unemployment is one of contracting lower occupations, contracting manufacturing employment, and of too many young people remaining attached to, or dependent upon, such occupations and industries. When unemployment is described as 'structural' it is proper to ask what are the constraints or rigidities which have prevented adaptation. In this case, barriers to vertical occupational mobility appear to offer a simple and sufficient answer. Over-supply of lower qualified workers cannot readily be corrected by a redistribution of occupations; workers unable to find manual jobs cannot, in general, switch to white-collar jobs. And young people who have difficulty in establishing themselves in employment find it still more difficult to get on upward career paths. When kept out of manual occupations through an imbalance of supply and demand, they have literally 'nowhere to go'.

Before passing on to the next stage of our explanation of long-term youth unemployment, it may be worth pausing briefly to recall some of the most significant findings from the present study which appear to support, or be consistent with, the account which we have given. These findings come both from our analysis of historical employment data for 20 local labour markets, and from the work histories of the sample of unemployed young people. We showed that over the period 1971-81, employment loss in most of the local labour markets was to an extremely high degree accounted for by the extent and structure of their manufacturing industries in 1971, together with general national trends in manufacturing employment. Similarly, employment loss was almost wholly concentrated in manual occupations. Even in areas experiencing the most dramatic contraction of total employment, we estimated that non-manual employment had expanded or at least remained constant relative to the total working population. Further, the local labour market analyses suggested that local employment contraction was so distributed by industry as to particularly affect the employment chances of 16-24 year olds.

In case the connection of these points with current youth unemployment may still seem dubious or circumstantial, we also showed that the local predominance of manufacturing employment in 1981 was as powerful a predictor of the employment record of our sample during 1975-84, as was their own educational and vocational qualifications.

But the simplest, and most important, evidence for our long-term structural view of long-term youth unemployment rests in the analysis of their occupational backgrounds and qualification levels. The sample came predominantly from manual, especially semi-skilled manual, and lower service occupations. It included only a sprinkling of those who had formerly entered intermediate or higher white-collar occupations, and clerical jobs were also greatly under-represented; and these, although under-qualified relative to young people in such occupations, had better than average success in getting back into new jobs. The great majority of young unemployed people from manual occupational backgrounds were, in terms of their qualification levels, fairly representative of the occupations from which they came.

The interpretation we put forward for these findings is that, first, young people are segregated into occupational levels by means of their qualifications; and that, subsequently, their chances of entering long-term unemployment vary primarily in terms of their occupation.

The long-term, structural view explains why unemployment differs between groups and why, in particular, it is concentrated upon young people within the lower strata of occupations. It does not by itself predict the total level of unemployment nor how changes in that level will affect young people. For that, one must turn to changes taking place in the medium-term, the time scale which reflects macro-economic demand.

The young people in our sample had entered the labour market at various times during 1975-83. In the centre of this period, and having central importance for the medium-term view of unemployment, was the second oil shock of 1979, and the alterations in economic policy which followed it in Britain, as elsewhere. During 1980-82 a particularly deep recession ensued, the facts of which are familiar enough to require little reminder. The long-term structural contraction in manufacturing was greatly accelerated, with many closures and redundancies taking place. Apprenticeship places, already declining in the latter part of the 70s, were further curtailed. The number of officially recorded vacancies fell, in the trough of the cycle, to less than one half the level of the preceding peak. Total unemployment and long-term unemployment rose steeply during 1980-81, followed with a short lag by youth unemployment and long-term youth unemployment.

There can be little doubt that these macroeconomic events and their expression in the youth labour market had major repercussions for the young people in our sample. These repercussions can be seen in the striking contrasts in patterns of labour market experience between 1975-79 on one hand and 1980-83 on the other.

Those in the sample who entered the labour market before 1980 tended to spend most of their time in jobs until 1980, and in many cases these jobs were reasonably stable or lasting. But, once a job had been lost in the early 80s, in the kinds of lower-level occupations from which most came, it was much more difficult to get back. Jobs became temporary or fragmented, jobs at lower levels and at lower wages than before were accepted, and yet long spells of unemployment ensued. Instead of the usual pattern of unstable work to begin, followed by progressively settled employment, these young people in many cases were experiencing the opposite.

Yet they fared much better than most of those in our sample who entered the labour market in 1980 or thereafter. The latter spent most of their time out of work. Indeed, many of them never succeeded in finding a job, even though, on average, they had better educational qualifications than the earlier entrants. And any jobs they got (those were relatively few) were short-lived. A fragmented work career with many changes was characteristic of large proportions both before and after 1980; but after 1980, the degree of fragmentation increased.

So marked were the differences between 1975-79 and 1980-83 that they would swamp most of the other influences identified in our analyses of the survey. We obviously have to pay the closest attention to the effects of macroeconomic demand in understanding the labour market history of the period. But we should also be cautious about the longer-term inferences or predictions which we draw from what happened in the early 80s. As we have already argued, the contraction of manufacturing employment and of manual employment preceded the economic recession by many years. What happened in 1980-82 was an accentuation of pre-existing trends, not a new development, and the longer-term trends seem likely to continue, slowly, beneath the surface of economic cycles. If one imagined that long-term youth unemployment was the creation of macroeconomic recession, then one might also presume that with the ending of recession in 1982/3, 'normal' employment conditions for young people would resume. That plainly has not been the case.

The macroeconomic recovery since 1983 seems to be reflected in some of the findings of our 1985 follow-up, small though that was in scale. Those young unemployed people getting new jobs were finding a degree of stability in their employment almost unknown to them in 1980-83. Moreover, those 18-20 year olds who had found it so difficult to get started did not, as a result, seem to be permanently disadvantaged. Indeed, they were more successful in getting back to work than the older age group (for reasons which we will shortly come to).

Yet the rate at which young people who had been unemployed *for one year or more* returned to new jobs did not seem to have improved since 1980/81, in the depths of the recession. There were great differences in the rate of job-finding by length of time in unemployment. More favourable economic conditions may accelerate the return to employment of those with relatively short unemployment histories, but seem to leave behind many with deeper-seated problems.

So, finally, it is to individual differences within the experience of long-term youth unemployment that we must turn.

This last level of explanation must consider how the young unemployed compete with one another: who get jobs, and who are left behind. This is the short-term view of youth unemployment, reflecting what happens in the 'here and now' once young people have become unemployed and in a set of circumstances which is given.

Our survey does not include young people with less than six months' unemployment and so cannot see what sorting-out occurs in that early phase. From six months onward, the lines of competition are clear enough. Jobs are much more likely to go to young unemployed people who have some certificated personal qualifications or attainments. And, although the graduations are not always clear, broadly speaking the higher the qualifications which a young person has, the better his or her chances of a new job. But possession of a driving licence is also important, carrying as much weight as many educational qualifications, or more, and perhaps permitting young people to consider jobs further afield than if they depend on public transport. Hence, as time goes on in unemployment, the qualified (however modestly qualified) tend to be sifted back into work, while those without certificates tend to remain in unemployment. Over and above any consideration of qualifications, moreover, the chances of getting a job diminish as the period of unemployment gets longer.

This process is reinforced by the way job search works. The young unemployed people who make more job applications are those with, objectively, the better chances of getting jobs: the qualified, car drivers, those with the shorter periods of unemployment. Conversely, those most likely to become discouraged and 'drop out' of seeking work are the young people without qualifications, non-drivers, and those with long periods of unemployment. (Here we must except young mothers, who leave unemployment for domestic roles, and have to be considered as a special group.) Their chances of getting work may have been low before, but once they drop out even those chances are gone. Hence the losers in competition form the hard-core unemployed, which, though a minority, is of considerable size. And, as time goes on, there seems to be a slow upward movement in the proportion dropping out.

Young unemployed people's competitive behaviour and success can be influenced from outside. Information from family members and from friends constitutes one of the important aids to finding jobs for this age group. This support helps to keep these young people looking for work, and also materially increases their chances of success. And because such help is given irrespective of the young person's advantages or lack of advantages in the job market, its impact is greater than would appear at first sight. The same can be said about support from Jobcentres, provided that this support takes the form of specific suggestions about possible vacancies. We found that Jobcentres had made progress since the beginning of the 1980s in their ability to help young people in long-term unemployment. But, whereas the majority of young long-term unemployed people had supportive contacts with family and friends, the Jobcentres at the time of the study still reached only a minority of the group in this way.

Some groups of young unemployed people have special problems in competition for jobs. In our sample, young Asian men and young Afro-Caribbean women, had among the highest qualification levels, and the lowest chances of getting jobs, of all the groups in the survey. Moreover, there was a sizable group of young women with particularly high qualifications, but particularly long periods of continuous unemployment: no comparable group of men could be found. Our study was not sufficiently specialized to tell how discrimination works within long-term youth unemployment. We can only point out that such discrimination plays a part.

Our list of influences upon competition for new jobs, to leave long-term unemployment, is now complete. But we must also point out some items missing from the list. Educational and vocational qualifications are there, as is the driving licence, another kind of qualification. But what of qualification in the wider sense: what of training, what of experience in work? For the young long-term unemployed, unlike many other groups, these types of human capital prove valueless in the job market. This was particularly the experience of the 21-24 year olds who had entered the labour market in 1975-79. Despite their much greater experience of employment, and higher levels of in-job training, they consistently lost out in 1984-85 to younger unemployed people with better educational qualifications. It seems that employers pay attention to experience and qualifications only when it is part of a current job (most vacancies being filled by people moving from an existing employment). Once a young person has been unemployed for a substantial period of time, his or her training and experience are devalued, and certificated qualifications are what counts.

Also missing from the explanation is anything to do with young unemployed people's flexibility in looking for jobs. One might have expected that those willing to take a lower wage, or move to a different occupation from their usual one, would have had an advantage over those who were less flexible. The reason why this did not turn out to make a difference may have been because most of these young people had already acquired the habit of being flexible, perhaps through the difficulties they had experienced. When most are flexible, there is no personal competitive advantage in being flexible.

So, if we were to sum up our explanation in terms of what it told young people themselves, it would be to emphasize the central importance of certificated qualifications. It is qualifications which permit or restrict entry to various occupational levels, more than anything else, and the risks of entering unemployment vary greatly by occupational level. Through qualifications, also, it becomes possible to seek jobs outside a home area in economic decline, and so become more mobile. Finally, if unemployment continues for a substantial period, certificated qualifications (including those of a practical kind, like driving) give the best chance of finding a way into work.

## The young long-term unemployed: issues for policy

As we indicated at the beginning of this chapter, our aim in turning to the policy implications of the research is not to review current youth labour market policies, but, more generically, to clarify some issues within broad policy domains. The findings of the study seem relevant to two such domains, which we propose to label, 'qualification policy' and 'remedial policy'. Each of these is now discussed separately, although there are points of connection between them to which we will draw attention.

## Qualification policy

In our explanation of long-term youth unemployment we have argued that qualifications play a role twice, and in two different ways. When young people are in prolonged unemployment, qualifications are highly important in deciding who gets back into jobs and who remains out of work.  But at an earlier stage, and more fundamentally, qualifications are involved in the process by which young people become sorted into occupational levels or strata:  and it is the lower strata which are particularly vulnerable to unemployment.  The questions to be posed, in the light of this, are whether policies to raise levels of qualification would help young people, either in relation to escaping from unemployment or in relation to avoiding it; and, if so, whether any particular considerations should be addressed in the design of the relevant policies.

In the first place, it is worth noting that since the late 1970s there has been a considerable increase in the attention paid to the qualifications of the labour force as an object of policy. International comparisons have repeatedly indicated that the British labour force is characterized by low levels of qualification by comparison with leading competitor nations.

The notion has emerged that qualification policy is likely to be an important element in the development of higher levels of economic competitiveness.  During the 1980s, a wide range of programmes has been initiated with the intention of raising levels of qualification or adapting qualification to economic needs.  It is not necessary, therefore, for us to debate the value of raising qualification levels, since development in that direction already receives a broad measure of assent. Rather, we take the increased priority given to qualification of the labour force as an established context.  The questions remain, however, as to how the efforts to raise qualification levels might be made most relevant to the young long-term unemployed.

A finding of considerable significance in our study is the difference between certificated qualifications and non-certificated training and experience.  Once a young person has been affected by prolonged unemployment, it appears that non-certificated training and experience have little or no value in the competition to return to employment, while certificated qualifications not only have considerable influence, but an influence which if anything grows with time.  It may be that when employers look for particular kinds of non-certificated training and experience in order to fill posts, they think in terms of young people already in employment, where the training and experience is 'fresh' and up-to-date. If that is the case, then young long-term unemployed people's training and experience will inevitably be devalued and they will find it difficult to compete.

In addition, the high degree of occupational, industrial and sectoral mobility which the young long-term unemployed display (a flexibility which, from another point of view, is highly desirable), may itself reduce the apparent value of previous non-certificated training and experience. Even if the skills previously gained would in reality be relevant to employment in different fields, the employers may not be able to assess the relevance or value; or perhaps the cost of finding out would be too great. Certificated qualifications, on the other hand, are more standardised and therefore easier to recognise and assess; and generic educational qualifications tell something about the individual who possesses them, irrespective of the line of work in which a job is being sought. Similarly, the effectiveness of a driving licence as a practical qualification is easy to appreciate. It embodies a national standard, is universally recognised and understood, and constitutes a competence which can be used as a component of many jobs.

In principle, then, it seems that there are two aspects of qualification policy which might help young people in their competition for jobs once they have become unemployed. The one is to increase the proportion of young people holding existing certificated qualifications. The other is to extend the scope of certification to cover various skills, training and experience which are at present non-certificated. The latter could include the certification of re-training following unemployment.

But how exactly would a broadening of certificated qualifications help? Let us assume both that there is an over-supply of young people relative to demand for labour in the lower part of the job market, and that there is an unavoidably high degree of instability in many of these lower-level jobs. In these conditions, many young people will find themselves in unemployment at some time. When half of these have certificated qualifications and half have none, the half without are in a sense at an unjust disadvantage. The injustice lies in the fact that what they do have to offer, in terms of non-certificated training and experience, is discounted, and their personal worth is not examined. Put another way, those with certificates gain on those without because they are able to reduce the information costs of recruitment for prospective employers. A broadening of certification to include more individuals in the lower strata, and more kinds of training and experience, would therefore (other things being equal) make job competition in long-term youth unemployment more equitable.

But would a broadening of certification also, through its effects on job competition within unemployment, lead to increased efficiency in the labour market and, in particular, to lower aggregate levels of youth unemployment? One possibility is that broader certification should increase real competition for available vacancies. It might then be argued that increased competition should improve allocation, in this case the allocation of people to jobs, and this should improve efficiency. But this argument requires rather strong assumptions about the working of the labour market to hold unequivocally. Other constraints on the labour market could prevent any real gains in efficiency being made. Most obviously, the fact that the labour market is to a considerable degree segmented, with under-supply for many higher-level occupations existing alongside over-supply for many lower-level occupations, makes it difficult to assess what the results of increased real competition in the over-supplied segment would be. If the growth of employment in the lower strata of occupations is constrained by under-supply in the upper strata (or if, indeed, it is otherwise constrained: for example, by capacity or capital shortages), then increased competition within those lower strata is unlikely to result in any reduction of unemployment or fuller utilization of labour capacity.

A more probable, though still not certain, gain in the efficiency of the labour market might come through reduced levels of discouragement and dropping out among the young long-term unemployed. Our analysis (in Chapter 8) showed that job search was sustained by the factors which improved chances of getting new jobs, with qualifications particularly prominent. If more young people have certificated qualifications, they may feel that there are more jobs for which they can apply, and that employers will be more likely to consider their applications, and these considerations may help to sustain their job-seeking. The economic and social costs of having many young workers in effect 'opt out' of the labour market are high, since this will affect the market clearing wage rate and will tend to reduce in the long term the ratio of producers to those dependent on state benefits. Anything which can be done to maintain activity in the labour market is, from this point of view, important. From the viewpoint of individual welfare, moreover, nothing so severely reduces chances of getting back into employment as cessation, or virtual cessation, of job search. The possession of qualifications by a greater proportion of young people affected by unemployment, or increased chances for them to gain qualifications in unemployment, might help to reduce some of the most serious individual and economic risks involved.

In discussing qualifications, we have implicitly assumed that they will be a 'good' recognized by employers and bestowing advantages upon those who hold them. In practice, different kinds of qualifications differ in their usefulness and in their relevance to individuals in different circumstances. It is worthwhile to consider what characteristics of qualifications are most relevant to the young people who are at risk of long-term unemployment. The findings of the present study draw attention to two desirable characteristics.

The qualifications need to be accessible to young people who have left the basic educational system without any educational certificates, or whose educational attainments have been at a relatively low level. This seems to indicate that they must be vocational or practical in character, and must be tested or examined in a way which does not bias them in favour of those already holding educational qualifications. Of course, this does not exclude the possibility that young people entering the labour market without educational qualifications may subsequently be capable of re-entering education, or moving on from perhaps relatively simple practical qualifications to attainment of more advanced skills. We would stress the potential advantages of seeking for more flexibility in systems of qualification; it is against such a development that a broadening of initial vocational and practical qualification is likely to be most useful.

The second point of particular importance to young people at risk of unemployment is that qualifications should be recognized and accepted by a wide range of employers. Of course, this is precisely what one is trying to achieve when establishing most types of qualification, especially those which are vocational. But as we have shown, once young people have become unemployed for a substantial period their chances of getting back to work are particularly dependent on certification of their past attainments. Moreover, because they have high rates of mobility across industries and occupations, certificates recognized only in a narrow section of the labour market will be of much less value than those which have wide acceptability. Hence, the broadening of qualifications of which we have spoken will be ineffectual unless supported by policies of standardizing, accrediting and disseminating the new qualifications.

So far we have talked of qualification policy in relation to the position of young people already in long-term unemployment, or with a substantial risk of falling into unemployment because of the insecure position which they occupy in the labour market. Could qualification policy affect the risks for young people of entering unemployment in the first place? One's answer to this question depends, of course, on one's view of the role played by qualifications in 'selection' for unemployment. Our view, argued in detail in Chapter 3, is that the effect of qualifications on entry into unemployment is indirect rather than direct. Qualifications influence occupational entry, but it is occupational levels which primarily influence vulnerability to unemployment. And youth unemployment results in part from too many young people offering themselves for employment within the lower occupational levels, which have for long been contracting, thereby creating a structural imbalance.

If this interpretation is correct, then the effect of increased qualification levels on youth unemployment is not a simple matter. The requirement is not merely that more young people should obtain qualifications, but also that they should as a result allocate themselves, or be allocated, differently across occupations. One consequence of wider educational qualification, without restructuring of occupational entry, can be plainly read in the results from the present study, for such an expansion of qualification was taking place during the 1970s through the influence of the Certificate of School Education. The consequence was that a greater proportion of qualified young people came into unemployment. The self-same qualifications which give them an important advantage when competing for jobs with other unemployed young people, do not prevent them from entering unemployment if they are in vulnerable occupations.

In short, qualification policy is unlikely to reduce entry to unemployment unless it forms part of occupational restructuring. If such a restructuring takes place, however, it is likely to constitute a particularly fundamental and genuine contribution to the reduction of youth unemployment in the long run. It is therefore in support of restructuring that qualification policy is particularly crucial for youth unemployment. This is too large a subject to be covered systematically here. All that we can do is to point out some of the ways in which increases in the qualifications of young people might be combined with other processes of change, to bring about a better balance between supply and demand across the entire occupational structure.

(i) The most obvious, but not necessarily most significant, path to restructuring would be a higher qualification level combined with alteration in the occupational entry proportions. Raising of qualifications should permit some upward shift at the entry point of occupations, but this would have to be combined with raised aspirations on the part of young people, so that more took steps to enter intermediate and higher level careers. In the British system, this would particularly involve more young people continuing into further and higher education after obtaining the initial qualifications (educational or vocational) which would open up this path.

Another possibility, which has been widely discussed in recent years, is that the system of further and higher qualifications should itself be made more flexible in terms of initial entry requirements, so that, for example, more young people could gain access after obtaining initial vocational qualifications in employment.

(ii) Higher standards of qualification, or greater opportunities for qualification through continuing education and training, can contribute to increased upward mobility throughout the occupational structure.

This can happen in a variety of ways. Better qualified young workers in lower occupations may be more able to make subsequent transitions to intermediate level occupations, for example supervisory or technical; and employers may be more willing to supply further training in support of this because the costs of training would be reduced.

Higher standards at any level of an organization permit that level to absorb some of the tasks of the level immediately above, and release the higher level for more productive activities. The literature on skill shortages in British industry contains many references to under-utilization of existing skills, and it has been inferred that this is partly a consequence of poor-quality support for skilled specialists as a result of the prevalent low qualification levels. To improve the overall balance, therefore, qualification policy external to the firm has to be combined with personnel development practices within the firm.

(iii) The flow of qualifications might be selectively directed towards areas where demand was strongest and where, accordingly, job expansion opportunities were most immediate. This is clearly more relevant in the field of vocational education and training. For example, it might be beneficial to make provision for and encourage increased rates of qualification in information technology and in related subjects, such as skills for the modern office.

Of course, any attempt to steer vocational education and training towards a better fit with demand faces thorny problems in interpreting and forecasting that demand. Those are difficulties which cannot be discussed here. However, our notion of imbalance in the occupational structure suggests at least one potentially useful way of assessing the provision of vocational education and training. We can be sure that demand will continue to shift in the direction of intermediate and higher level skills. Vocational education and training needs to offer a sufficient increase in pathways to those levels to meet the demands created by this shift. General goals of upgrading and upward linking should not be incompatible with the highest degree of flexibility and responsiveness in the choice of the particular courses or pathways to be offered.

To sum up the implications of the research in this field of policy, we first of all see considerable scope for a broadening of qualifications which will reduce inequitable disadvantage for many of the young unemployed, and help to keep them as productive members of society. But we also see, in the light of our findings, a larger task for qualification policy, and one which will involve other aspects of policy in combination. That task is to reduce the over-supply of young people to lower occupational levels, and to increase the supply to intermediate and higher levels on which economic competitiveness and growth depend. Reducing the present occupational imbalance will involve qualification policy not only at the more basic levels, but in further and higher education and in advanced training. It will also require consideration of how the various elements of the qualification system can become more flexible in order to yield higher rates of upward mobility.

**Remedial policy**
The notion of 'remedial policy' may need some explanation. The metaphor is medical, and suggests that there are groups whose

members have suffered some condition which weakens or handicaps them, so that special steps have to be taken to help return them to a normal way of life.

It is not our view that young people in long-term unemployment are, as a whole, a particularly handicapped group requiring remedial treatment. On the contrary, the assumption of our preceding discussion of qualification policy was that the young long-term unemployed form a fairly representative cross-section of young people in manual and lower service occupations, and can benefit from a broadening of opportunities for qualification without being treated as a special problem group. Nevertheless, it is certainly true that among those in long-term unemployment there are groups of young people with special problems. It is also true that unemployment if sufficiently protracted creates its own problems: young people who formerly held normal employment may in time come to be seen as unemployable because of the length of time they have spent out of work, and they themselves may become so discouraged that they hold the same view. Remedial policies may need to be developed for particular groups of young unemployed people in order to cope with these problems.

Qualification policy may itself create problems for those who, for whatever reason, fail to take advantage of the available opportunities. It seems likely that an effect of this kind has resulted from the reduced proportions of school leavers, in recent years, with no school examination qualifications. The unqualified residue become, as a result, both more conspicuous and, from employers' viewpoint, easier to bar from entry. The success of any policy to broaden the attainment of qualifications or to raise the average standards achieved, carries with it a correspondingly greater disadvantage for those who fail. The clearest evidence of this problem comes from the Federal German Republic, with its well established apprenticeship system bringing three quarters of the work force a respected vocational qualification. Even there, about one in 10 of young people fail to complete any qualification, and these represent a problem which has so far proved intractable. Hence, the more successful a qualification policy, the more clearly will a residual group, standing in need of remedial help, be defined.

These considerations lead to more general notions of 'selection and signalling' in the formation of groups needing remedial attention. As individuals are passed through a process of selection, those rejected form a residue who have to try other means of entering employment. But the very fact of having been rejected, if it is highly visible, may count against them and deter other employers from considering them. Their past failure becomes a signal which influences their future selection. Selection and signalling can also be cumulative. Young people rejected at one selection stage may then enter a remedial programme which gives them a further chance. But if at the end of this remedial programme they are rejected again, their 'failure' is doubly signalled to potential employers. (First, they were on a programme for young people already rejected; second, the programme apparently did not work for them.) Evidence for the operation of such processes has been discussed in Chapter 5 of this report.

Two possible types of remedial programmes for young unemployed people are programmes of training and programmes of economically sheltered or subsidized employment. At the time of writing, emphasis is being placed within government policy upon training for the young long-term unemployed, but during the period to which our study relates, economically sheltered employment was playing the leading role. There is also considerable public interest in the notion of 'workfare', that is, in linking welfare payments for the unemployed to work on sheltered employment programmes. Our analysis suggests that any scheme of remedial training or economically sheltered employment will be subject to the processes of selection and signalling which we have described. However, the precise way in which these processes work will depend on the details of operation of each particular scheme. A few examples may help to clarify the range of possibilities.

(i)   In some schemes, entry may be guided by assessment of individuals' chances of re-employment. In this case, the better prospects from within the remedial group are being, so to speak, re-launched into normal employment by way of training or sheltered employment. While such a scheme will probably be highly effective for those selected for entry, it will also probably reduce employment chances both for those left outside the scheme and for those entering but, eventually, failing to take advantage of the opportunity.

(ii)  At the opposite pole, a scheme may be provided for those with the lowest chances of employment (for example, those having certain specific handicaps). The danger with such a scheme is that it sends out a strong signal about the employability of any person admitted to it. Its effectiveness therefore depends upon the accuracy with which individuals' chances of employment can be assessed. If indeed individuals' chances are extremely low, then admission to the scheme can hardly reduce them, and some may gain sufficiently from the scheme to make their way into normal employment.

(iii) A third possibility is a scheme with automatic entry criteria, sometimes called a 'universal' scheme. For example, all unemployed below a certain age and with a certain period of unemployment might be admitted to re-training or sheltered employment. In principle, such a scheme minimizes both the advantages and the disadvantages of selection and signalling processes: the larger the group to which it applies, the more this will be the case. As in this case re-training or sheltered employment becomes the norm for young long-term unemployed people, individuals' chances of moving into normal employment thereafter should not be affected one way or another. However, in practice it might be natural, within a universal scheme, for local, more specialized sub-schemes to develop, some selecting the higher employment prospects and some the lower. In this case, subsequent employment chances would depend upon initial selection into a particular type of sub-scheme.

These observations suggest that schemes need to be examined carefully to determine the selection and signalling processes which they are likely to generate. And they should be assessed not only in terms of the proportions selected into employment, but also in terms of the subsequent effect on those who are not initially successful.

Ideally, what one is seeking in a remedial measure is to increase the opportunities of selection for disadvantaged individuals, while minimizing the adverse signals given to employers in the process. From this point of view, we suggest that the ideal remedial scheme would be 'invisible'. Clearly, no scheme of economically sheltered employment is likely to be invisible, because any such scheme will involve public collective action. It might be that a more individual approach is more likely to meet the needs of the most disadvantaged young people in long-term unemployment.

The present survey showed, as we earlier noted in this chapter, that both support from Jobcentres and support from family and friends helped to sustain job search and materially increased the chances of finding a new job. By support, we here mean specifically the provision of information about possible job vacancies. Such support was provided independently of the characteristics of the young people, and so would be of particular value to those with the greatest disadvantages. Personal support for disadvantaged individuals, hence with a remedial element to it, is from the outside indistinguishable from support given to others, and hence meets our criterion of 'invisibility'.

Although it lies outside the scope of our discussion to review the work of the government employment services, there seems to be little doubt that there remains considerable scope for providing more job information and guidance on an individual basis to the young long-term unemployed, and to specially disadvantaged groups among them. Information technology, the role of which is developing within both the employment and social services, might make such specialized and personalized support feasible without undue increase in administrative costs. There might also be scope to do more to mobilize and back up the resources of young people's families. Family counselling has been incorporated into many branches of medical and social services practice, but seems so far to have been neglected in regard to youth unemployment.

Another type of remedial measure which meets our criteria is, of course, individual self-help. A striking finding, although with small-scale data, from our follow-up survey was that nearly all the young people entering self-employment lacked any educational or vocational qualifications. Although self-employment has been receiving a great deal of attention as a means of reducing unemployment, its potential for helping young people in particularly disadvantaged circumstances might be worth separate consideration. The kind of support of value to such young people, when they consider self-employment, might be quite different from the kinds of support suitable for the generality of those entering self-employment. The area of self-employment and small business formation may also offer scope to assist young members of ethnic minority groups facing discrimination in the labour market. Here too, however, the standard kind of support for those considering self-employment might not be effective.

Finally, the role of remedial policy for long-term youth unemployment needs to be kept in perspective. We reiterate that it would be misleading to regard all the young people in this position as a separate and handicapped stream within the labour market. Only minorities within the young long-term unemployed would fit that description. The majority have either been displaced from normal and stable employment, or have achieved at least a moderate level of qualification from our education system, or both. In the aggregate, they are hardly distinguishable from young people holding the lower-level jobs in our economy. These considerations indicate that remedial policy can deal only with the margins of the task of restoring young people to normal employment. That task demands a long perspective, and can only be achieved by a progressive upgrading and restructuring of the whole labour force to meet the needs of modern technology and economic competition.

# Appendix 1

## Sampling and response

### 1.  Sample design

The sample design was shaped by the aim of obtaining sufficient respondents in particular localities to permit a series of separate analyses.

A stratified design was used, with 11 strata, as follows:

(a)  Seven metropolitan areas formed strata 1-7:

Greater London
West Midlands
Greater Manchester
Merseyside
West Yorkshire
Tyne & Wear
City of Glasgow

In each of these strata, *four* unemployment benefit offices were randomly selected, with probability proportional to numbers of people aged 18-24 in long-term unemployment. The frame was an alphabetically ordered list of benefit offices supplied by the Department of Employment, together with statistics, as at December 1983, of unemployment by age within jobcentre area (jobcentre areas being associated with benefit offices). From this list, however, benefit offices were first removed if they were within localities classified as 'suburban and growth areas' under the area classification scheme developed by Webber and Craig[1]. These were transferred to stratum 10 below. Thus the remaining benefit offices in the metropolitan areas represent inner city, industrial, and low-income residential localities while excluding higher-income metropolitan localities.

(b)  Stratum 8 consisted of four large industrial or service centre towns/cities (population greater than 75,000 at the 1981 Census of Population), randomly selected with probability proportional to numbers aged 18-24 in unemployment, from a frame of all such towns/cities. The definition of 'industrial or service centre' corresponds to families 3-5 in Webber and Craig (with the addition here of a size criterion). Within each of the four selected towns/cities, two benefit offices were selected at random, if there were more than two, otherwise both benefit offices were included. The towns/cities selected were as follows:

Newport, Nottingham, Sheffield, Southampton.

It will be noted that Sheffield was included as a large town/city; it had been decided *not* to include South Yorkshire as a metropolitan region, since it lacks the characteristics of an extensive conurbation found in the other metropolitan regions.

(c)  Stratum 9 consisted of one benefit office from each of nine smaller industrial towns (less than 75,000 population at the 1981 census), randomly selected with probability proportional to numbers aged 18-24 in unemployment, from a frame of all benefit offices in such towns. (A few of the towns had more than one benefit office.) The towns were again drawn from families 3-5 of the Webber and Craig classification.

(d)  Stratum 10 consisted of nine benefit offices, in suburban, growth (including rural growth), resort and retirement areas. The areas included in the frame corresponded to family 1 and clusters 11-12 of the Webber and Craig classification. The benefit offices were selected as in stratum 9.

(e)  Stratum 11 consisted of six benefit offices drawn from rural areas other than those covered in stratum 10. The definition corresponded to clusters 7-10 of the Webber and Craig classification. The selection method was as previously described.

In total, then, the survey covered 60 benefit offices, out of a total of approximately 750. However, by use of the 'probability proportional to size' method, the benefit offices in the sample represented a higher proportion of young unemployed people than would have been obtained by simple random selection.

Individuals to be included in the sample were drawn within each unemployment benefit office through the National Unemployment Benefit System computers. Those aged 18-24 on the reference date (8 February 1984) and recorded as having either (a) six up to 12 months of unemployment in their current period of registration for benefit, or (b) 12 months or more of unemployment, were randomly selected to fill quotas which varied by sample strata, larger numbers being selected in strata 1-8. The ratio between duration groups (a) and (b) were always fixed at 2:3. The sex of the individual was not taken into consideration in the sampling plan.

The lists drawn from the computer files were sufficiently large to allow for subsequent wastage. Letters were sent to the individuals in the sample by the Department, explaining the purpose of the survey and the conditions of confidentiality under which it was conducted, and affording the option of withdrawing from the survey by contacting the Department's head office. In total, seven per cent of the original sample chose to 'opt out' from the survey, and their names were withdrawn, prior to issue of the sample to the fieldwork agency (Social and Community Planning Research).

## 2. Response

The following table shows the sample numbers issued and the interviews completed and analysed (13 interviews were rejected as insufficiently complete). The table also shows the response rate at fieldwork, and the interviews as a fraction of the population of 18-24 year olds with six months or more of unemployment.

| | Issued | Interviews | Gross response rate (%) | Interviews as fraction of population |
|---|---|---|---|---|
| Greater London | 240 | 126 | 52 | 0.0036 |
| West Midlands | 240 | 189 | 79 | 0.0058 |
| Greater Manchester | 240 | 168 | 70 | 0.0084 |
| Merseyside | 240 | 187 | 78 | 0.0067 |
| West Yorks | 240 | 172 | 72 | 0.0103 |
| Tyne & Wear | 240 | 177 | 74 | 0.0101 |
| Glasgow | 240 | 185 | 77 | 0.0071 |
| Large industrial/service centre towns/cities | 720 | 541 | 75 | 0.0071 |
| Other industrial towns | 378 | 288 | 76 | 0.0028 |
| Suburban/growth/resort/ retirement | 378 | 252 | 67 | 0.0038 |
| Rural (low-growth) | 252 | 187 | 74 | 0.0120 |
| *Total* | *3408* | *2472* | *73* | *0.0060* |

The *net response rate* (after elimination of untraceable addresses, individuals moved from area, and so on) was 82 per cent.

It can be seen from the table that response was much lower in the Greater London area than elsewhere.

In terms of the national population of 18-24 year olds in long-term unemployment, those interviewed represented 0.6 per cent. The sample precision, in the statistical sense was *greater* for metropolitan areas (except Greater London), Glasgow, large industrial or service centre towns/cities, and rural (low-growth) areas; and *lesser* for Greater London, smaller industrial towns, and suburban/ growth/resort/retirement areas.

# Appendix 2

**Secondary data sources**
The secondary data analysis was confined to those localities where substantial sub-samples had been drawn in the 1984 survey: that is, the five metropolitan areas *excluding* Greater London, the City of Glasgow, and the four large industrial towns. Because of this focus, the secondary data analysis relates only to *urban* areas. Greater London was excluded because it is impossible to divide it into separate travel-to-work areas.

The survey sample was selected from computer records organised by unemployment benefit office. These offices are, in their turn, linked to 'Jobcentre areas'; definitions of these links were supplied by the Department of Employment. Finally, Jobcentre areas can in most cases be allocated to CURDS functional regions or Department of Employment travel-to-work areas. The Jobcentre areas are usually smaller then the latter, and more than one Jobcentre area may fall within a single functional region or travel-to-work area.

Contextual information about local labour markets can most usefully be examined at the level of functional regions or travel-to-work areas, since these are to a reasonable degree self-contained. The 36 Jobcentre areas in the main urban centres of the survey fell within a total of 20 CURDS functional regions, which are listed below.

For each travel-to-work area, data were collected from the following sources: Annual Census of Population, 1971 and 1981; Annual Census of Employment, 1971 and 1981 (with industries classified by the 1968 Standard Industrial Classification); Regional Office Information System, 1975 and 1981.

## Coverage of the local labour market analysis

| Metropolitanregion or industrial city | No of UBOs sampled | Functional region | CURDS reference |
|---|---|---|---|
| West Midlands | One | Coventry | VCV5 |
|  | One | Smethwick | BWU5 |
|  | One | Walsall | BWS5 |
|  | One | Wolverhampton | BWV5 |
| Greater Manchester | Two | Bolton | MBL5 |
|  | Two | Manchester | MMC5 |
| Merseyside | One | Birkenhead | LWL5 |
|  | Two | Liverpool | LLV5 |
|  | One | Southport | LSV5 |
| West Yorkshire | One | Bradford | OBD5 |
|  | One | Huddersfield | OHD5 |
|  | Two | Leeds | YLS5 |
| Tyne & Wear | Three | Newcastle | NNE5 |
|  | One | Sunderland | OSR5 |
| Glasgow | Three | Glasgow | GGG5 |
|  | One | Motherwell | GML5 |
| Newport | One | Newport | JNP5 |
| Nottingham | One | Nottingham | FNG5 |
| Sheffield | One | Sheffield | SSH5 |
| Southampton | One | Southampton | OSO5 |

In addition, educational data were obtained by local authority area from the statistics for England and Wales published by the Department of Education and Science and the Welsh Office.

It should be noted that the ROIS data were based on travel-to-work area definitions slightly different from those of the CURDs functional regions. In addition, the local authority areas used for educational statistics can be related to travel-to-work areas only in a crude manner.

# Appendix 3

**Multivariate analyses**
The chief method of analysing relationships between sets of four or more variables has been the fitting of log-linear models to multiway tables. Such a table contains the counts of individuals for each element or cell of the complete factorial combination of variables. For instance, if there are four variables, three of which have two possible responses (for example, yes-no, male-female) and one of which has three possible responses, than the multiway table will have 2 x 2 x 2 x 3 = 24 cells. The aim of the analysis is to establish that some simpler set of relationships among the variables will satisfactorily account for the complete table. For example, if there are four variables and they are labelled A,B,C and D, then we might hypothesize that the complete multiway table is accounted for by the pairwise associations among the variables, of which there are six (AB,AC,AD,BC,BD,CD). The analysis tests specific hypotheses of this type, first finding the maximum likelihood weights for the hypothesized explanatory relationships, and then assessing how close a fit this solution gives to the actual data. The test of fit is provided by referring the residual variation or 'scaled deviance' to the chi-square distribution.

The analyses were performed using the Generalised Linear Interactive Modelling (GLIM) system[1], on a Research Machines PC186 microcomputer. For further explanation of the statistical and computational basis of the method, see Everitt[2].

It should be remarked that, in many discussions of statistical model fitting, the objective is seen in terms of a search strategy leading to a best-fitting model. While we would not argue against the suitability of that approach for certain research tasks, that has not been the approach adopted here. Rather, we have selected variables for the analyses because of their hypothesised relationships with one another, and have then directly tested out hypothesis through the analysis. If, upon completion of the analysis, we find that a satisfactory fit to the data has been achieved, but one of the relationships included in the model is non-significant, we do not proceed to a further analysis with that relationship dropped from the model. In terms of our research objectives, this further analysis would yield no information.

In some cases our hypothesis has included interactions involving three or more variables. In all such cases, we have also compared this model with a simplified model omitting the higher-order interaction terms.

A practical problem with this form of analysis can be the occurrence of numerous zero cells in the multiway table. Such an occurrence can lead to spuriously impressive model fits: although in the future, such problems may be overcome by the application of multivariate exact test methods. We have aimed to avoid these situations by careful selection of variables and, where necessary, the collapsing of multiple categories into two or three categories. The choice of variables and the representation of variables are the areas where the researcher's judgement plays a crucial part. It must be stressed, equally, that the availability of model-fitting statistical procedures does not dispense with the need for judgement in the interpretation of the results.

We now proceed to provide details of the main analyses referred to in the text of the report.

## M1. Qualifications, social variables, and return to work

The variables, and values of variables, for this analysis were as follows (the labels at the left are as shown in the computer-produced table).

MS =      Sex (1 = Male, 2 = Female)

MC =      Car driving licence (1 = Yes, 2 = No)

MT =      Tenure (1 = Owner-occupier household, 2 = other)

MQS =    Qualifications (1 = No qualification; 2 = Certificate of school Education (CSE) below grade 1; 3 = CSE grade 1, or General Certificate of Education Ordinary level (GCE 'O') at any grade; 4 = GCE Advanced (A) leevel at any grade, or CSE below grade 1 with Vocational qualification;

5 = higher (tertiary) qualification, or O/A level with additional vocational qualification)

MI =     In work at 1984 interview (1 = Yes, 2 = No)

The complete five-way table was formed, with 80 cells, and a log linear analysis conducted. The model consisted of all 10 pairwise associations of the five variables, and required 31 parameters. The parameter estimates, and standard errors of the estimates, are shown below. The scaled deviance was 58.8 on 49 degrees of freedom, indicating a satisfactory fit. It should be noted, however, that the associations between 'sex' and 'in work', and between 'tenure' and 'in work', were relatively small.

scaled deviance = 58.821
d.f. = 49

| estimate | s.e | parameter |
|---|---|---|
| 2.201 | 0.1673 | 1 |
| -1.135 | 0.1634 | MS(2) |
| 0.09467 | 0.1978 | MQS(2) |
| 0.3059 | 0.1875 | MQS(3) |
| -0.2821 | 0.2495 | MQS(4) |
| 0.3197 | 0.2039 | MQS(5) |
| -0.2006 | 0.1583 | MC(2) |
| 0.7674 | 0.1502 | MT(2) |
| 1.630 | 0.1602 | MI(2) |
| 0.1009 | 0.1269 | MS(2).MQS(2) |
| 0.3068 | 0.1191 | MS(2).MQS(3) |
| 0.6248 | 0.1731 | MS(2).MQS(4) |
| 0.8391 | 0.1464 | MS(2).MQS(5) |
| 1.051 | 0.1099 | MS(2).MC(2) |
| -0.3046 | 0.1371 | MQS(2).MC(2) |
| -0.5023 | 0.1286 | MQS(3).MC(2) |
| -0.9395 | 0.1794 | MQS(4).MC(2) |
| -1.201 | 0.1519 | MQS(5).MC(2) |
| -0.5194 | 0.09724 | MS(2).MT(2) |
| -0.7529 | 0.1294 | MQS(2).MT(2) |
| -0.7422 | 0.1234 | MQS(3).MT(2) |
| -1.250 | 0.1718 | MQS(4).MT(2) |
| -0.9144 | 0.1481 | MQS(5).MT(2) |

| | | |
|---|---|---|
| 0.8690 | 0.1006 | MC(2).MT(2) |
| -0.1826 | 0.1286 | MS(2).MI(2) |
| -0.3719 | 0.1742 | MQS(2).MI(2) |
| -0.3774 | 0.1657 | MQS(3).MI(2) |
| -0.3407 | 0.2340 | MQS(4).MI(2) |
| -0.7002 | 0.1849 | MQS(5).MI(2) |
| 0.7097 | 0.1291 | MC(2).MI(2) |
| 0.1626 | 0.1295 | MT(2).MI(2) |

## M2. Qualifications, 'time', and return to work

The variables, and values of variables, for this analysis were:

QB = Qualifications (1 = No qualifications; 2 = CSE or GCE 'O' at any grade; 3 = GCE 'A', or higher, or any educational qualification combined with vocational qualification)

CB = Car driving licence (1 = yes, 2 = no)

PB = Period of entry to labour market (1 = 1975-79, 2 = 1980-83)

UB = Unemployment duration at sampling (1 = up to one year, 2 = 13-24 months, 3 = 25 months or more)

IB = In work at 1984 interview (1 = yes, 2 = no)

The complete five-way table was formed, with 72 cells, and a log linear analysis conducted. The model consisted of all 10 pairwise associations of the five variables, and required 27 parameters. The analysis resulted in a satisfactory fit, but it should be noted that the association between 'period of entry' and 'in work' was near zero.

scaled deviance = 46.247
d.f. = 45

| estimate | s.e. | parameter |
|---|---|---|
| 2.281 | 0.1620 | 1 |
| 0.5973 | 0.1589 | QB(2) |
| 0.6360 | 0.1778 | QB(3) |
| 0.4651 | 0.1473 | CB(2) |
| -0.3520 | 0.1470 | PB(2) |
| -0.3360 | 0.1594 | UB(2) |
| -0.6821 | 0.2061 | UB(3) |
| 1.365 | 0.1582 | IB(2) |

| | | |
|---:|---:|---|
| -0.4891 | 0.1056 | QB(2).CB(2) |
| -1.096 | 0.1239 | QB(3).CB(2) |
| 0.2417 | 0.09367 | QB(2).PB(2) |
| 0.3025 | 0.1184 | QB(3).PB(2) |
| 0.3846 | 0.09482 | CB(2).PB(2) |
| -0.2830 | 0.1057 | QB(2).UB(2) |
| -0.6205 | 0.1196 | QB(2).UB(3) |
| -0.6231 | 0.1290 | QB(3).UB(2) |
| -1.448 | 0.1759 | QB(3).UB(3) |
| 0.08770 | 0.1046 | CB(2).UB(2) |
| 0.3217 | 0.1266 | CB(2).UB(3) |
| 0.08931 | 0.09394 | PB(2).UB(2) |
| -0.9779 | 0.1150 | PB(2).IB(2) |
| -0.3217 | 0.1410 | QB(2).IB(2) |
| -0.4680 | 0.1630 | QB(3).IB(2) |
| 0.6825 | 0.1250 | CB(2).IB(2) |
| -0.06212 | 0.1226 | PB(2).IB(2) |
| 0.4183 | 0.1338 | UB(2).IB(2) |
| 0.8805 | 0.1845 | UB(3).IB(2) |

## M3. Qualifications, area and return to work

The variables, and values of variables, for this analysis were:

B =     Qualifications (1 = Any qualifications; 2 = No qualification)
C =     Car driving licence (1 = Yes; 2 = No)
A =     Area (11 area-types as defined in Appendix 1)
D =     In work at 1984 interview (1 = yes, 2 = no)

The complete four-way table was formed, with 88 cells, and a log linear analysis conducted. The model consisted of all six pairwise associations between the variables, and required 47 parameters. The model resulted in a satisfactory fit, but it should be noted that the standardized estimates relating to the associations between 'area' and the other variables were generally small, especially between 'area' and 'in work'.

scaled deviance = 33.637
d.f. = 41

| estimate | s.e. | parameter |
|---|---|---|
| 1.958 | 0.2523 | 1 |
| 0.1305 | 0.3345 | A(2) |
| -0.01417 | 0.3390 | A(3) |
| -0.1930 | 0.3475 | A(4) |
| -0.3521 | 0.3620 | A(5) |
| -0.3571 | 0.3643 | A(6) |
| -0.4961 | 0.3495 | A(7) |
| 1.105 | 0.2799 | A(8) |
| 0.7174 | 0.3014 | A(9) |
| 1.026 | 0.2894 | A(10) |
| 0.2199 | 0.3302 | A(11) |
| -0.9229 | 0.2170 | B(2) |
| -0.05691 | 0.2243 | C(2) |
| 0.9009 | 0.2517 | D(2) |
| -0.3023 | 0.2353 | A(2).B(2) |
| 0.05865 | 0.2399 | A(3).B(2) |
| -0.4398 | 0.2363 | A(4).B(2) |
| 0.0007335 | 0.2386 | A(5).B(2) |
| -0.5094 | 0.2398 | A(6).B(2) |
| 0.6344 | 0.2402 | A(7).B(2) |
| -0.2090 | 0.2017 | A(8).B(2) |
| 0.01767 | 0.2178 | A(9).B(2) |
| 0.2026 | 0.2227 | A(10).B(2) |
| -0.1920 | 0.2354 | A(11).B(2) |
| 0.03067 | 0.2569 | A(2).C(2) |
| 0.06473 | 0.2652 | A(3).C(2) |
| 0.5585 | 0.2714 | A(4).C(2) |
| 0.1648 | 0.2670 | A(5).C(2) |
| 0.4455 | 0.2713 | A(6).C(2) |
| 0.6870 | 0.2841 | A(7).C(2) |
| 0.1194 | 0.2218 | A(8).C(2) |
| -0.4084 | 0.2345 | A(9).C(2) |
| -0.4533 | 0.2388 | A(10).C(2) |
| -0.1240 | 0.2549 | A(11).C(2) |
| 0.7111 | 0.09471 | B(2).C(2) |
| 0.4570 | 0.3274 | A(2).D(2) |

| | | |
|---|---|---|
| 0.2485 | 0.3289 | A(3).D(2) |
| 0.4254 | 0.3303 | A(4).D(2) |
| 0.6279 | 0.3506 | A(5).D(2) |
| 0.6778 | 0.3501 | A(6).D(2) |
| -0.01821 | 0.3168 | A(7).D(2) |
| 0.4266 | 0.2725 | A(8).D(2) |
| 0.4355 | 0.2975 | A(9).D(2) |
| -0.1725 | 0.2855 | A(10).D(2) |
| 0.4103 | 0.3249 | A(11).D(2) |
| 0.4317 | 0.1259 | B(2).D(2) |
| 0.7187 | 0.1247 | C(2).D(2) |

## M4. Individual variables, local labour market structure, and proportion of time in work, 1975-84

This analysis differed from the remainder in this appendix in that it used multiple regression methods. The objective was to consider whether measures of local labour market structure affected individual experience of the labour market, as opposed to the alternative hypothesis, that individual experience would depend entirely on characteristics measured at the individual level. (If the latter were the case, it would not rule out the possibility that individual-level attributes might be influenced by local structural circumstances).

The dependent variable selected for this purpose was the proportion of time spent in work by each individual since entering the labour market, excluding from that calculation any period other than those in work, in registered unemployment, or on a government scheme. This variable is referred to by the label WPC.

The analysis was performed on that sub-sample of the whole sample whose members were located in one of the 20 travel-to-work areas defined in Chapter 2 and Appendix 2. The sub-sample size was 1619 individuals, about two-thirds of the whole sample.

The individual-level independent variables considered were:

- Qualifications (QS) defined as a three-category discrete variable (1 = no qualification; 2 = CSE or O level; 3 = A level or higher qualification, or educational and vocational qualification combined).
- Car driving licence (C) (1 = Driving licence, 2 = No licence)
- Gender (GEN) (1 = Male, 2 = Female)

- Unemployed parent (UNP) (1 = One or both parents unemployed, 2 = Neither parent unemployed). This variable was included here since it was found to be significant in a similar analysis carried out at the Centre for Educational Sociology, Edinburgh (Raffe, D., Personal communication).
- Period of entry to the labour market (YLM) (1 = 1975-79; 2 = 1980-83)

The measures of local labour market structure were defined in relation to CURDS functional regions, as described in Chapter 2 and Appendix 2. They were:
- the proportion of economically active aged 16-24 in 1981 (YPC)
- the proportion of economically active in social classes IV and V (semi-skilled and unskilled manual) in 1981 (USK)
- the proportion of households not owning a car in 1981 (NCH)
- manufacturing employment in 1981 as a proportion of 1971 (MCH)
- service employment in 1981 as a proportion of 1971 (SCH)
- manufacturing employment in 1981 as a proportion of total employment (MPC).

An initial analysis including all the variables revealed a high degree of collinearity. Accordingly, the procedure adopted was to specify a reduced model incorporating the variables which appeared most important on a priori grounds. The remaining variables were then tested for inclusion one at a time, and each was adopted into the model only if: (a) it did not introduce collinearity, (b) it significantly imporoved the fit of the model.

The 'core' model was:

WCP = constant + QS+C+YLM.MPC

where the term YLM.MPC indicates that separate slopes are estimated for MPC at each of the two levels of YLM. As described in Chapter 4, there were great differences in the work experience of those who entered the labour market before 1980 and those who entered in 1980-1983. On the basis of the material discussed in Chapter 2, it seems reasonable to associate this particularly with the decline in manufacturing employment at the turn of the decade. Hence the model represents the change in the labour market as a change in the influence of manufacturing employment. This representation was supported since, upon adding YLM as a separate term, the fit of the model was not improved.

The deviance of the null model (constant term only) was 1,222,300 on 1618 degrees of freedom. The scaling factor for the deviance was estimated from the model incorporating all variables, at 524.0.

The final selected model is shown below. The variables omitted from the final model were UNP and NCH (no significant improvement of fit); YPC, USK and MCH (collinearity). In addition, an alternative formulation in which all other terms were crossed with GEN (i.e. gender was considered as an interaction with the model) was tried, but the increase in model fit was non-significant. The improvement of fit of the selected model over the null model was estimated as 648.9 on 7 degrees of freedom (p<0.001). The proportion of deviance accounted for was 27.8 per cent. The correlation matrix of parameter estimates shows that the model had a low level of collinearity.

| estimate | s.e. | parameter |
|---|---|---|
| 10.57 | 7.176 | 1 |
| -9.025 | 1.398 | C(2) |
| 2.784 | 1.276 | GEN(2) |
| 0.1638 | 0.06209 | SCH |
| 7.120 | 1.312 | QS(2) |
| 7.517 | 1.661 | QS(3) |
| 0.3125 | 0.05625 | MPC.YLM(1) |
| -0.3096 | 0.05724 | MPC.YLM(2) |

Correlations of parameter estimates

| | | | | | | |
|---|---|---|---|---|---|---|
| 1.000 | | | | | | |
| -0.1489 | 1.0000 | | | | | |
| -0.0318 | -0.1949 | 1.0000 | | | | |
| -0.9231 | -0.0126 | 0.0211 | 1.0000 | | | |
| -0.0273 | 0.1087 | -0.0561 | -0.0853 | 1.0000 | | |
| -0.0610 | 0.2103 | -0.1600 | -0.0364 | 0.3837 | 1.0000 | |
| -0.2580 | 0.0371 | -0.0119 | -0.0700 | 0.0523 | 0.0308 | 1.0000 |
| -0.2334 | 0.0198 | -0.0358 | -0.0856 | 0.0195 | 0.0002 | 0.8868 |
| 1 | 2 | 3 | 4 | 5 | 6 | 7 |

## M5. Basic model of the associates of job search

The variables, and values of variables, for this analysis were as follows:

SA =     Sex (1 = Male, 2 = Female)
QA =     Qualifications (1 = No qualification, 2 = Any qualification)
CA =     Car driving licence (1 = Yes, 2 = No)
CHA =   Children (1 = None, 2 = One or more)
UA =     Unemployment duration of time of sampling (1 = up to one year, 2 = 13-24 months, 3 = 25 or more months)
JAA =   Number of job applications in past year (1 = None, 2 = 1-10, 3 = 11 or more).

    The full six-way table was formed, consisting of 144 cells, and a log-linear analysis conducted. The model fitted consisted of (a) the four three-way interactions involving 'sex' and 'children', and each of the other variables, (b) the six pairwise associations between the four variables other than 'sex' and 'children'. In addition, a simplified model consisting of the 15 pairwise associations among all six variables was fitted for comparison.

    The model including the three-way interaction terms yielded a satisfactory fit (see below); however, the simplified model resulted in an increase of scaled deviance of 151.1 for a reduction in the number of parameters of six, and was clearly not a satisfactory alternative.

scaled deviance = 101.04
d.f. = 103

| estimate | s.e. | parameter |
|---|---|---|
| 2.374 | 0.1488 | 1 |
| -1.300 | 0.1617 | SA(2) |
| 0.4315 | 0.1330 | QA(2) |
| 1.196 | 0.1377 | CA(2) |
| -1.490 | 0.2081 | CHA(2) |
| 0.1874 | 0.1456 | UA(2) |
| 0.04441 | 0.1619 | UA(3) |
| 0.6712 | 0.1507 | JAA(2) |
| 0.6615 | 0.1572 | JAA(3) |
| 0.3154 | 0.09939 | SA(2).QA(2) |
| 0.9449 | 0.1168 | SA(2).CA(2) |

| | | |
|---:|---:|:---|
| -0.7203 | 0.09858 | QA(2).CA(2) |
| 1.526 | 0.3532 | SA(2).CHA(2) |
| -0.5615 | 0.1361 | QA(2).CHA(2) |
| -0.06755 | 0.1411 | CA(2).CHA(2) |
| -0.06312 | 0.1089 | SA(2).UA(2) |
| -0.09200 | 0.1256 | SA(2).UA(3) |
| -0.3082 | 0.09917 | QA(2).UA(2) |
| -0.7655 | 0.1123 | QA(2).UA(3) |
| 0.1739 | 0.1060 | CA(2).UA(2) |
| 0.3859 | 0.1267 | CA(2).UA(3) |
| 0.2981 | 0.1605 | CHA(2).UA(2) |
| 0.7103 | 0.1661 | CHA(2).UA(3) |
| -0.1441 | 0.1208 | SA(2).JAA(2) |
| -0.2633 | 0.1300 | SA(2).JAA(3) |
| 0.5566 | 0.1076 | QA(2).JAA(2) |
| 0.9051 | 0.1170 | QA(2).JAA(3) |
| -0.1984 | 0.1244 | CA(2).JAA(2) |
| -0.5127 | 0.1298 | CA(2).JAA(3) |
| 0.03160 | 0.1642 | CHA(2).JAA(2) |
| 0.001865 | 0.1768 | CHA(2).JAA(3) |
| -0.05188 | 0.1248 | UA(2).JAA(2) |
| -0.3999 | 0.1332 | UA(2).JAA(3) |
| -0.4030 | 0.1365 | UA(3).JAA(2) |
| -0.6741 | 0.1468 | UA(3).JAA(3) |
| 1.026 | 0.2547 | SA(2).QA(2).CHA(2) |
| -0.5514 | 0.2638 | SA(2).CA(2).CHA(2) |
| -1.822 | 0.2961 | SA(2).CHA(2).UA(2) |
| -3.149 | 0.4660 | SA(2).CHA(2).UA(3) |
| -0.8932 | 0.2715 | SA(2)CHA(2).JAA(2) |
| -2.171 | 0.3687 | SA(2).CHA(2).JAA(3) |

## M6. Relationship of number of children with job seeking

The purpose of this analysis requires some introduction. Analysis M5 showed the importance of interviews involving the sex and parental status of respondents. However, while distinguishing between parents and non-parents, the analysis did not represent the possible influence of number of children on job seeking. This could be important since, for the 18-24 age group, number of children was much the largest determinant of variation in the amount of supplementary benefit received.

Only 45 people in the sample had three or more children. Accordingly, the chief practical distinction was between those with only one child and those with two or more children, and this led to a three-category representation of number of children. It was not possible to introduce this elaboration along with the complete set of six variables from analysis M5, as this resulted in a table with many empty cells. Instead, we separately analysed two subsets of M5. One consisted of sex, number of children, unemployment duration, and job applications. The other consisted of sex, number of children, qualifications, car driving licence, and job applications. Here we report only the former. The latter produced a relatively poor fit (scaled deviance 55.2, degrees of freedom 37). However, both analyses produced broadly similar results with regard to 'number of children'.

In examining the results shown below, we find two features of particular interest. First, focussing upon the 'sex, children and job applications' interaction, we see that there was no difference in the parameters as one moved from 'one child' to 'two children'. In other words, for women, the presence of a single child reduced the relative odds of making frequent job applications as much as having two or more children. To see the corresponding result for men, we look at the parameters relating to the association between number of children and number of job applications. Three of these four parameters have estimated values much smaller than their standard errors, and the fourth is also clearly non-significant. Neither the presence of children, nor the number of children, appears to be related to number of job applications among this group of men.

The variables, and values of variables, used in the analysis below were:
SA = Sex (1 = Male, 2 = Female)
CHA = Children (1 = None, 2 = One, 3 = Two or more)
UA = Unemployment duration (1 = up to one year, 2 = 13-24 months, 3 = 25 months or more)
JAA = Job applications in past year (1 = None, 2 = 1-10, 3 = 11 or more).

The full four-way table was formed, with 54 cells, and a log-linear analysis performed. The model fitted required 34 parameters and consisted of (a) the two three-way interactions of 'sex' and 'children' with each of the other two variables (b) the association of the other two variables. The fit was satisfactory; its main features have been discussed above.

scaled deviance = 14.819
d.f. = 20

| estimate | s.e. | parameter |
|---|---|---|
| 4.495 | 0.09062 | 1 |
| -0.4129 | 0.1150 | SA(2) |
| -2.292 | 0.2272 | CHA(2) |
| -2.662 | 0.2373 | CHA(3) |
| 0.1747 | 0.1121 | UA(2) |
| 0.03394 | 0.1182 | UA(3) |
| 0.8447 | 0.1039 | JAA(2) |
| 0.8886 | 0.1056 | JAA(3) |
| 1.953 | 0.2882 | SA(2).CHA(2) |
| 0.6021 | 0.4216 | SA(2).CHA(3) |
| -0.04685 | 0.1069 | SA(2).UA(2) |
| -0.06742 | 0.1223 | SA(2).UA(3) |
| 0.04607 | 0.2156 | CHA(2).UA(2) |
| 0.4471 | 0.2216 | CHA(2).UA(3) |
| 0.6368 | 0.2214 | CHA(3).UA(2) |
| 1.161 | 0.2225 | CHA(3).UA(3) |
| -0.1447 | 0.1184 | SA(2).JAA(2) |
| -0.3045 | 0.1260 | SA(2).JAA(3) |
| 0.03135 | 0.2220 | CHA(2).JAA(2) |
| -0.3072 | 0.2471 | CHA(2).JAA(3) |
| -0.1098 | 0.2142 | CHA(3).JAA(2) |
| 0.03122 | 0.2207 | CHA(3).JAA(3) |
| -0.1032 | 0.1237 | UA(2).JAA(2) |
| -0.5004 | 0.1307 | UA(2).JAA(3) |
| -0.5259 | 0.1341 | UA(3).JAA(2) |
| -0.9091 | 0.1428 | UA(3).JAA(3) |
| -1.825 | 0.3582 | SA(2).CHA(2).UA(2) |
| -2.860 | 0.4885 | SA(2).CHA(2).UA(3) |
| -1.552 | 0.5099 | SA(2).CHA(3).UA(2) |

| | | |
|---|---|---|
| -12.01 | 39.35 | SA(2).CHA(3).UA(3) |
| -0.8057 | 0.3174 | SA(2).CHA(2).JAA(2) |
| -1.763 | 0.4296 | SA(2).CHA(2).JAA(3) |
| -0.6544 | 0.4993 | SA(2).CHA(3).JAA(2) |
| -1.783 | 0.6993 | SA(2).CHA(3).JAA(3) |

## M7. The basic model of job search applied to withdrawal from the labour market

This analysis differs from M5 only in the substitution, for 'number of job applications', of 'withdrawal from the labour market', with individuals being classified as either remaining in the labour market or as having withdrawn.

The variables and values of the variables are as M5, except for:

OA = Withdrawal from the labour market (1 = Has withdrawn, 2 = Remains in labour market)

The full six-way table was formed, consisting of 96 cells, and a log-linear analysis conducted. The model fitted consisted of (a) the four three-way interactions of 'sex' and 'children' with each of the other variables, (b) the six pairwise associations among the other four variables. The number of parameters required was 33, and the fit obtained was satisfactory. A simplified model, consisting of the 15 pairwise associations among the six variables, was also analysed, but the scaled deviance increased by 134.5 for a decrease of five degrees of freedom, and the fit was clearly unsatisfactory.

scaled deviance = 67.395
d.f. = 63

| estimate | s.e. | parameter |
|---|---|---|
| 1.330 | 0.2128 | 1 |
| -1.259 | 0.2024 | SA(2) |
| 0.7407 | 0.1679 | QA(2) |
| 1.157 | 0.1843 | CA(2) |
| -1.432 | 0.2665 | CHA(2) |
| 0.06098 | 0.1936 | UA(2) |
| 0.05904 | 0.2085 | UA(3) |
| 2.559 | 0.2027 | OA(2) |

273

| | | |
|---|---|---|
| 0.2893 | 0.09810 | SA(2).QA(2) |
| 0.9587 | 0.1165 | SA(2).CA(2) |
| -0.7740 | 0.09738 | QA(2).CA(2) |
| 1.953 | 0.4176 | SA(2).CHA(2) |
| -0.5598 | 0.1346 | QA(2).CHA(2) |
| -0.06745 | 0.1406 | CA(2).CHA(2) |
| -0.04943 | 0.1085 | SA(2).UA(2) |
| -0.07611 | 0.1251 | SA(2).UA(3) |
| -0.3528 | 0.09784 | QA(2).UA(2) |
| -0.8357 | 0.1108 | QA(2).UA(3) |
| 0.2050 | 0.1054 | CA(2).UA(2) |
| 0.4234 | 0.1259 | CA(2).UA(3) |
| 0.2995 | 0.1601 | CHA(2).UA(2) |
| 0.7082 | 0.1656 | CHA(2).UA(3) |
| -0.2137 | 0.1627 | SA(2).OA(2) |
| 0.3420 | 0.1421 | QA(2).OA(2) |
| -0.2439 | 0.1648 | CA(2).OA(2) |
| -0.04891 | 0.2226 | CHA(2).OA(2) |
| -0.04084 | 0.1689 | UA(2).OA(2) |
| -0.4489 | 0.1777 | UA(3).OA(2) |
| 0.8678 | 0.2528 | SA(2).QA(2).CHA(2) |
| -0.4646 | 0.2632 | SA(2).CA(2).CHA(2) |
| -1.734 | 0.2961 | SA(2).CHA(2).UA(2) |
| -3.090 | 0.4671 | SA(2).CHA(2).UA(3) |
| -1.547 | 0.3272 | SA(2).CHA(2).OA(2) |

**M8. 'Jobcentre support' added to the basic job search model**
This analysis differed from M5 in the *addition* of a variable to indicate whether the individual had received support from Jobcentre staff concerning job vacanicies; and in the removal of 'car driving licence' from the model.

The variables, and values of variables, in the analysis were:

SA = Sex (1 = Male, 2 = Female)
QA = Qualifications (1 = No qualifications,
2 = Any qualifications)
CHA = Children (1 = No children, 2 = One or more children)
UA = Unemployment duration at sampling (1 = up to one year,
2 = 13-24 months or more)

JAA =   Job applications in the past year (1 = None, 2 = 1-10, 3 = 11 or more)

JSA =   Jobcentre support in past year (1 = Yes, 2 = No)

The full six-way table assisting of 144 cells was formed, and a log-linear analysis was conducted. The model fitted, which required 40 parameters, consisted of (a) the three-way interactions of 'sex' and 'children' with each of the other variables *except* Jobcentre support, (b) the six pairwise associations between the other four variables. This model provided a satisfactory fit and the estimated associations involving 'Jobcentre support' were particularly interesting: only that with 'Job applications' was significant. The simpler model, consisting of all 15 pairwise associations, increased the scaled deviance by 146.3 for a reduction of five degrees of freedom, and was unsatisfactory.

scaled deviance = 113.79
d.f. = 104

| estimate | s.e. | parameter |
|---|---|---|
| 1.440 | 0.1859 | 1 |
| -0.5331 | 0.1583 | SA(2) |
| 0.1685 | 0.1458 | QA(2) |
| -1.723 | 0.2194 | CHA(2) |
| 0.4537 | 0.1581 | UA(2) |
| 0.4966 | 0.1730 | UA(3) |
| 1.353 | 0.1788 | JAA(2) |
| 1.350 | 0.1854 | JAA(3) |
| 2.298 | 0.1677 | JSA(2) |
| 0.1979 | 0.09729 | SA(2).QA(2) |
| 1.048 | 0.2795 | SA(2).CHA(2) |
| -0.5429 | 0.1343 | QA(2).CHA(2) |
| -0.03088 | 0.1072 | SA(2).UA(2) |
| -0.02841 | 0.1238 | SA(2).UA(3) |
| -0.3393 | 0.09819 | QA(2).UA(2) |
| -0.8248 | 0.1112 | QA(2).UA(3) |
| 0.3006 | 0.1605 | CHA(2).UA(2) |
| 0.7110 | 0.1658 | CHA(2).UA(3) |
| -0.1696 | 0.1201 | SA(2).JAA(2) |
| -0.3456 | 0.1297 | SA(2).JAA(3) |
| 0.5466 | 0.1074 | QA(2).JAA(2) |

| | | |
|---|---|---|
| 0.9262 | 0.1171 | QA(2).JAA(3) |
| 0.05800 | 0.1650 | CHA(2).JAA(2) |
| 0.04282 | 0.1777 | CHA(2).JAA(3) |
| -0.07705 | 0.1256 | UA(2).JAA(2) |
| -0.4452 | 0.1344 | UA(2).JAA(3) |
| -0.4367 | 0.1374 | UA(3).JAA(2) |
| -0.7418 | 0.1482 | UA(3).JAA(3) |
| 0.02193 | 0.1045 | SA(2).JSA(2) |
| -0.2593 | 0.1025 | QA(2).JSA(2) |
| 0.1958 | 0.1357 | CHA(2).JSA(2) |
| -0.1458 | 0.1124 | UA(3).JSA(2) |
| -0.1627 | 0.1297 | UA(3).JSA(2) |
| -0.9679 | 0.1506 | JAA(2).JSA(2) |
| -1.257 | 0.1550 | JAA(3).JSA(2) |
| 1.083 | 0.2520 | SA(2).QA(2).CHA(2) |
| -1.840 | 0.2959 | SA(2).CHA(2).UA(2) |
| -3.183 | 0.4654 | SA(2).CHA(2).UA(3) |
| -0.8771 | 0.2711 | SA(2).CHA(2).JAA(2) |
| -2.123 | 0.3673 | SA(2).CHA(2).JAA(3) |

## M9. 'Support of family and friends' added to the basic job search model

This analysis differed from M8 in the replacement of 'Jobcentre support' by a variable indicating whether the individual had obtained job information from family or friends. The new variable and its values were defined as follows:

FA = Family support in job seeking (1 = Yes, 2 = No).

The other variables SA, QA, CHA, VA, JAA were as in M8.

The full six-way table was formed, consisting of 144 cells, and a log-linear analysis was conducted. The model fitted, which required 40 parameters, consisted of (a) the four three-way interactions of 'sex' and 'children' with each of the other variables, (b) the six pairwise associations among the other variables. The model yielded a satisfactory fit, and the estimated associations involving 'family support' were particularly interesting. The simplified model, consisting of all 15 pairwise associations, resulted in an increase of the scaled deviance of 146.3 for a decrease of five degrees of freedom, and was unsatisfactory.

scaled deviance = 103.55
d.f. = 104

| estimate | s.e. | parameter |
|---|---|---|
| 3.025 | 0.1275 | 1 |
| -0.6206 | 0.1381 | SA(2) |
| -1.524 | 0.1914 | CHA(2) |
| -0.1092 | 0.1259 | QA(2) |
| 0.2769 | 0.1358 | UA(2) |
| 0.4375 | 0.1443 | UA(3) |
| 1.116 | 0.1330 | JAA(2) |
| 0.9242 | 0.1405 | JAA(3) |
| 0.2195 | 0.1280 | FA(2) |
| 1.048 | 0.2795 | SA(2).CHA(2) |
| 0.1943 | 0.09724 | SA(2).QA(2) |
| -0.5511 | 0.1342 | CHA(2).QA(2) |
| -0.03419 | 0.1073 | SA(2).UA(2) |
| -0.02344 | 0.1239 | SA(2).UA(3) |
| 0.2962 | 0.1604 | CHA(2).UA(2) |
| 0.7048 | 0.1657 | CHA(2).UA(3) |
| -0.3339 | 0.09804 | QA(2).UA(2) |
| -0.8155 | 0.1110 | QA(2).UA(3) |
| -0.1038 | 0.1249 | SA(2).JAA(2) |
| -0.2755 | 0.1341 | SA(2).JAA(3) |
| 0.02256 | 0.1700 | CHA(2).JAA(2) |
| -0.004338 | 0.1824 | CHA(2).JAA(3) |
| 0.6097 | 0.1126 | QA(2).JAA(2) |
| 1.006 | 0.1221 | QA(2).JAA(3) |
| -0.02909 | 0.1312 | UA(2).JAA(2) |
| -0.3864 | 0.1398 | UA(2).JAA(3) |
| -0.4741 | 0.1438 | UA(3).JAA(2) |
| -0.7743 | 0.1542 | UA(3).JAA(3) |
| 0.1867 | 0.09962 | SA(2).FA(2) |
| -0.03051 | 0.1241 | CHA(2).FA(2) |
| 0.07771 | 0.09922 | QA(2).FA(2) |
| 0.07793 | 0.1099 | UA(2).FA(2) |
| -0.1637 | 0.1269 | UA(3).FA(2) |
| -1.637 | 0.1131 | JAA(2).FA(2) |
| -1.824 | 0.1271 | JAA(3).FA(2) |
| 1.085 | 0.2521 | SA(2).CHA(2).QA(2) |

| | | |
|---|---|---|
| -1.839 | 0.2958 | SA(2).CHA(2).UA(2) |
| -3.182 | 0.4654 | SA(2).CHA(2).UA(3) |
| -0.8776 | 0.2711 | SA(2).CHA(2).JAA(2) |
| -2.123 | 0.3674 | SA(2).CHA(2).JAA(3) |

**M10. Relationships between job search and return to work**

These analyses were carried out on a subset of the whole sample, the following groups being excluded: (i) mothers, (ii) those who had withdrawn from the labour market. The reduced sample size was 2127.

*(a)  Analysis incorporating 'Jobcentre support'*

The variables, and values of variables, for this analysis were as follows:

QA =    Qualifications (1 = No qualification, 2 = Any qualification)
CA =    Car driving licence ( 1 = Yes, 2 = No)
UA =    Unemployment duration at sampling (1 = up to one year, 2 = 13-24 months, 3 = 25 months or more)
JAA =   Job applications (1 = 0-1, 2 = 2-10, 3 = 11 or more)
JSA =   Jobcentre support (1 = Yes, 2 = No)
IA =    In work at 1984 interview (1 = Yes, 2 = No).

The full six-way table was formed, consisting of 144 cells, and a log-linear analysis conducted. The model fitted, which required 35 parameters, consisted of the 15 pairwise associations among the six variables. The fit was somewhat less satisfactory than with the preceding log-linear analyses.

scaled deviance = 138.03
d.f. = 109

| estimate | s.e. | parameter |
|---|---|---|
| -1.275 | 0.3131 | 1 |
| 0.9804 | 0.1981 | QA(2) |
| 1.040 | 0.2060 | CA(2) |
| 0.03885 | 0.2172 | UA(2) |
| -0.5045 | 0.2617 | UA(3) |
| 1.902 | 0.2757 | JAA(2) |

| | | |
|---|---|---|
| 2.173 | 0.2785 | JAA(3) |
| 1.440 | 0.2084 | JSA(2) |
| 1.607 | 0.2671 | IA(2) |
| -0.6055 | 0.1032 | QA(2).CA(2) |
| -0.2932 | 0.1052 | QA(2).UA(2) |
| -0.7344 | 0.1189 | QA(2).UA(3) |
| 0.08385 | 0.1115 | CA(2).UA(2) |
| 0.2583 | 0.1329 | CA(2).UA(3) |
| 0.3962 | 0.1206 | QA(2).JAA(2) |
| 0.7442 | 0.1261 | QA(2).JAA(3) |
| -0.2248 | 0.1419 | CA(2).JAA(2) |
| -0.5664 | 0.1433 | CA(2).JAA(3) |
| -0.1465 | 0.1409 | UA(2).JAA(2) |
| -0.4588 | 0.1456 | UA(2).JAA(3) |
| -0.3922 | 0.1533 | UA(3).JAA(2) |
| -0.6084 | 0.1595 | UA(3).JAA(3) |
| -0.3471 | 0.1053 | QA(2).JSA(2) |
| -0.1559 | 0.1159 | CA(2).JSA(2) |
| -0.1257 | 0.1159 | UA(2).JSA(2) |
| -0.1505 | 0.1336 | UA(3).JSA(2) |
| -0.3581 | 0.1457 | JAA(2).JSA(2) |
| -0.5829 | 0.1485 | JAA(3).JSA(2) |
| -0.2719 | 0.1347 | QA(2).IA(2) |
| 0.6408 | 0.1294 | CA(2).IA(2) |
| 0.4593 | 0.1392 | UA(2).IA(2) |
| 0.8808 | 0.1858 | UA(3).IA(2) |
| -0.8727 | 0.2188 | JAA(2).IA(2) |
| -0.9356 | 0.2210 | JAA(3).IA(2) |
| 0.4473 | 0.1342 | JSA(2).IA(2) |

## (b) Analysis incorporating 'support of family and friends'

In this analysis, 'Jobcentre support' was replaced by 'support of family and friends'. All other details of the analysis were the same as with analysis (a). The new variable and its values were defined as follows:

FA = Support of family and friends in job seeking (1 = Yes, 2 = No)

The analysis resulted in a satisfactory fit.

scaled deviance = 111.37
d.f. = 109

| estimate | s.e. | parameter |
|---|---|---|
| -0.02832 | 0.2734 | 1 |
| 0.7124 | 0.1834 | QA(2) |
| 0.8584 | 0.1904 | CA(2) |
| -0.1199 | 0.2018 | UA(2) |
| -0.5706 | 0.2442 | UA(3) |
| 1.782 | 0.2547 | JAA(2) |
| 1.912 | 0.2572 | JAA(3) |
| -0.7126 | 0.2112 | FA(2) |
| 2.095 | 0.2469 | IA(2) |
| -0.5956 | 0.1030 | QA(2).CA(2) |
| -0.2852 | 0.1049 | QA(2).UA(2) |
| -0.7245 | 0.1186 | QA(2).UA(3) |
| 0.08237 | 0.1115 | CA(2).UA(2) |
| 0.2673 | 0.1329 | CA(2).UA(3) |
| 0.4178 | 0.1207 | QA(2).JAA(2) |
| 0.7813 | 0.1261 | QA(2).JAA(3) |
| -0.1977 | 0.1423 | CA(2).JAA(2) |
| -0.5297 | 0.1434 | CA(2).JAA(3) |
| -0.1205 | 0.1414 | UA(2).JAA(2) |
| -0.4245 | 0.1458 | UA(2).JAA(3) |
| -0.3998 | 0.1538 | UA(3).JAA(2) |
| -0.6114 | 0.1597 | UA(3).JAA(3) |
| 0.005501 | 0.1114 | QA(2).FA(2) |
| 0.1788 | 0.1234 | CA(2).FA(2) |
| 0.1758 | 0.1227 | UA(2).FA(2) |
| -0.1695 | 0.1472 | UA(3).FA(2) |
| -0.5657 | 0.1358 | JAA(2).FA(2) |
| -0.6579 | 0.1443 | JAA(3).FA(2) |
| -0.3031 | 0.1342 | QA(2).IA(2) |
| 0.6367 | 0.1292 | CA(2).IA(2) |
| 0.4584 | 0.1390 | UA(2).IA(2) |
| 0.8573 | 0.1855 | UA(3).IA(2) |
| -0.9405 | 0.2193 | JAA(2).IA(2) |
| -1.030 | 0.2213 | JAA(3).IA(2) |
| -0.3493 | 0.1481 | FA(2).IA(2) |

# Notes and References

## Chapter 1

1. Under the 1984 European Social Fund Guidelines, nearly one half of the budget was designated for initiatives relating to the under 25s. See: European Social Fund, *Employment Gazette*, May 1984.
2. For details of most of the major schemes to assist young people with difficulties of employment, see Annual Reports of the Manpower Services Commission.
3. Moylan, S., Millar, J. and Davies, B. *For Richer, for Poorer? DHSS Cohort Study of Unemployed Men*, Department of Health and Social Security, Research Report 11, 1984.
   White, M. *Long-term Unemployment and Labour Markets*, Policy Studies Institute, 1983.
4. The definition of period of unemployment used in this study is the same as used for the official unemployment statistics at the time of sampling (February 1984). Computerisation of benefit records makes it possible to treat as continuous spells any for which registration is broken for very short periods. For further details see: Compilation of the unemployment statistics, *Employment Gazette*, September 1982.
5. Myrdal, G. *Challenge to Affluence*, Gollancz, 1963.
6. See, for example: *Employment changes in Greater Manchester 1965-81*, GMC County Planning Department, Policy background paper 85/4; *Local Unemployment in Greater Manchester: Analysis by age and duration*, GMC County Planning Department, Policy background paper 85/1; *Unemployment in Tyne and Wear*, Tyne and Wear County

Council, April 1984. Also, for more general discussions, see: Mawson, J. and Miller, D. Interventionist approaches in local employment and economic development: the experience of labour local authorities, in: Hausner, V.A. (ed.) *Critical Issues in Urban Economic Development*, Clarendon Press/Economic and Social Research Council, 1986; Pay, J. *The Response of Local Labour Market Agencies to the Problem of Long Term Unemployment*, School for Advanced Urban Studies, University of Bristol (mimeo), 1983.

7. Ashton, D.N. and Maguire, M.J., *Young Adults in the Labour Market*, Department of Employment Research Paper No. 55, 1986.
   Manpower Services Commission, *London Employment Review 1984*.
   McIntosh, A. and Keddie, V. *Industry and Employment in the Inner City*, Department of the Environment, Inner Cities Research Programme No. 1, 1979.

8. See, for example, Fothergill, S. and Gudgin, G., *Unequal Growth: Urban and Regional Employment Change in the UK*, Heinemann, 1982.
   Owen, D.W., Gillespie, A.E. and Coombes, M.G., 'Job Shortfalls' in British Local Labour Market Areas: A Classification of Labour Supply and Demand Trends, 1971-1981. *Regional Studies*, vol.18, no.6, 1985.

9. Pahl, R. *Divisions of Labour*, Blackwell, 1984.
   Roberts, B., Finnegan, R. and Gallie, D. (eds.) *New Approaches to Economic Life*, Manchester University Press, 1985.

10. Statistics of vacancies, as reported in *Employment Gazette* series, cover only those vacancies notified to Jobcentres (or in earlier years Employment Offices) and to the Professional and Executive Register. It is customary to state that these account for about one third of all vacancies, but it is doubtful whether this is a wholly reliable figure. However, the change in the vacancy statistics may still be reliable. Between early 1980, just before the main increase in unemployment, and mid-1981, published vacancies decreased by one half.

11. Between December 1979 and December 1982, employment in manufacturing fell by 1.33 million, a decline of 19.2 per cent. See *Employment Gazette*, Table 1.2. While precise statistics on

all redundancies are not compiled, redundancies affecting 10 or more workers are reported by employers to the Manpower Services Commission. This indicator showed a rise from 186,800 to 493,800 between 1979 and 1980, and a further rise to 532,000 in 1981. See *Employment Gazette*, May 1982, page 219.

12. Between June 1982 and June 1983, employment in manufacturing fell by 5.0 per cent while employment in services remained constant. Over the subsequent 12 months, employment in manufacturing fell by 1.6 per cent, while employment in services rose by 2.0 per cent. Finally, between June 1984 and June 1985, manufacturing jobs remained constant while service jobs rose by a further 2.4 per cent.

13. Owen, D.W., Gillespie, A.E. and Coombes, M.G. *op.cit.*

14. Roberts, K., Dench, S. and Richardson, D. *The changing structure of youth labour markets*, Department of Employment Research Paper No. 59, 1986.

15. Wells, W. *The relative pay and employment of young people*, Department of Employment Research Paper No. 42, 1983.

16. For a discussion of the differences between studies of the stock and of the flow, see: Daniel, W.W. Unemployment, *Policy Studies*, Spring, 1979.

17. For details of the improved flow statistics becoming available in the early 1980s, see: Hughes, P. Flows on and off the unemployment register, *Employment Gazette*, December 1982; Regional and age variations in unemployment flow, *Employment Gazette*, November 1983; Unemployment flows: detailed analysis, *Employment Gazette*, August, 1984.

18. Weels, W. *op.cit.*

19. Casson, M. *Economics of Unemployment*, Martin Robertson, 1983.

20. Manpower Services Commission, *Young People and Work*, 1977.
Rees, A. An essay on youth joblessness. *Journal of Economic Literature*, vol. 24, June, 1986.
Thurow, L. *Generating Inequality*, Macmillan, 1975.
White, M. *op.cit.*

21. Myrdal, G. *op.cit.*

22. Goldthorpe, J.H. with others, *Social Mobility and Class Structure*, Clarendon Press, 1980. Goldthorpe, J.H. and

Payne, C.W. Trends in intergenerational class mobility in England and Wales 1972-83, *Sociology*, no.1, 1986.

23. There is a large academic literature contesting whether technological development leads to increases or decreases in skill requirements, but it appears that most evidence of de-skilling rests upon the study of particular cases, while a broader perspective leads to the conclusion that skill demands have been increasing. See, for example: Fuchs, V.R. *The Service Economy*, Basic Books, 1968;
   Sorge, A. and others, *Microelectronics and Manpower in Manufacturing*, Gower, 1983.
   Wood, S. (ed) *The Degredation of Work?* Heinemann, 1982.

24. A satisfactory term to cover 'all higher level' jobs still appears to be lacking. Such a term should encompass the professions, scientists and technologists, managers, and administrative or 'white collar' staff on career ladders.

25. Ashton, D.N, Maguire, M.J. and Garland, V. *Youth in the Labour Market*, Department of Employment Research Paper No. 34, 1982.

26. Webber, R. and Craig, J. *Socio-economic Classification of Local Authority Areas*, HMSO, 1978.

27. Martin, J. and Roberts, C. *Women and Employment: a Lifetime Perspective*, HMSO, 1984.

28. This (unpublished) analysis was conducted by Social and Community Planning Research as part of their initial work on the survey (see Acknowledgements).

## Chapter 2

1. Coombes, M.G. and others, Functional Regions for the Population Census of Great Britain, in: Herbert, D.T. and Johnston, R.J. *Geography and the Urban Environment: Progress in Research and Applications*, Volume V, Wiley, 1982.

2. For such a study, see: Buck, N.H., Gordon, I.R., and Young, K. *The London Employment Problem*, Oxford University Press, 1986.

3. Shift share analysis is outlined and exemplified in Fothergill, S. and Gudgin, G. *op.cit.*

4. Sizer, J. *An Insight into Management Accounting*, Penguin, 1969.

5.  Owen, D.W., Gillespie, A.E. and Coombes, M.G., *op.cit*; Fothergill, S., and Gudgin, G. o*p.cit.*
6.  The 1968 Standard Industrial Classification (SIC) was used for this purpose. The classification was changed in 1980, but where necessary, the 1980 classification was translated (approximately) to the 1968 classification by means of a table prepared by CURDS.
7.  Owen, D.W., Gillespie, A.E., and Coombes, M.G., *op.cit*; Centre for Urban and Regional Development Studies, *Long-term Unemployment*, Functional Regions Factsheet 6, December 1983.
8.  Cross, M. *New Firm Formation and Regional Development,* Gower, 1981.
    Fothergill, S. and Gudgin, G. *op.cit.*
    Johnson, P. and Cathcart, D.G. The founders of new firms: A note on the size of their incubator plants. *Journal of Industrial Economics*, vol.28, 1979.
9.  The conventional argument is that the growth of local economies depends upon the multiplier effect of 'exports' beyond the local economy, and such exports are provided by manufacturing while services are, for the most part, locally consumed. Changes in communications, transport, and the nature of services (e.g. the growth of producer services) could all tend to reduce differences between manufacturing and services in this respect, and so weakens the conventional argument.
10. In 1981, according the the *Labour Force Survey*, only two per cent of economically active men were engaged in part-time work, while the proportion was 47 per cent for married women and 16 per cent for those not married.
11. Bowen, W.G. and Finegan, T.A., *The Economics of Labour Force Participation*, Princeton University Press, 1969.
12. An increase in earlier retirement for men, *Employment Gazette*, April, 1980.
    Labour force outlook for Great Britain, *Employment Gazette*, June 1984; see especially the chart on page 262.
13. *Census 1981 Regional Migration* - various reports by region.
14. Green, A.E. and others, 'What contribution can labour migration make to reducing unemployment?' in: Hart, P.E. (ed) *Unemployment and Labour Market Policies*, Gower, 1986.

**Chapter 3**

1.  It might be argued that a year as close as possible to the time of the survey should have been used for this comparison, as proportions of non-qualification were steadily decreasing over the period. However, after 1979 the pattern of qualification by occupational level for young people was likely to be distorted by youth unemployment itself, rendering causal interpretation difficult. In fact, from 1980 onwards the General Household Survey has published tables of qualification by occupational level only for age groups aged 25 upwards. The suitability of 1979 as a year for comparative purposes consists both in being the last year in which the youth labour market functioned normally, and also in being positioned in the middle of the period during which our sample was entering the labour market.

2.  See note 1.

3.  Payne, J. and Payne, C.W. Youth unemployment 1974-81: the changing importance of age and qualifications, *Quarterly Journal of Social Affairs*, 1985.

4.  Halsey, A.H., Heath, A.F. and Ridge, J.M., *Origins and Destinations*, Clarendon Press, 1980.

5.  Fogelman, K. (ed.), *Growing up in Great Britain*, Macmillan, 1983.

6.  No single study has focused upon tendencies for spouses' employment status to change together. The evidence from a variety of studies, however, suggests that there is a tendency for wives to work when their husbands are working, and to become unemployed or economically inactive when their husbands have been unemployed for a considerable period. See, for instance: Moylan, S., Millar, J. and Davies, B. *op.cit.*; Pahl, R., *op.cit*; White, M., *op.cit.*

7.  White, M., *op.cit.*

8.  'Childhood housing experiences and school attainment', in: Fogelman, K. *op.cit.*

9.  'Single parent families', *ibid.*

10. Brown, C., *Black and White Britain*, Heinemann, 1984.

11. *Ibid.*

## Chapter 4

1. Two main procedures were used to improve the quality of information from the work histories. First, after completion of the work history in the interview, each individual was prompted to think of any other short spells which might have been missed out. These were then separately noted. A computer programme was written to insert these extra short spells where this could be done consistent with the sequence already obtained. This procedure added about 10 per cent of spells in the aggregate.

   The second procedure used was based upon the development of a computer programme to check the internal consistency of the work histories. Inconsistencies revealed by this method were checked with the original interview records, and more than 100 were satisfactorily resolved and corrected. In total 13 interviews were discarded because the work history was grossly incomplete or unintelligible.

2. There was a difficult choice concerning the base for this proportion. Employment and unemployment (where the individual continues to seek work) are generally counted as economic activity, while full-time education, illness, or withdrawal into a domestic role, are regarded as inactivity; but participation in government training schemes or special labour market schemes have an intermediate status. On grounds of practical interpretation, it seemed best on balance to count periods on such schemes as part of economic activity.

3. Ashton, D.W. and Maguire, M.J. *op.cit.*

4. Daniel, W.W. and Hogarth, T., *Pay Expectations of Wage and Salary Earners*, Policy Studies Institute, forthcoming.

5. The chief limitations of the New Earnings Survey, for comparison with out data, are that they cover only full-time workers, and report gross rather than net earnings. An adjustment has been made for deductions from earnings, but not for the effect of part-time work on the comparison. But see Table 4.11 also.

6. Ashton, D.W. and Maguire, M.J. *op.cit.*

## Chapter 5

1. Greaves, K. *The Youth Opportunities Programme in Contrasting Local Areas*, Manpower Services Commission, Research and Development Series: No.16, 1983.
2. *ibid.*
3. *ibid.*
4. Roberts, K. Dench, S. and Richardson, D. *op.cit.*
   Sako, M. and Dore, R. How the Youth Training Scheme helps employers, *Employment Gazette*, June 1986.
5. Collins, M., Crompton, S. and Courtenay, G., *Employment after YOP*, Social and Community Planning Research (mimeo) May 1983.
6. Daniel, W.W. *The Unemployed Flow*, Interim Report, Policy Studies Institute, 1981.
7. Greaves, K. *op.cit.*
8. *Community Programme Postal Follow-up Survey*, Employment Division, Manpower Services Commission, December 1984.
9. Turner, P. After the Community Programme - results of the first follow-up survey, *Employment Gazette*, January 1985.

## Chapter 6

1. Daniel, W.W. and Hogarth, T. *op.cit.*
2. Ashton, D.W. and Maguire, M.J. *op.cit.*

## Chapter 7

1. For a review, see: Spence, M. 'Signaling, screening and information', in: Rosen, S. (ed.) *Studies in Labour Markets*, National Bureau of Economic Research, 1981.
2. Blau, P.M. and Duncan, O.D., *The American Occupational Structure*, Wiley, 1967.
3. McRae, S.M., Ethnic Minorities. Unpublished working paper, Policy Studies Institute, December, 1985.
4. Bartel, A.P. and Borjas, G.J. 'Wage growth and job turnover: an empirical analysis', in : Rosen, S. *op.cit.*
5. Blau, P.M. and Duncan, O.D. *op.cit.*
6. Pahl, R. *op.cit.*
7. For some recent evidence see: Crowley-Bainton, T., Discriminating employers, *New Society*, 27 November 1987.

**Chapter 8**
1. McRae, S. *Young and Jobless*, Policy Studies Institute, 1987.

**Chapter 9**
1. Goldthorpe, J.H. and Hope, K. *The Social Grading of Occupations*, Clarendon Press, 1974.
2. The New Earnings Survey publishes data by occupations within sex only where the number obtained in the sample is at least 100. Also, it excludes part-time workers. As a result, the data for women's pay by occupation is incomplete. Whereas five per cent of young men in our survey came from occupations where NES data were lacking, the proportion in the case of young women was 22 per cent.

**Appendix 1**
1. Webber, R. and Craig, J. *op.cit.*

**Appendix 3**
1. Payne, C.D. (ed.) *The GLIM System Release 3.77 Manual*, Numerical Algorithms Group, 1985.
2. Everitt, B.S. *The Analysis of Contingency Tables*, Chapman and Hall, 1977.